Perverse Modernities

A series edited by

Judith Halberstam

and Lisa Lowe

TIME BINDS

Queer Temporalities,

Queer Histories

ELIZABETH FREEMAN

Duke University Press

Durham and London 2010

Printed in the United States
of America on acid-free paper ∞
Designed by Amy Ruth Buchanan
Typeset in Carter & Cone Galliard
by Keystone Typesetting, Inc.
Library of Congress Cataloging-
in-Publication Data appear on the
last printed page of this book.

Duke University Press gratefully
acknowledges the University of
California, Davis, who supported
the publication of this book.

For the Frog and the Fly

And for my mother,

who needs more time

contents

Preface   ix

Acknowledgments   xxv

Introduction:
Queer and Not Now   1

1. Junk Inheritances, Bad Timing:
   Familial Arrhythmia in Three Working-
   Class Dyke Narratives   21

2. Deep Lez: Temporal Drag and
   the Specters of Feminism   59

3. Time Binds, or, Erotohistoriography   95

4. Turn the Beat Around: Sadomasochism,
   Temporality, History   137

Coda   171

Appendix: Distributors for Films
and Videos   175

Notes   177

Bibliography   193

Index   209

preface

In 1915, the British poet Robert Graves wrote a poem, "It's a Queer Time." Popularly understood as a lighthearted, topical ballad about the trauma of trench warfare, the poem sets up a counterpoint between images of gory battle and of the hallucinatory utopias the second-person speaker encounters when he loses consciousness. "It's hard to know if you're alive or dead," the poem opens, "When steel and fire go roaring thro' your head." It's also hard to know if being "alive" consists of fighting the war or blacking out. Here is a sample stanza, the third of five:

> You're charging madly at them yelling "Fag!"
> When somehow something gives and your feet drag.
> You fall and strike your head; yet feel no pain
> And find . . . . you're digging tunnels through the hay
> In the Big Barn, 'cause it's a rainy day.
> Oh, springy hay, and lovely beams to climb!
> You're back in the old sailor suit again.
> It's a queer time.[1]

Here, the homophobia necessary to fuel masculine violence gives way to another version of the trench: tunnels in a haystack. The speaker finds himself back on the farm, where rain, "springy" hay, and wood suggest life. He also appears to be dressed as a gay icon.

Lest I be accused of reading "sailor suit" and even "queer" anachronistically, let me summarize the other stanzas. All but the first two-line closed couplet end with the refrain "It's a queer time." In the second stanza, the speaker is wounded ("you're clutching at your chest," line 5) and astrotravels to the homosocial Treasure Island, which is some amalgam of Orientalized Eastern tropical romance ("spice winds blow / To lovely groves of Mango, quince, and lime —," lines 7–8) and dime-novel western ("Breathe no good-bye, but ho! for the Red West!," line 9). In the fourth stanza, when a bomb hits the speaker as he's sleeping in a trench, he finds himself "struggling, gasping, struggling, then . . . hullo! / Elsie comes tripping gaily down the trench / Hanky to nose [. . .] Getting her pinafore all over grime" (lines 21–24). Given the campiness of Elsie's attire and gestures, it's hard not to read Elsie "gaily," as a bit of a queen. But she is also an apparition — "Funny! because she died ten years ago" (line 25) — so "queer time" appears haunted. And in the last stanza, the speaker remarks that the trouble with war is that "things happen much too quick" (line 27): whereas queer time elongates and twists chronology, war simply forecloses it. He tells us that "even good Christians don't like passing straight / From Tipperary or their Hymn of Hate / To Alleluiah-chanting and the chime / Of golden harps . . . and . . . I'm not well today . . . / It's a queer time" (lines 30–34). The line break suggests that the speaker himself might be "passing [for] straight," but the next enjambed line rewrites the verb to condemn the direct route to Heaven. Here the speaker prefers to dwell in some other temporal regime than either the foreshortened time of the patriot or the eschatological scheme where death leads directly to salvation. He breezily dismisses his own mortal end, preferring to be merely "not well today," and remains in "queer time."

This poem seemingly sets straight and queer temporalities, life and death, military nation and hallucination against one another: but it also suggests that the pleasures of queerness can be found in the interstices of national-political life, and that they are definitely worth living for. Its "queer time" is at once temporal (a phantasm in the first stanza, a black-out in the second, an apparitional encounter in the third, and the whole scene "fading" away in the fourth, as the speaker nears death) and historical (the "it" in "it's a queer time" is clearly World War I, situated by the poem's references to trenches and dugouts, the chemical explosive lyddite, and the "Boches," French slang for "krauts"). So not only is the time of fantasy queer here, so also is the time of world history and politics proper.

This isn't exactly news to anyone who has read any gay and lesbian history; the First World War saw the rise of a nascently gay subculture in port cities where sailors and rough trade met one another, and in the urban areas that expanded to accommodate any number of migrations.[2] But more than telling a story of how gay and global histories intertwine, this poem narrates military history's failure to fully organize time toward nationalist ends. The speaker is a soldier who refuses to die for the glory of his country but comes back for more and more of the pain that will give him access to a queer world of his own making. Queer time overtakes both secular and millennial time. And within the lost moments of official history, queer time generates a discontinuous history of its own, which includes colonialist endeavors (the source material for the novel *Treasure Island*), the homosocial nationalism of boys' culture (the cultural work to which *Treasure Island* was put), cowboy culture and manly Manifest Destiny in the "Red West" of the Americas, the aforementioned ports of homosexual call, drag culture, and even the Church itself, each of which fostered erotic contact between men. In other words, these dreams may be dreams of an escape from history, but they also give access to an alternative history. And they are more than reveries: they are moments of extreme bodily sensation. As the soldier's presumably masculine, figuratively impenetrable body is ripped by "steel and fire" (line 2), struck in the head, suffocated with lyddite, and shot with a German rifle, he enters queer time, which makes a queer history he can enter too.

Throughout this book, I try to think against the dominant arrangement of time and history that would ordinarily guide the understanding of this poem, in which historical narrative (here, the First World War) organizes various temporal schemae into consequential sequence (such that eventually, the speaker's hallucinations will be readable as harbingers of his glorious sacrifice for this country).[3] Instead, I track the ways that nonsequential forms of time (in the poem, unconciousness, haunting, reverie, and the afterlife) can also fold subjects into structures of belonging and duration that may be invisible to the historicist eye. This poem prefigures my chapters in many ways. For instance, "It's a Queer Time" juxtaposes the precise timings of military incursions, perhaps the nation's most explicit form of synching up bodies and time, with "travers[ing] . . . dozing . . . struggling . . . stagger[ing]" movements that bring past and present together (lines 4, 19, 21, 29). In chapter 1, I argue that even non-nationalist cultural belonging is a matter of affects that inhere, in many ways, in shared timings, and I stake my claim for a counterpolitics of encounter in which bodies, de-composed by the workings of experimental film and literature, meet one another by chance, forging — in the sense of both making and counterfeiting — history differently. In "It's a Queer Time," "Elsie," mincing along in her Victorian regalia, appears as an anachronism both in her costuming and in terms of the calendar. In chapter 2, I examine a mode of campy and yet yearning queer archivalism that turns feminist, sometimes fat, sometimes dowdy, always unruly female bodies into irreverent living museums. In "It's a Queer Time," a certain splattering of the speaker's body causes him to jump the timeline. In chapter 3, I demonstrate that this fantasy of rubbing up against the past has, itself, a past, and I trace its uneven movement from an eighteenth- and early-nineteenth-century homosocial mode of sentimental history: in an avowedly erotic and lesbian twentieth-century version of this, I argue, touches that are both painful and pleasurable break open the past, slicing it into asynchronous, discontinuous pieces of time. I have remarked that the speaker of "It's a Queer Time" keeps coming back for more pain; he also "mow[s] heaps down half in fun," perhaps playing at wartime to find a history not yet recognized as such (line 4). In chapter 4, I take up the sadomasochistic play that emerged from the French Revolution, arguing that s/m reorganizes the body's microtemporalities enough to let in histories of pleasure as well as pain, preserving fugitive and resistant delights and transmitting them unevenly across time.

But "It's a Queer Time" also engages with what is seen by traditional literary critics as the inaugural event of twentieth-century modernity, the First World War. With its pointed reference to an event that nobody would argue is *not* historical, the poem allows me to inquire upon the official narrative of modernity as the by-product of global deterritorializations. Instead, "It's a Queer Time" imagines a more intimate strategy of reterritorialization, which I take up in my introduction. There I argue that corporations and nation-states seek to adjust the pace of living in the places and people they take on: to quicken up and/or synchronize some elements of everyday existence, while offering up other spaces and activities as leisurely, slow, sacred, cyclical, and so on and thereby repressing or effacing alternative strategies of organizing time.[4] Thus being normatively "modern" is a matter not only of occupying an imagined place at the new end of a sequence but also of living a coordinated, carefully syncopated tempo between a quick time that seems to be enforced and a slow time that seems to be a matter of free choice. In this sense, the soldier-speaker of "It's a Queer Time" is simply an ordinary avatar of modern time, a time whose violence offers up queer possibilities despite itself.

If queer time appears within as well as in counterpoint to modern time, temporality has inflected queer theory from its outset. Take, for instance, Michel Foucault's interest in "lowly lives reduced to ashes in a few phrases that have destroyed them," in the infamous who are also unfamous, the archive's stray dogs.[5] Or Eve Sedgwick's focus on the queer "inner child" with whom the sexually dissident adult has a complexly narcissistic, avowing and disavowing, even pedophiliac relation.[6]

Or Douglas Crimp's moving cry for "mourning *and* militancy" during a moment when rage seemed the predominant modality for AIDS activism.[7] Or the gradual emergence of melancholia in Judith Butler's work, a figure of psychic fixation or stuckness that troubles the smooth machine of gender performativity.[8] Or the many undead referents of Cherríe Moraga's play *Giving Up the Ghost* (1986), in which time and history appear as borders, too, alongside the borders between Anglo and Chicana, Spanish and English, the United States and Mexico, all of which the play complicates and violates.[9] These and other works confront, on an affective register irreducible to traditional historical inquiry, what has been forgotten, abandoned, discredited, or otherwise effaced.

Yet until recently the dominant strains of queer theory have tended to privilege the avant-garde. At one point in my life as a scholar of queer culture and theory, I thought the point of queer was to be always ahead of actually existing social possibilities. On this model, it seemed that truly queer queers would dissolve forms, disintegrate identities, level taxonomies, scorn the social, and even repudiate politics altogether (and indeed, there is one wing of queer theory that does privilege this kind of negating work).[10] But this version of "queering" the social text strikes me as somewhat akin to Eve Sedgwick's notion of paranoid criticism: it's about having the problem solved ahead of time, about feeling more evolved than one's context.[11] Now I think the point may be to trail behind actually existing social possibilities: to be interested in the tail end of things, willing to be bathed in the fading light of whatever has been declared useless. For while queer antiformalism appeals to me on an intellectual level, I find myself emotionally compelled by the not-quite-queer-enough longing for form that turns us backward to prior moments, forward to embarrassing utopias, sideways to forms of being and belonging that seem, on the face of it, completely banal.[12] This is the essence of what I think Sedgwick means by reparative criticism: that because we can't know in advance, but only retrospectively if even then, what is queer and what is not, we gather and combine eclectically, dragging a bunch of cultural debris around us and stacking it in idiosyncratic piles *"not necessarily like any preexisting whole,"* though composed of what preexists.[13] For queer scholars and activists, this cultural debris includes our incomplete, partial, or otherwise failed transformations of the social field: like the speaker of "It's a Queer Time," we never hear the "Alleluia." But perhaps that is a state to enjoy, rather than just mourn.

Thus this book is organized not around the great wars of the twentieth century and beyond, but around a series of failed revolutions in the 1960s and 1970s — political programs not only as yet incompletely realized but also impossible to realize in their original mode — that nevertheless provide pleasure as well as pain. I consider class revolution as it dead-ends again and again not only in post-Fordist America but also in wayward daughters; second-wave feminism's lost possibilities; the unfinished, mutually intertwined projects of black emancipation and gay freedom. Derrida reminds us that with nostalgia, the *return* is acceptable provided that "the *revolt*, which initially inspired uprising, indignation, insurrection, revolutionary momentum, does not come back."[14] In the projects I take up here, particularly the visual texts, the 1970s appear as a "revolting" decade in a slightly different way: they glimmer forth as an embarrassment, as something that remains to be thought, as the text's indigestible material, and/or as a point of departure for resistance but not for grand revolution. In other words, "uprising, indignation, insurrection, revolutionary momentum" reappear, but not in a one-to-one correspondence with the original scenes of dissent that inspire them. The 1970s emerge as the scene of mass socialist, feminist, and gay-liberationist projects retrospectively loved or hated but also used as placeholders for thinking beyond the status quo of the 1990s and early years of the twenty-first century.

A simpler way of putting this might be: all of the texts I analyze in this book engage with historical "post-ness." All of this book's visual artists (though not all of the novelists whose work I intertwine with films and videos) were born between 1960 and 1970, meaning that they were at most young teenagers during the height of "the sixties," the period between the escalation of the Vietnam War in 1965 and the resignation of Richard Nixon in 1974. These artists, coming of age in the afterlife of the sixties, are the successors to mass movements whose most radical elements were often tamed, crushed, or detoured into individualistic projects as they were disseminated through the mainstream media. These artists are more likely to have participated in the more pragmatic, coalitional movements of the 1980s and 1990s — AIDS and queer activism, pro-sex and/or Third World/women of color feminism, and culture-jamming — than in projects that explicitly named capitalism as the root enemy. Their political experience unfolded in and moved outward from the 1980s, when the feminist, lesbian/gay, and AIDS movements met continental theory in the foundation of groups like the feminist Guerrilla Girls and the anti-homophobic ACT UP, in mergers that made mass culture itself the popular front for the semiotic warfare eventually known as "queering." In particular, they witnessed how ACT UP's understanding of AIDS as an "epidemic of signification" brought deconstructive reading practices and grassroots activism together, laying the groundwork for Queer Nation's clever detournements and for queer theory.[15] Indeed, most of these artists have worked within the academy as well as beyond it: all hold MFAS or PhDs and quite a few are professors. At the same time, though, they lived to see lesbian and gay identity mainstreamed and trivialized into just one of many possible "lifestyles"; AIDS normalized in the United States as new drugs made HIV a chronic rather than terminal condition and as it spread beyond urban gay enclaves; feminism morphed into a commodified "Girl Power" and "queer" into the premise for cable TV shows; ACT UP, Queer Nation, and the Guerrilla Girls archived in libraries and turned into museum exhibits; and queer theory become an academic subspecialty.

During the period I cover, the horizon of expectation has also changed dramatically for straight women, adult lesbians and gay men, and queer youth. It is now possible to imagine (1) each constituency as having a history; (2) each member of each adult constituency as having to negotiate a future in which "work time" and "family time" alternate or overlap, or more precisely, in which women have entered the wage-time of the professions, and lesbians and gay men have entered the repronormative time of parenting; and (3) each "queer youth" as having a future as a queer adult and/or a future in which he or she might move among gay, bi, or straight identities (or abandon them), or between or beyond genders. These changes seem praiseworthy to many, yet all of the works I treat — like our soldier-speaker above — view one or more of these forms of history and futurity without much enthusiasm, preferring to elaborate ways of living aslant to dominant forms of object-choice, coupledom, family, marriage, sociability, and self-presentation and thus out of synch with state-sponsored narratives of belonging and becoming. Even so, their project is less to negate than to prevaricate, inventing possibilities for moving through and with time, encountering pasts, speculating futures, and interpenetrating the two in ways that counter the common sense of the present tense.

Schematically, then, we could say this: these artists exist in a moment unavailable to the soldier-speaker, in which their history seems to be already written. Having encountered history (thought as collective movement for change) through the mass-mediated detritus of "the sixties," through their own participation in 1980s projects that struggled to find new forms of political action, and through the institutionalization and commodification of these projects, the artists I treat here engage the temporal politics of deconstruction (thought as an antirepresentational privileging of delay, detour, and deferral) to arrive at a different modality for living historically, or putting the past into meaningful and transformative relation with the present. Pure nostalgia for another revolutionary moment, their works seem to argue, will not do. But nor will its opposite, a purely futural orientation that depends on forgetting the past. Instead, the queerness of these artists consists in mining the present for signs of undetonated energy from past revolutions.

Crucially, the texts I discuss here see queerness as a powerful site from which we might read another kind of failure: not just that of progressive movements but the failure of Western "modernity" and the capitalist system that organizes it to completely overwrite or take up all of the meanings and energies that they aim for. Indeed, this is one version of what I mean by the word "bind": in Freud, "binding" is a way to manage excess; yet this very binding also produces a kind of rebound effect, in which whatever it takes to organize energy also triggers a release of energy that surpasses the original stimulus.[16] The artists I examine work from within what looks like a fully "bound," commodified postfeminist, postgay, postsocialist, postnational world in which we are told our problems are solved now that our market niche has been discovered. Within that world, the artists I discuss cherish not only history's flotsam and jetsam but also the excess generated by capital, its castoffs, and the episodes it wishes us to forget. Aware that the activist and artistic energies indexed and inspired by this material are also potentially available for recapture, they read and write for more than the infinite play of meaning, yet also for less than the total transformation of culture. In their own version of trench warfare, they collect and remobilize archaic or futuristic debris as signs that things have been and could be otherwise. That capitalism can always reappropriate this form of time is no reason to end with despair: the point is to identify "queerness" as the site of all the chance element that capital inadvertently produces, as well as the site of capital's potential recapture and incorporation of chance.[17]

Methodologically, their work involves something that might at first glance look rather rearguard or recalcitrant: close readings of the past for the odd detail, the unintelligible or resistant moment. Reading closely means fixating on that which resists any easy translation into present-tense terms, any "progressive" program for the turning of art into a cultural/historical magic bullet or toxin. To close read is to linger, to dally, to take pleasure in tarrying, and to hold out that these activities can allow us to look both hard and askance at the norm. But in the works I have gathered here, close reading is a way into history, not a way out of it, and itself a form of historiography and historical analysis.[18] These artists see any sign as an amalgam of the incommensurate: of dominant uses in the present, of obsolete meanings sensible only as a kind of radiation from the past, of new potential, and, more simply, of different points in time as meanings accrue and are shed. Like the speaker of "It's a Queer Time," their works all seize anachronisms large and small, each of which constitutes a fragment of the queer past: mining towns, Hollywood weepies, obsolete slang, macramé, women's lib, a pair of gold lamé disco shorts. They bring out the latent dreams and lost power that dwell within these silly details. Thus what I'd like to identify as perhaps the queerest commitment of my own book is also close reading: the decision to unfold, slowly, a small number of imaginative texts rather than amass a weighty archive of or around texts, and to treat these texts and their formal work as theories of their own, interventions upon both critical theory and historiography. Though I am trained as a literary critic, my texts are not primarily novels — even though Bertha Harris's *Lover*, Mary Shelley's *Frankenstein*, and Virginia Woolf's *Orlando* make appearances — but instead minor visual works by minor artists in a minor key. The cult texts I discuss are "minor" because they are contemporary, short and/or experimental, and made by emerging artists disconnected from large funds or dominant modes of production and distribution: where I do treat canonical works such as *Frankenstein*, I reverse the canonical/noncanonical relationship of priority, treating the canonical works as ways into noncanonical ones rather than vice versa. Many of the works I discuss are also made in ephemeral media or media subordinate to literature in academic English departments: film, video, and installation art.

Film and video are, in part, a minor literature because they are still associated with mindless (and hence overly embodied) absorption, and this charge holds particularly for the direct-to-video subgenres such as horror movies, thrillers, tearjerkers, home movies, and pornography, within which several of my texts traffic.[19] Mobilizing both fiction and a risky corporeality, the works I treat here may seem even more minor when considered as examples of a mode of historiography: if a few die-hard academic literary critics are still disinclined to see new media as literature, even fewer disciplinary historians tend to accept nondocumentary filmmaking as a method of doing history. Yet as Philip Rosen argues, film and disciplinary history have several things in common. As with any writing about other times, the photographic media negotiate the relationship between past and present: a photographic image consists of the trace of an object and presents that object in a moment other than the moment of recording. Photographic media, like works of historiography, inevitably posit "a different *when* from that of the spectator" and thus "participate in a cultural terrain of historicity," the latter term describing the state of being recognizably historical to a given public.[20] Rosen stresses that as with the texts written by disciplinary historians, the dominant modes they write in, and the way these modes construct and concatenate the objects of their text, filmic texts aim to put past and present into some stable relationship to one another even as the medium puts forth a model of reality as change itself.[21] The photographic media, in Rosen's analysis, are unthinkable without "history" — the modern assumptions that the present differs from the past and thus the past must be recorded, and the understanding of reality as protean, or at least potentially so. Last, Rosen claims, film intersects with the aspect of history that involves collective experience. As a medium, film emerged during the era of a reorganization of the social along temporal lines. There is much in the medium that mimics the segmenting and sequencing of time achieved in the era of industrial capitalism. As an institution, the mass cinema certainly borrowed the assembly line and other forms of rationalized time-space, but its institutionalization also depended on the corollary to organized labor time — organized leisure time.[22] Only when workers had disposable income and disposable time, only when the days and weeks of the masses were segmented into workdays and off-days, work-hours and off-hours, could such products as the matinee or the two-hour feature film become standard.

Film, then, creates a historically specific shared temporality, setting limits on how long the spectator can dwell on any one object or experience any one story, and thus socializing (or, we might say, binding) the gaze.[23] Thus, to pause on a given image, to repeat an image over and over, or to double an existing film in a remake or reshoot become productively queer ways to "desocialize" that gaze and intervene on the historical condition of seeing itself. The "time arts" of film, video, and installation are, then, a mode of both close reading and historiography, an optical and visceral unconscious encoding what is at once lost and foreclosed. Yet this aesthetic is not just desocializing but resocializing, as it also refuses to abandon the terrain of basic bodily need. Deleuze and Guattari's "What Is a

Minor Literature?," though it treats the question of writing in relation to a dominant national language, is a useful text for thinking about this queer politics of cinematic style, for this essay describes semiotic insurgency in terms of bodily pain and pleasure: teeth and tongues, bloated or hungering stomachs.[24] Deleuze and Guattari write that one form of minor literature dislodges referentiality by overloading the dominant language to the point of explosion via neologism, hypotaxis, or semantic overpacking, as in the work of James Joyce. This is a kind of "fat" aesthetic that rebinds fixed meanings and allows new associative chains to form. Another form strips the dominant language down to a bare minimum; parataxis, repetition, and pronominal ambiguity, among other techniques, rob language of the sensory pleasures of referentiality, as in the work of Gertude Stein or Samuel Beckett. This might be called a "thin" aesthetic and produces the same ultimate effect of restringing the signifying chain. In these models of gorging and purging, bloating and wasting the language, style — a mode of embodying language itself — also performs a relationship *to* rather than a mere duplication *of* what Foucault called discourse and New Historicists referred to as "cultural logic": in any given culture at any given time, the dominant paradigms within which not only art but also lived experience itself could take shape.[25] As several critics have argued, Foucauldian and New Historicist analyses have tended to flatten out the relationship between imaginative texts and the historical formations within which they are produced: whether imaginative texts are perceived as mere effects of larger cultural forces, as equal to them, or as indistinguishable from them, the result is a certain homogenizing of matters aesthetic. But style — by which I mean not only or not even primarily figures of speech but all of the compositional elements of literature, the visual arts, and live performance — encodes and enacts the bending of dominant form. Whether fat, thin, or something else, style neither transcends nor subsumes culture but pries it open a bit, rearranges or reconstitutes its elements, providing glimpses of an otherwise-being that is unrealizable as street activism or as blueprint for the future.

This book follows its texts' hunch that hermeneutics, the property of art as well as criticism, indirectly feeds the making of new social forms across space and time. What Dipesh Chakrabarty writes of the analytic social sciences aligned with Marx is also true for paranoid-style criticism in the humanities: that it attempts to "demystify ideology in order to produce a critique that looks toward a more just social order." To this Chakrabarty opposes the "hermeneutic tradition," which "produces a loving grasp of detail in search of an understanding of the diversity of life worlds. It produces what may be called 'affective histories' . . . [It] finds thought immediately tied to places and to particular forms of life. It is innately critical of the nihilism of that which is purely analytic."[26]

Of course, to do queer theory and textual criticism without some relationship to social justice seems impossible; merely to name queer texts as such registers an impulse toward not only understanding but promoting "the diversity of life worlds." But also, to take seriously that "a loving grasp of detail . . . produces affective histories" entails thinking that a bodily motion (a grasp, a clutch, a refusal to let go) might have something to do with knowing and making history — with continuities, contacts, and contradictions among past, present, and future — through both physical sensation and emotional response. And indeed, Chakrabarty's "History 2" seems especially ripe for queering: while History 1, the history-with-a-capital H that subtends Graves's poem, is part of "the modernizing narrative(s) of citizenship, bourgeois public and private . . . the nation-state" and especially the operations and perceived inevitability of capitalism, History 2 emerges within the logic of capital as a manifestation of its contradictions, frequently as seemingly archaic material not yet fully vanquished.[27] Lesbians and gays, John D'Emilio reminds us, emerged in just such a way: capitalism broke up the family economy, producing subjects available for projects other than the heterosexual coupling and reproduction necessary to sustain that economy — yet they were troped as people who had not yet arrived to civilization and/or individual maturity.[28] Moreover, History 2 consists especially of dispositions that enable other subject-positions than that of a worker. These are, Chakrabarty writes, "partly embodied in the person's bodily *habits*, in unselfconscious collective practices, in his or her reflexes about what it means to relate to objects in the world as a human being and together with other human beings in his given environment."[29] Put simply, History 2 suggests that habitus, Bourdieu's term encompassing both individual dispositions and collective modes of belonging sedimented by rituals of timing that accrete over time, not only consolidates but potentially disrupts dominant class positions.[30] Affective histories, then, are, in Chakrabarty's words, "narratives of human belonging where life forms, although porous to one another, do not seem exchangeable through a third term of equivalence such as abstract labor" (and, we might add, sexual identity).[31] They are not only or even primarily narratives but also practices of knowing, physical as well as mental, erotic as well as loving "grasps" of detail that do not accede to existing theories and lexicons but come into unpredictable contact with them: close readings that are, for most academic disciplines, simply too close for comfort.[32]

This commitment to overcloseness also informs my sense of another other-organizing term for this book: queer. To me, "queer" cannot signal a purely deconstructive move or position of pure negativity. In enjoining queers to operate as agents of dis- or de-figuration, critics like Lee Edelman (whose compelling *No Future* follows the Lacanian injunction that there is no sexual relationship) risk evacuating the messiest thing about being queer: the actual meeting of bodies with other bodies and with objects.[33] Contact with other bodies demands, and will generate, a figure, as happens over and over in the battle scenes of "It's a Queer Time." Indeed, sex may unbind selves and meanings, but these must relatively quickly rebound into fantasies, or the sexual agents would perish after only one release of energy. The fact that the secondary figure may be false, or in a belated relationship to the movement of desire, is less compelling to me than the fact that it is often so beautiful and weird. Thus my first book, *The Wedding Complex*, began with my fascination over a polymorphous white child finding the wedding, of all things, a suitable figure and focus for her multiple vectors of longing and repulsion, particularly in relation to her black nursemaid.[34] And *Time Binds* began when I understood someone else's self-presentation as drag, if drag can be seen as the act of plastering the body with outdated rather than just cross-gendered accessories, whose resurrection seems to exceed the axis of gender and begins to talk about, indeed talk back to, history. This drive to figure, along with our drive to love, survive, and mourn, is part of "our history," or at least our way of becoming and being historical. As much as sexual dissidents have suffered, lived as objects of contempt or oblivion, endured physical and emotional punishment, we have also risked experimentation with our bodies and those of others, with affiliation, and with new practices of hoping, demanding, and otherwise making claims on the future, and this has entailed an enormous commitment to the pleasure and power of figuration.

For instance, among all the blocks of the AIDS Memorial NAMES Quilt, that extraordinary tribute to those who died from complications of HIV and AIDS, only one persists in my visual memory: it said, "I had a FABUlous time," the word "fabulous" emerging from the label of a bright orange bottle of laundry detergent. Queers have, it is fair to say, fabricated, confabulated, told fables, and done so fabulously — in fat and thin art, and more — in the face of great pain. This is the legacy I wish to honor here, that of queers as close enough readers of one another and of dominant culture to gather up, literally, life's outtakes and waste products and bind them into fictitious but beautiful (w)holes. Because in taking care of our own we have also been forced to stay close, to wash one another's sweat-soaked sheets in Fab when no one else would, I am hard pressed to give up on sex and sociability, especially sociability and even erotics with the dead, as ways of knowing and making.

Each chapter in this book, then, explores not only the shrapnel of failed revolutions but also one or more moments when an established temporal order gets interrupted and new encounters consequently take place: whether or not I use the proper rhetorical terms, I focus on textual moments of asynchrony, anachronism, anastrophe, belatedness, compression, delay, ellipsis, flashback, hysteron-proteron, pause, prolepsis, repetition, reversal, surprise, and other ways of breaking apart what Walter Benjamin calls "homogeneous empty time."[35] Though Benjamin used this phrase to describe the spatialized, featureless calendrical time across which the history of nations supposedly marches forward, I take it to be the case that there are, in fact, multiple discursive regimes not reducible to nationhood that depend on empty homogeneous time. These consist not only of history "proper" but also coming out, consummation, development, domesticity, family, foreplay, genealogy, identity, liberation, modernity, the progress of movements — all key concepts for gay and lesbian as well as other social justice projects and theories, and all of which take their meanings from, and contribute to, a vision of time as seamless, unified, and forward moving.[36] Queer temporalities, visible in the forms of interruption I have described above, are points of resistance to this temporal order that, in turn, propose other possibilities for living in relation to indeterminately past, present, and future others: that is, of living historically.

After an introduction theorizing time and history in relation to one another, my first two chapters focus on the familial times that organize the durational and the everyday in supposedly universal or at least Western experience: generationality and intimacy.[37] Both focus on white women, who have traditionally been in charge of maintaining both intergenerational ties and the household rhythms that mark middle-class belonging. Chapter 1, "Bad Timing, Junk Inheritances," focuses on what I call *chrononormativity*, the interlocking temporal schemes necessary for genealogies of descent and for the mundane workings of domestic life. It centers on three texts by lesbians in the 1970s and 1990s—Cecilia Dougherty's eighty-minute experimental Pixelvision video *Coal Miner's Granddaughter* (1991), Diane Bonder's twenty-four-minute experimental 8mm video *The Physics of Love* (1998), and Bertha Harris's novel *Lover* (1976)—all of which use the wayward temporalities of the female body to foil both diachrony and synchrony and to articulate a working-class dyke politics of the chance encounter. In this chapter, the title phrase "Bad Timing, Junk Inheritances" names both the effect of modern, which is to say heteronormative, time on laboring and pleasuring bodies, and the strategies these artists use to imagine alternatives. Chapter 2, "Deep Lez," turns from temporality to the question of historiography, from the incomplete and flawed project of class solidarity to the afterlife of white second-wave feminism. This chapter focuses on Elisabeth Subrin's feature-length independent video *Shulie* (1997) alongside the art installations of Allyson Mitchell from 2003 to 2005, in order to proffer the classically queer practice of drag performance as one of these alternatives, that is, as a countergenealogical practice of archiving culture's throwaway objects, including the outmoded masculinities and femininities from which usable pasts may be extracted. My name for this practice, as well as for the set of feelings that informs it, is *temporal drag*.

The second part of this book focuses even more closely on historiography, in part to introduce the question of racial difference. Chapter 3, "Time Binds," moves outward again to coin a new term that can capture the centrality of pleasure, especially sexual pleasure, in queer practices of encountering and documenting the past. Establishing a genealogy of sorts for what I call *erotohistoriography*, this chapter moves from Mary Shelley's novel *Frankenstein* (1831) to Virginia Woolf's novel *Orlando* (1928) to the analytic centerpiece, Hilary Brougher's independent feature-length 35mm time-travel film *The Sticky Fingers of Time* (1997). This film, I argue, picks up on the latent racializing logic of both of the novels, for in *Sticky Fingers* a black woman both figures and blocks the sentimental translation of feelings across temporally disparate bodies, precisely because such time traveling seems to depend on white amnesia. Chapter 4, "Turn the Beat Around," takes up the problematic racializing logic apparent in my erotohistoriographic texts by turning to Isaac Julien's eight-minute film *The Attendant* (1992). In this work, I argue, Julien uses role-playing s/m as a formal device for a new historiography, one that alternates between suspense and surprise to break up the horrifying tableau of the slave auction, thus opening up the bodies of its actors toward a queer and black "bottom historiography" in which they might lay claim to the homoerotics of the slave trade on their own terms.

Taken together, these chapters are, in some ways, nothing more than a series of thought experiments. Looking backward, I can see how the crisscrossing energies of postcolonial studies, studies in medieval and other so-called premodern periods, and critical race theory made the questions of time's sexual politics (and the temporal politics of sex), if not inevitable, at least already asked in several different idioms. Since then, my own work has emerged in fits and starts alongside, and often in conversation with, many excellent rethinkings of temporality in the name of sexual dissidence, to which I feel deeply indebted.[38] It is my hope that there's still something to say on the subject (although as my writing schedule lagged further and further behind my best-laid plans, I decided that the book must somehow establish that belated is the new "now"). But what I can't offer is that which would, in any case, follow the kind of projective logic that queer cultural productions so often derail: a neat translation of theory into policy, a program for better and more radical living. Instead, I offer the most complicated gamble on tomorrow and thereafter — writing. To write, after all, is only to hazard the possibility that there will be a future of some sort, a "Queer Time" off the battlefield of everyday existence, in which the act of reading might take place some-how, somewhere. This book is my bet.

acknowledgments

Counting one's intellectual and personal debts is a bittersweet form of time travel, for it reminds me of both my great fortune and some losses along the way. François Meltzer's and Harry Harootunian's seminar "History and Literature" at the University of Chicago in 1991 got me thinking about *Orlando*, and portions of the paper I wrote for them appear in chapter 3, "Time Binds, or, Erotohistoriography." This book, though, really began with an invitation from Ann Pellegrini to write a review of Lynda Hart's *Between the Body and the Flesh* for GLQ, portions of which became chapter 4, "Turn the Beat Around." Lynda has since died of cancer, and though I did not know her well, her book launched me into thinking about sex and time in ways that make me wish I could have conversed with her. Luckily for me, Heather Love asked me, on the basis of that review, to contribute to a special issue of *New Literary History* on the "afterlives" of cultural studies. With faith and insight, she shepherded along the essay that eventually became part of chapter 2, "Deep Lez," and she continues to be a prince of a friend and colleague. At that point, too, I was lucky to be taking part in a reading/workshop group at New York University, whose members gave the draft a necessary and for the most part loving kick in the pants: I am especially indebted to Ann Cvetkovich, Lisa Duggan, Janet Jakobsen, Ann Pellegrini, and Patty White for their interventions and continued friendship, and to Ed Cohen and Douglas Crimp for attending to the piece on their visits to the workshop. Judith Halberstam had faith in the project early and saw several versions of things, always offering me her own special brand of enthusiasm and tough love. Her critique and editing, as well as those of José Muñoz and David Eng, were invaluable in the process of writing what became chapter 3 for their special issue of *Social Text* on the new queer studies. All three continue to help and inspire. Mike Goode generously shared the proofs of his book with me before chapter 3 went to press, and bore with my citing his dissertation in the meantime. Ellen Rooney, along with Anne Cheng and another anonymous reader, helped bring chapter 4 to fruition by way of publishing an earlier version of it in *differences*. Ann Cvetkovich and Annamarie Jagose kindly invited me to do a special issue of GLQ on queer temporalities; I am especially grateful to them for their help with the introduction, parts of which traveled to this book, and to the contributors to that special issue for their ideas.

Each of these chapters owes a great deal, too, to audiences at conferences and invited lectures. I want particularly to thank audiences at the University of California, Berkeley's Center for Gender and Sexuality, especially Daniel Boyarin and Michael Lucey; Penn State University English Department's "Rising Scholars" Symposium, especially Scott Herring; my Dartmouth Humanities Institute "Futures of American Studies" plenary session, especially Don Pease; the University of Pennsylvania Speaker Series on Sexuality, especially Heather Love (and Amy Kaplan for the tough questions); and the Harvard University "Sexualities across the Disciplines" Group, especially Brad Epps and Orit Halpern; as well as fellow participants and audience members at the "Disciplining Time" roundtable of the Pembroke Center for Research on Women at Brown University, especially Jane Elliott and Rebecca Schneider. I owe a great deal, also, to audiences closer to home, at the UC Davis Department of English Fall Lecture, Performance Studies Research Cluster (special thanks to Karen Shimakawa and Sophie Volpp), Queer Research Cluster, and English Department Scholars' Symposium.

Beyond those captive audiences, I've been very lucky to have colleagues who are friends enough to read drafts of things and offer their comments, encouragement, and inspiring examples. Molly McGarry still reigns supreme in this category; her generosity, loyalty, smarts, and sense of fun have sustained me more than she knows. Steven Blevins, Peter Coviello, Rebecca Gordon, Dana Luciano, H. N. Lukes, Timothy Morton, Ann Pellegrini, Alison Shonkwiler, Kathryn Bond Stockton, and Kara Thompson are friends, comrades, colleagues, and my go-to people for stupidity checks, though when they are done with anything, the remaining stupidity is solely my own. Stephen Bruhm, Michael Cobb, Gayatri Gopinath, Bishnu Ghosh, E. L. McCallum, Marcia Ochoa, Michael O'Rourke, Juana María Rodriguez, Michael Snediker, Bethany Schneider, Kat Sugg, Karen Tongson, Kate Thomas, and Mikko Tuhkanen also lent me their minds and hearts at various moments, knowingly or not. Eileen Joy patiently engaged with what became chapter 4 on the blog "In the Medieval Middle." Jean-Christophe Castelli of Good Machine Productions kindly spoke with me when I first began thinking about *The Sticky Fingers of Time*, and for that I thank him.

At UC Davis, I've been fortunate to have smart colleagues whom I like very much. Margaret Ferguson has been an exemplary mentor through this stage of my career, and David Robertson and David Simpson looked after this book's emergence early on. I'm grateful to all the other members of my department too, but particularly to Seeta Chaganti, Joshua Clover, Lucy Corin, Greg Dobbins, Fran Dolan, Mark Jerng, Kathleen Frederickson, Desirée Martín, Colin Milburn, Elizabeth Carolyn Miller, Linda Morris, Catherine Robson, Parama Roy, Matthew Stratton, David Van Leer, Claire Waters, Evan Watkins, Karl Zender, and Mike Ziser for their generosity with matters intellectual, administrative, or both. Our department staff, headed up by Terry Antonelli and then Darla Tafoya, contributed to my research program in countless ways. In general, the University of California and the Davis campus have been extraordinarily supportive: I could not have written this book without a President's Research Fellowship in the Humanities in 2006–7, a UC Davis Chancellor's Fellowship from 2004 to 2009, and several UC Davis Small Grants for Research. A fellowship at the Penn Humanities Forum at the University of Pennsylvania in 1999–2000 also enabled me to complete a first draft of chapter 2, the first piece I wrote for this book.

I thank my graduate research assistants at UC Davis, too, for their alienated labor and scholarly input: Melissa Bender, April Boyd, Catherine Fung, Anett Jessop, Samaine Lockwood, Vanita Reddy, Melissa Strong, Julie Wilhelm, and especially the magnificent Kara Thompson all helped with this book immensely. Katrin Greim did some important archival sleuthing as my predoctoral fellow at UC Davis. Students in my graduate seminar "Sexuality and Temporality in Twentieth-Century American Literature" in 2005 and 2009 pushed my thinking. Two undergraduates, Meg Kavanagh and Selene Stewart, asked the right questions a long time ago. Finally, the artists I've worked with have been unstintingly kind and patient: I'm grateful to Cecilia Dougherty, Sharon Hayes, Allyson Mitchell, Nguyen Tan Hoang, and Elisabeth Subrin for allowing me to print images of their work and helping me obtain them, Mona Jimenez for images from *The Physics of Love*, Hans Sundquist at Video Data Bank for images from *Shulie*, Tamsin Wright for images from *The Attendant*, and to Nick Penrose at UC Davis Academic Techology Services for his work on several other images.

Ken Wissoker has been an amazing editor, unfailingly kind and efficient; the staff at Duke University Press has made producing this book a pleasure. I also want to extend my thanks to Christopher Nealon and another anonymous reader for Duke for their extremely helpful comments on the manuscript. Lauren Berlant gets credit for helping me get over myself and approach Ken with my second book. And special thanks to Lynn Langmade for the index.

Finally, I am lucky to have such generous friends: here in San Francisco, godmamas Lori Lamma and Rachel Robson, honorary aunties Liz Rodriguez and Melissa Green, and fellow lesbian mamas Heather Hadlock and Kathy Veit have saved me from any number of time binds. Audrey Genet, Birgitte Gilliland, Emily Hilton, Daphne Magnawa, Kylie Owen, Jenny Sagstrom-Warnes, and Lisa Schiller Tehrani have also performed heroic rescues and plied me with cocktails. Sarah Lawton and Alexandra Gordon have given advice and comfort. My dear Oberlin friends A. K. Summers, Deb Schwartz, Annie Piper, and Camilla Enders continue to inspire. Then there are those who have had the misfortune of trying to make *famille* with me while I am on "book time." B. J. Wray was an early sufferer and I thank her for her fortitude. Amy Robinson reminded me of what else there was. Diane Bonder, whose life was cut short by cancer, was a steady presence, and I miss both her and the work she could have done. My parents and their partners, Caroline Freeman and Glenn Hoffman, and Donald C. and Margaret Freeman, buoyed me up. My brother Roger Freeman and his partner Mi-Sun gave help without being asked. Jac Cherry deserves a medal, or at least my undying and humble thanks. And Caroline "Firefly" Freeman-Cherry has taught me everything I know about slowing down. To Jac and Firefly, especially, I owe the world. And a bit more of my time.

Portions of this manuscript have appeared elsewhere as follows: preface: "Still After," in the special issue "After Sex?," ed. Andrew Parker and Janet Halley, *South Atlantic Quarterly* 106, no. 3 (summer 2007): 495–500; introduction: "Introduction," in the special issue "Queer Temporalities," ed. Elizabeth Freeman, GLQ: *A Journal of Lesbian and Gay Studies* 13, nos. 2–3 (winter/spring 2007): 159–76; chapter 2: "Deep Lez: Temporal Drag and the Specters of Feminism," in the special issue "Is There Life After Identity Politics?," ed. Bill Albertini, Ben Lee, Heather Love, Mike Millner, Ken Parille, Alice Rutkowski, and Bryan Wagner, *New Literary History* 31, no. 4 (autumn 2000): 727–44; chapter 3: "Time Binds, or,

Erotohistoriography," in the special issue "What's Queer about Queer Studies Now?," ed. David Eng, Judith Halberstam, and José Esteban Muñoz, *Social Text* 84–85 (October 2005): 57–68; and chapter 4: "Turn the Beat Around: Sadomasochism, Temporality, History," *differences* 19, no. 1 (2008): 32–70.

introduction: Queer and Not Now

In Nguyen Tan Hoang's video *K.I.P.* (2002), a young man faces a past
that may or may not be his. The video opens with a series of grainy,
flickering, blurry shots of body parts flashing across the screen; eventually
it's clear that the scene shows two white men having sex. The men's
shaggy haircuts and sideburns and the low-res quality of the video images
suggest that the period is the 1970s or early 1980s. For the full four-
minute duration of Nguyen's piece the scene skips and stutters, with
dropouts, black frames, or smears of color occasionally interrupting the
action. The slight distortion of the images, occasional glare, and falling
static "snow" indicate that we are not seeing the scene directly but rather
through the curved glass front of an old-fashioned cathode ray tube television. Reflected on the surface of the TV monitor floats the ghostlike face
of a young male — the director himself, as it turns out — expression blank,
glasses glinting a bit, mouth occasionally opening slightly, as if to eat, to
suck, to speak, or as if simply surprised (see figure 1).

K.I.P. explicitly connects experimental video's temporal dissonance to
queer sexual dissidence: it links the malleability of filmic time to the
sexually experimental body. To be sure, it has any number of qualities that
are merely generic to experimental film and video. Eschewing the narrative conventions of classical Hollywood cinema, this genre foregrounds
the medium's status as a "time art" and emphasizes the constructedness of
its images, the materiality of the production process, and/or the historical contingency of its apparatus.[1] But Nguyen's piece also speaks to mass-
popular ways of using filmic temporality to expand bodily possibilities,
and of using the body's rhythms to reimagine what film can say and do.
The original porn tape's intended audience of home video watchers, who
may or may not have been gay but were certainly participating in the
stigmatized sexual practice of viewing gay sex acts, had presumably got-
ten their pleasures from just the kind of remix that video technology itself enables. For they could zoom the tape backward to the money shot
as often as they wanted, witnessing multiple climaxes far beyond the

1. Still from *K.I.P.*
Copyright Nguyen Tan Hoang, 2002. Courtesy of the artist.

capacity of the male body to produce them. And apparently this is exactly what these viewers did. The temporal reshufflings particular to the fragmented sex scene between the two hunky actors actually came from a specific history of consumption, rather than solely from Nguyen's manipulations at the level of production, as is generally the case with experimental film.[2] In his notes for *K.I.P.*, which appear on the DVD of his complete works, Nguyen describes finding a videotape titled "Kip Noll Superstar, Part I" (1981), a compilation of the then-iconic porn star Kip Noll's best sex scenes put together by the prolific pornography director William Higgins.[3] Nguyen's copy of the tape, which he reports renting at Tower Video in San Francisco's Castro district, was damaged. It had apparently been rewound too many times to the most explicit sex scene, so that the images now skipped and repeated, and entire frames were blurred or erased. In other words, "the hottest part of the tape," as Nguyen's note puts it, appeared in his viewing of it as instances returning to themselves over and over, and as a series of leaps across the bodily gestures or sexual choreographies that we are ordinarily supposed to experience as smooth, continuous, and natural.

K.I.P., then, follows video pornography's logic of interactive spectatorship: the reflected face becomes a figure for the way this genre enables the viewer to derail the normative progression of sexual intercourse from foreplay to penetration to climax. In fact, Nguyen's reshoot and the overlay of an almost motionless face disconnect gesture from response, action from consequence, by separating them in time.[4] Far from consolidating the spectacle and naturalizing power differentials, *K.I.P.* suggests, the medium of video, and especially the genre of pornography, produce powerful sexual disorientation—not the least of which is dis-integrating the so-called sex act (as if there could be only one). In keeping with this derangement of bodies and pleasures, even Nguyen's title breaks down the unity of "Kip" Noll's muscular body into the alphabetic, recombinatorial "K.I.P." The reshoot itself then uses this logic of fragmentation and remixing to open up gaps in the sexual dyad, inviting in not only a third party in the figure of the spectator but also, potentially, any number of viewers or even participants. In short, Nguyen seems to recognize that a hiccup in sequential time has the capacity to connect a group of people beyond monogamous, enduring couplehood—and this awareness, I would argue, is crucial to revitalizing a queer politics and theory that until fairly recently has focused more on space than on time.[5]

By portraying the reciprocal derangement of bodies and sequences, *K.I.P.* offers a through-the-looking-glass view of how time *binds* a socius. By "binds," I mean to invoke the way that human energy is collated so that it can sustain itself.[6] By "time binds," I mean something beyond the obvious point that people find themselves with less time than they need. Instead, I mean that naked flesh is bound into socially meaningful embodiment through temporal regulation: binding is what turns mere existence into a form of mastery in a process I'll refer to as *chrononormativity*, or the use of time to organize individual human bodies toward maximum productivity. And I mean that people are bound to one another, engrouped, made to feel coherently collective, through particular orchestrations of time: Dana Luciano has termed this *chronobiopolitics*, or "the sexual arrangement of the time of life" of entire populations.[7]

Chrononormativity is a mode of implantation, a technique by which institutional forces come to seem like somatic facts. Schedules, calendars, time zones, and even wristwatches inculcate what the sociologist Evitar Zerubavel calls "hidden rhythms," forms of temporal experience that seem natural to those whom they privilege.[8] Manipulations of time convert historically specific regimes of asymmetrical power into seemingly ordinary bodily tempos and routines, which in turn organize the value and meaning of time. The advent of wage work, for example, entailed a violent retemporalization of bodies once tuned to the seasonal rhythms of agricultural labor.[9] An even broader description of chrononormativity appears in Pierre Bourdieu's discussion of habitus—a social group's cultivated set of gestural and attitudinal dispositions. Bourdieu argues that "the durably installed generative principle of regulated improvisations" structuring the norms of embodiment, personhood, and activity in a culture takes shape within the rhythms of gift exchange.[10] For Bourdieu, cultural competence and thus belonging itself are matters of timing, of coming to inhabit a culture's expectations about the temporal lapses between getting and giving such that they seem inborn. More recently, Judith Butler has shown how the rhythms of gendered performance—specifically, repetitions—accrete to "freeze" masculinity and femininity into timeless truths of being.[11] Zerubavel's "hidden rhythms," Bourdieu's "habitus," and Butler's "gender performativity" all describe how repetition engenders identity, situating the body's supposed truth in what Nietzsche calls "monumental time," or static existence outside of historical movement.[12] But Bourdieu alone allows us to see that subjectivity emerges in part through mastering the cultural norms of withholding, delay, surprise, pause, and knowing when to stop—through mastery over certain forms of time. In temporal manipulations that go beyond pure repetition, his work suggests, institutionally and culturally enforced rhythms, or timings, shape flesh into legible, acceptable embodiment.

In chronobiopolitics, this process extends beyond individual anatomies to encompass the management of entire populations: people whose individual bodies are synchronized not only with one another but also with larger temporal schemae experience belonging itself as natural. In a chronobiological society, the state and other institutions, including representational apparatuses, link properly temporalized bodies to narratives of movement and change. These are teleological schemes of events or strategies for living such as marriage, accumulation of health and wealth for the future, reproduction, childrearing, and death and its attendant rituals. Indeed, as the anthropologist John Borneman's work clarifies, so-called personal histories become legible only within a state-sponsored timeline.[13] This timeline tends to serve a nation's economic interests, too. In the United States, for instance, states now license, register, or certify birth (and thus citizenship, eventually encrypted in a Social Security ID for taxpaying purposes), marriage or domestic partnership (which privatizes caretaking and regulates the distribution of privatized property), and death (which terminates the identities linked to state benefits, redistributing these benefits through familial channels), along with sundry privileges like driving (to jobs and commercial venues) and serving in the military (thus incurring state expenditures that often serve corporate interests). In the eyes of the state, this sequence of socioeconomically "productive" moments is what it means to have a life at all. And in zones not fully reducible to the state — in, say, psychiatry, medicine, and law — having a life entails the ability to narrate it not only in these state-sanctioned terms but also in a novelistic framework: as event-centered, goal-oriented, intentional, and culminating in epiphanies or major transformations.[14] The logic of time-as-productive thereby becomes one of serial cause-and-effect: the past seems useless unless it predicts and becomes material for a future. These teleologies of living, in turn, structure the logic of a "people's" inheritance: rather than just the transfer of private property along heteroreproductive lines, inheritance becomes the familial and collective *legacy* from which a group will draw a properly political future — be it national, ethnic, or something else.

Chronobiopolitics harnesses not only sequence but also cycle, the dialectical companion to sequence, for the idea of time as cyclical stabilizes its forward movement, promising renewal rather than rupture. And as Julia Kristeva argues, the gender binary organizes the meaning of this and other times conceived as outside of — but symbiotic with — linear time.[15] Kristeva claims that Woman, as a cultural symbol, comes to be correlated with the endless returns of cyclical time, as well as the stasis of monumental time: the figure of Woman supplements the historically specific nation-state with appeals to nature and eternity. Luciano dates a particularly Anglo-American version of this arrangement to the early nineteenth century, when "separate spheres" were above all temporal: the repetitions and routines of domestic life supposedly restored working men to their status as human beings responding to a "natural" environment, renewing their bodies for reentry into the time of mechanized production and collective national destiny.[16] In the wake of industrialization in the United States, she writes, mourning was newly reconceptualized as an experience outside of ordinary time, as eternal, recurrent, even sacred — and so, I would argue, were any number of other affective modes. Mid-nineteenth-century writers figured maternal love, domestic bliss, romantic attachments, and eventually even bachelorhood as havens from a heartless world and, more importantly, as sensations that moved according to their own beat. The emerging discourse of domesticity, especially, inculcated and validated a set of feelings — love, security, harmony, peace, romance, sexual satisfaction, motherly instincts — in part by figuring them as timeless, as primal, as a human condition located in and emanating from the psyche's interior. In this sense, the nineteenth century's celebrated "heart," experienced by its owner as the bearer of archaic or recalcitrant sensations, was the laboring body's double, the flip side of the same coin of industrialization. The fact that the wage system privatized domestic activities also meant that they could be experienced as taking place in a different time zone. In the home, time bound persons "back" to "nature," a state of innocence that could be understood as restorative only if women's domestic labor were fully effaced. If time becomes history through its organization into a series of discrete units linked by cause and effect, this organization in turn retrospectively constructs an imagined plenitude of "timeless" time to which history can return and regroup.

Thus the monumental or sacred time that Kristeva also describes as "Women's Time" does not escape chronobiopolitical regulation either. Luciano's crucial extension of and intervention into Kristeva's work demonstrates that nations and other public forms of engroupment depend not only on progressive, linear time and the cyclical time that buttresses it but also on the illusion that time can be suspended. Pauses or interruptions in the routinized rhythms of everyday life, in the sequences expected to unfold naturally from one another, become the material for a peoplehood experienced as pre- or a-political, as merely human. In describing the narrative texture of modern nationality, Homi Bhabha too refines the distinction between linear-historical time and the more static times of cyclic and monumental time: he describes the dialectic between a "pedagogical" time in which historical events seem to accrete toward a given destiny, and a "performative" time in which a people recreates itself as such through taking up a given activity simultaneously.[17] Soliciting the masses to stop and feel together, activities done in tandem with strangers seen and unseen, like singing the national anthem or watching the Olympics, revivify national belonging as a matter of shared emotion rather than civic action. Bhabha claims that within performative strategies of national belonging, fissures can open up to suggest other historical moments or ways of living. And indeed, as Luciano points out, in counterpoint to the time of factory life in the antebellum United States, a set of "performative" sensations and corporeal forms was imagined, or even felt, not just as a contribution to national destiny but also as an impediment to or bulwark against the pedagogical time of history proper. Mourning and romance, empathy and affection were not segmented into clock-time, even if highly ritualized public performances like courtship and grieving did follow timelines; the sentiments and their perceived rhythms countered "work time" even as they were also a product of it. So did the time of specific bodily needs. As Eli Zaretsky writes, "The family, attuned to the natural rhythms of eating, sleeping, and child care, can never be wholly synchronized with the mechanized tempo of industrial capitalism."[18] Emotional, domestic, and biological tempos are, though culturally constructed, somewhat less amenable to the speeding up and micromanagement that increasingly characterized U.S. industrialization.

Time's Wounds

As Luciano puts it, in the dialectic between linear-national history and cyclical-domestic time, history appears as damaged time; time appears as the plentitude that heals the historical subject.[19] Time, then, not only "binds" flesh into bodies and bodies into social but also appears to "bind" history's wounds. But the figure of damaged time also became the signature of late-nineteenth-century decadence and modernism. Of course, the appearance of sexual identity as a field of knowledge and self-description was part of a more general movement toward the abstraction and taxonomizing of human qualities, the reification of both space and time, that began with industrial capitalism.[20] In this sense, homosexual identity was simply the product *of* a historical moment in time. But sexual dissidents have also in many ways been produced by, or at least emerged in tandem with, a sense of "modern" temporality. The double-time of the late nineteenth and early twentieth centuries was somewhat different from the highly gendered, sacred time of antebellum domesticity: rather than evoking timelessness, it trafficked in signs of fractured time. Its signature was interruptive archaisms: flickering signs of other historical moments and possibilities that materialized time as always already wounded. Thus gay men, lesbians, and other "perverts" have also served as figures *for* history, for either civilization's decline or a sublimely futuristic release from nature, or both.[21] Here we might cite, for instance, the poet Renée Vivien's Sapphic vampires, the novelist Djuna Barnes's hybrid animal/child/lesbian Robin Vote, or T. S. Eliot's sexually alienated J. Alfred Prufrock declaring himself to be "Lazarus, come from the dead!"[22] Sexual dissidents became figures for and bearers of new corporeal sensations, including those of a certain counterpoint between now and then, and of occasional disruptions to the sped-up and hyperregulated time of industry.

Freud's concept of the unconscious acknowledged exactly this doubled time: it relocated modernity's temporal splittings into the psyche's interior (and thus from their moorings in historically specific changes). Freud theorized the "normal" self as a temporal phenomenon, the ego as a manifestation of displaced and disavowed past experiences. The Freudian unconscious refused to make an experience obsolete or to relegate it to the past; within the Freudian paradigm that Laplanche and Pontalis term *Nachträglichkeit*, or deferred action, the mind recorded the signs of an event when the subject could not consciously process its meaning, and preserved these signs for future uses.[23] So even as an emerging consumer market and what Foucault calls the "incitement to discourse" about sexual types put an ever greater premium on novelty, the interlaced models of the unconscious and *Nachträglichkeit* insisted on a certain semiotic recalcitrance. And in Freud, what we might now claim as a queer intempestivity evidenced itself in and with the body as well as the emotions. The repetitions and returns that disturb the Freudian subject appear not as pictorial or narrative memories per se but in forms that are at once metaphorical and *visceral*: a "slip of the tongue," repetitive bodily acts, lingering symptoms with no apparent physical etiology. In this sense, the "perverse" Freudian body itself became the scene of and catalyst for encountering and redistributing the past.

This was particularly true of the body erotic. As early as the eighteenth century, Henry Abelove and Paul Morrison have argued, erotic life began to assume the contours of mechanized productivity, and specific sexual practices came to be seen as "foreplay," acceptable en route to intercourse but not as a substitute for it.[24] In Freud's update, these practices were remnants of childhood itself, not merely adult means to an orgasmic end. Psychologizing what had once been biological paradigms, Freud identified taboo sexual practices as normal childhood behavior in which the pathological adult subject was simply stuck or frozen due to an inability to remember, conceptualize, or narrate past events. Orality, anality, fetishism, and so on became, in the Freudian itinerary, places that children visited on their way to reproductive, genital heterosexuality, but not places to stay for long.

This stubborn lingering of pastness (whether it appears as anachronistic style, as the reappearance of bygone events in the symptom, or as arrested development) is a hallmark of queer affect: a "revolution" in the old sense of the word, as a turning back. Heather Love's *Feeling Backward*, for instance, astutely diagnoses the "backwards" emotions elaborated by artists for whom the birth of the modern homosexual identity-form was constraining rather than liberating: shame, passivity, melancholy, and recoil, to name but a few, were ways of refusing the progressive logic by which becoming ever more visible was correlated with achieving ever more freedom.[25] Late-nineteenth-century perverts, melancholically attached to obsolete erotic objects or fetishes they ought to have outgrown, or repeating unproductive bodily behaviors over and over, also used pastness to resist the commodity-time of speedy manufacture and planned obsolescence.

History's Holes

Interestingly, the dialectic between time and history has been characteristic of not only Euro-American modernity but also queer theory, or at least one particular caricature of queer theory. "Ludic" queer theory, as it has been called, tends to align itself with deconstruction, with the play of signifiers and the possibilities opened up by understanding identities as relational, constructed, and endlessly detoured to meanings outside themselves.[26] Insofar as deconstruction depends on the endless penetration of the whole by the other, current meanings by prior ones, it has dismantled the fiction of a time fully present to itself and accessible as such; its detotalization of time has been useful to a queer theory concerned with desire and fantasy. But according to some critics, ludic queer theory has not always concerned itself with history understood as a collective consciousness of the significance, singularity, and sheer pain of exploitation, or as collective agency toward relief from that pain.[27] A more somber queer theory, on the other hand, tends to align itself with Marxism, with social conflict and sufferings inflicted by powerful groups, with a politics attuned to need—with histories and even with History.[28] But this version of queer theory has not always attended to the vagaries of temporality, as practiced and as embodied, that make new conceptions of "the historical" possible.

Jacques Derrida's *Specters of Marx* has been a key text for bringing these two strains of queer theory into conversation, insofar as it explicates the "hauntological" properties of Marxist thought: Marx, Derrida argues, theorizes an ethics of responsibility toward the other across time—toward the dead or toward that which was impossible in a given historical moment, each understood as calls for a different future to which we cannot but answer with imperfect and incomplete reparations. In this Marx, the present is thereby always split, but split by prior violence and future possibility rather than simply by the nature of signification.[29] As Derrida argues, we are thereby bound not only to history (that is, we do not make it just as we please), but also, and crucially, to the other who always takes precedence and has priority and thus splits our selfhood, detours our forward-moving agency. Here, time does not heal but further fissures history.

Specters of Marx, then, contributes to queer theory the idea that time can produce new social relations and even new forms of justice that counter the chrononormative and chronobiopolitical. This call for a more sensate, sensory historical method also appears in other important critical theories, whether explicitly Marxist or not: Walter Benjamin's concept of "shock," for instance, suggests that modernity reorganizes the human sensorium.[30] Raymond Williams's phrase "structures of feeling" suggests that social change can be felt as well as cognitively apprehended, and that it appears alongside dominant structures in the uncanny persistence of obsolete formations and the proleptic, partial emergence of new ones.[31] Jameson's famous dictum that "history is what hurts" offers another example: in his analysis, large-scale social structures set limits on individual desires, even as works of imaginative fiction repress the fact of those limits and provide formal resolutions to irresolvable social conflicts.[32] In Lyotard's formulation of the *differend* is yet another version of history as hurt: occurrences earn their historical eventness by delegitimating both the existing methods for knowing the past and the forms that that knowledge can take: in this sense, traumatic experiences productively humiliate and discombobulate the knower into new epistemologies, or at least into feelings that intimate the possibility of new modes of apprehension.[33] Yet none of these formulations engages with what might be called vulgar physical pleasure. Even Derrida consistently displaces his radically porous ghost-host into a visual and occasionally aural economy (seeing and being seen, calling and responding), and *Specters of Marx* also insists that the ghost can only be, at best, a prosthetic body.

Indeed, in contemporary critical theory the body itself seems an impossible object with which or through which to think historically. Jameson suggests that "body theory" is actually the symptom of a certain loss of time itself, specifically the deeply comparativist time of modernity.[34] In the moment of modernity's emergence, he argues, prior modes of production had survived alongside industrial capitalism to produce a sense of living in two different time zones. There was something to compare modern temporality *to*, though Luciano's work importantly suggests that the alternative times were not so much prior to industrialization as they were co-constructed within it. For Jameson, temporal heterogeneity has been replaced by the instaneity of the Internet, cell phones, and so on, and "it seems clear enough that when you have nothing left but your own temporal present, it follows that you have nothing left but your own body."[35] To do body theory, he suggests, is to reduce history to something timeless and permanent, to heal history with bodily plenitude in the way Luciano describes denizens of antebellum sentimental culture doing — and unfortunately, gender and queer theory are Jameson's straw-girl examples of disciplines clinging to the fiction of a timeless, monolithic referent. Yet Jameson also reminds us that the body is an insistently nonpresent, nonunified nonentity: "We experience the body through our experience of the world and of other people, so that it is perhaps a misnomer to speak of the body at all as a substantive with a definite article, unless we have in mind the bodies of others, rather than our own phenomenological referent."[36] Queer theory and feminist theory have answered to calls for poststructuralist and affective historiography by foregrounding *just this kind* of body, that is, one intelligible only through its encounters with other bodies. *Pace* Jameson, though, what makes queer theory *queer* as opposed to simply deconstructionist is also its insistence on risking a certain vulgar referentiality, its understanding of the sexual encounter as precisely the body and ego's undoing.[37]

Queer theory, then, pays attention to gaps and losses that are both structural and visceral: the all-too-real limits presented by the stigmatization of AIDS, by violence against lesbians and gays, by the unbearable heaviness of the gender binary. Queer theory also describes how specific forms of knowing, being, belonging, and embodying are prevented from emerging in the first place, often by techniques that intimately involve the body. However, even in these descriptions pain has taken center stage. Queer melancholia theory, an especially lush account of how the mourning process bodies forth gendered subjects, insists that subjectivity itself is a record of partings and foreclosures, cross-hatched with the compensatory forms these absences engender. Within this paradigm, queer becoming-collective-across-time and even the concept of futurity itself are predicated upon injury — separations, injuries, spatial displacements, preclusions, and other negative and negating forms of bodily experience — or traumas that precede and determine bodiliness itself, that make matter into bodies. This paradigm is indebted, via Judith Butler's *The Psychic Life of Power*, not only to Derrida but also to Freud's theory that a bodily *imago* and eventually the ego itself emerge from raw suffering. With Freud, we gain the understanding that hurt is what morphologizes; it congeals inchoate sensations into personally and culturally legible forms of embodiment — we might even say that to Freud, hurt is what histories. In "On Narcissism," Freud describes how the libido invests in an uncomfortable local sensation such as a toothache, by which means it doubles back upon itself to delineate body parts as such; Freud suggests that the genitals are perhaps the most insistent locale for such hypochondriacal fixations.[38] In "The Ego and the Id," he argues that from within this Möbius loop of libidinal self-attachment to sensitive areas, an increasingly unified sense of bodily contours emerges, and these contours materialize the ego that is "at first, a bodily ego," an interconnected set of perceived surfaces and boundaries.[39] Opening these terms out into the social, we might think of engroupment — the collective form of the ego forged beyond familial ties — as engendered by this process as well as by, or alongside, chrononormativity. Bodily experiences of pain inflicted on a population, or indeed the agony of being socially reduced to a misreading of one's own body, may inform queer social contours, a wounded morphology of the social following a wounded morphology of the individual. Individual bodily *imagos*, in short, are nascent collective and historical formations in that they may arise from contingent, institutionalized forms of hurt that are experienced simultaneously and survive over time yet *cannot be reduced to* the social relations of the mode of economic production. We might call these collectively held morphologies the raw material for a queerly inflected consciousness that can hold deconstructionism and historical materialism in productive tension.

But why is it that even in queer theory, only pain seems so socially and theoretically generative? Turning back to Freud, we might ask why physical sensation, which he sees as the ground for body and psyche, must always be unpleasant, and even why this originary bodily displeasure is eventually recast as the kind of tumescence or engorgement that only penises experience. In order to become "ego," that is, Freud's wound must effectively be turned inside out into a phallus: as Judith Butler puts it, "The gaping hole in the mouth, the panoply of organic and hypochondriacal ailments, are synthesized in and summarized by the prototypical male genitals."[40] But even Butler's revision of Freud via the lesbian phallus only suggests that the primary tumescence from which the ego emerges might be productively relocated onto arms, hipbones, and other sites as a way of theorizing a lesbian ego; it doesn't challenge the phallicizing construction of "sensation" itself. Where goes that interestingly aching hole, symptom of a certain desire to be filled up by—let us risk—a vulgar referent?

One figure for that hole might be the open mouth of *K.I.P.*'s simultaneously mourning and lusting spectator, who seems to want to have sex with history—with dead men, with men older than he, with an era and place barred by both linear time and racial politics. Thus *K.I.P.*'s hauntological imaginings actually revise and go beyond *Specters of Marx*—and much of the queer work that has followed from it—by centering on erotic pleasure. In this light, we can reread *K.I.P.* as more than a gay-affirmative experimental film: it is also a queer hauntological exercise. For Nguyen's videographic double exposure exploits *Kip Noll*'s user-generated discombobulation of *filmic* and *erotic* sequence, in order to jam *historical* sequence. In the remake, the reflection of Nguyen's own face hovers over a scene of plenitude he did not witness directly, a time that he never experienced but nevertheless clearly mourns for: the exuberant moment when urban gay men in the 1970s and early 1980s could pursue and enjoy casual sex without latex. Too young, too racialized, too "foreign"—that is, too queer by more than half—Nguyen could not have literally joined the pre-AIDS white urban gay male scene for which *Kip Noll, Superstar* is a metonym. But by superimposing his own image *as* a spectator onto a scene already containing a trace of earlier spectators, with that trace in turn present only in the negative as gaps and repetitions, Nguyen figuratively joins a community of past- and present-tense viewers, some of whom we can presume died in the AIDS epidemic or are now seropositive. And he does so without ever presenting those people or that community as complete or fully apprehensible, for "K.I.P.," I presume, is a riff not only on Kip Noll's name but also on R.I.P., or "Rest in Peace," indicating both the desire to enliven the dead and the understanding that this is never wholly possible.[41] *K.I.P.* acknowledges that while physical contact across time may be—like the sexual relation itself—impossible, the very wish for it demands and enacts formal strategies and political stances worth taking seriously.

Longing produces modes of both belonging and "being long," or persisting over time.[42] Yet this is more than desire, for desire is a form of belief in the referential object that the subject feels s/he lacks and that would make him or her whole (and insofar as this referential object is often posited in terms of a *lost* object, desire is "historiographical," a way of writing that object into the present). Erotics, on the other hand, traffics less in belief than in encounter, less in damaged wholes than in intersections of body parts, less in loss than in novel possibility (will this part fit into that one? what's my gender if I do this or that to my body?). *K.I.P.* proffers a productive *disbelief* in the referential object, a disbelief strong enough to produce some kind of pseudo-encounter with it that isn't worried about the pseudo. Here, artifice is part of the pleasure: the fetishistic belief in the lost object is less important than the titillation of "but all the same . . . ," of the performance of substitution itself. *K.I.P.*'s queer subject would thus feel a encounter with what looks like a historical index not as a restored wholeness but as a momentary reorganization or rezoning of parts, even of the part-whole relation (will this part of a collective past fit into my present, remake it in some interesting way? how does this part of my personal past estrange a collective present?). He or she would refuse to write the lost object into the present, but try to encounter it already in the present, by encountering the present itself as hybrid. And he or she would use the body as a tool to effect, figure, and perform that encounter. By confronting the erotics of hauntology, *K.I.P.* intervenes not only on *Specters of Marx* but also on the occasion for that text: Shakespeare's *Hamlet*. Or rather, *K.I.P.* allows us to restore to *Hamlet* a *pleasurably* visceral sense of temporal and historical dissidence that even Derrida for the most part skirts.

O, O, O, O that Shakespearean Drag

Following *K.I.P.*, we might read Shakespeare a bit more literally. For when Prince Hamlet says that "the time is out of joint," he describes time as if its heterogeneity feels like a skeletal, or at least deeply somatic, dislocation.[43] In this famous phrase, time has, indeed *is*, a body; the disruption of present by past and the resulting disunity of the present seem visceral. And so it was in the early modern period of English history, where kinship articulated — in both the discursive and the physiological senses of the term — the body politic.[44] That is, the fleshly bonds of marriage and parentage (the latter sealed through a religious or eventually civil ceremony that would legitimize an eventual heir) not only metaphorized asymmetrical power relations but also directly regulated transfers and mergers of authority. Here and throughout *Hamlet*, then, the body is less a metaphor for time than it is the means for and effect of convoluting time, and consequently the smooth machinery of political power, or the mode of the state's *re*production. As Hamlet recognizes, time as body, and "the times," or the sphere of official politics and national history, form a joint: the body and the state are, rather than mere metaphors for one another, mutually constructing.

But *Hamlet* the play and Hamlet the Prince stick the gears of this machine. Centered on a protagonist who eschews the marriage plot or even its alternative, the revenge plot, Shakespeare's play freezes narrative movement, political/historical progression, and psychic development. As John Hunt argues, *Hamlet* is a fantasia of corporeal disfigurement and fragmentation, reducing the human form to "a collection of pieces whose morbidity intimates their violent dissolution."[45] Hamlet's disarticulated body, as well the bodies of those around him, both registers and performs time's heterogeneity. Indeed, the very manner in which Claudius murders King Hamlet effects generational disarray and somatic disintegration. As the Ghost tells it:

> Sleeping within my orchard,
> My custom always of the afternoon,
> Upon my secure hour thy uncle stole,
> With juice of cursed hebenon in a vial,
> And in the porches of my ears did pour
> The leperous distilment; whose effect
> Holds such an enmity with blood of man
> That swift as quicksilver it courses through
> The natural gates and alleys of the body,
> And with a sudden vigour doth posset
> And curd, like eager droppings into milk,
> The thin and wholesome blood: so did it mine;
> And a most instant tetter bark'd about,
> Most lazar-like, with vile and loathsome crust,
> All my smooth body. (1.5.59–73)

In this twisted Edenic tale, Claudius, whom the King has already called "the serpent that did sting thy father's life" (1.5.39), pours a poisonous liquid into the sleeping King's ear, so that the King is feminized not only in the implicit analogy to Eve but also in terms of the "natural gates and alleys" of his body. The Ghost goes on to compare the King's blood to milk, another female fluid, and the poison to curds in the milk. Given that Hamlet himself later makes the pun of his mother lying in an "enseamed" bed (3.4.92), this supposedly female milk looks suddenly and suspiciously like semen. The "leperous" poison Claudius administers, and the fact that the King's body erupts in "tetters" and "crust," also make the transmission look venereal. The story of Adam and Eve has here been transformed into a story of Adam and Steve, a scene of what looks very much like male-on-male oral or anal sex causing the royal house to fall from health into disease, timeless glory into sordid history.

Perhaps, too, Hamlet is complicit with at least part of this story: given his disinterest in marrying Ophelia, obsession with Claudius, and passion for Laertes, it's not unreasonable to read the entire play as — like *K.I.P.* — a melancholic wish for the homoerotic Eden that is this play's primal scene. In historical terms, that lost Eden might even be the era prior to the establishment of the Church of England, when Catholic monasteries sheltered passions between men. For Hamlet, the time for love between men is, indeed, out of joint, as it is for Nguyen, whose *K.I.P.* imagines a different articulation between past and present, body and collectivity. Through *K.I.P.* we might imagine a different *Hamlet*, in which the Prince would have figured out a way to answer his cross-generational and same-sex desires and, as the opening lines of Shakespeare's play put it, "stand, and unfold yourself" toward other times (1.1.2).

But the Shakespearean referent for *K.I.P.*, with its more exuberantly sensual effects of temporal alterity and its vision of how temporal dislocation might produce new orientations of desire, might be less the ponderous *Hamlet* than the spritely *A Midsummer Night's Dream*, in which nighttime and the nonsequential logic of dreams enable all kinds of illicit alliances. The latter play puts forth a model of time as embodied, of bodies and their *pleasures* as at once the vessels, figures, and even causes of temporal (dis)orientation. Indeed, the servant Philostrate initiates the comedy of mistimed erotic encounters — of people waking up suddenly and falling instantly in love with forbidden or ridiculous objects — solely for the purpose of speeding up the four days and nights preceding Theseus and Hippolyta's wedding. *Midsummer* follows the conventions of comedic closure with a wedding near the end, where everyone pairs off appropriately and the fairies' blessing explicitly ensures that the royal children will have none of the physical deformations that run through *Hamlet*. But like *K.I.P.*, the play also suggests that temporal misalignments can be the means of opening up other possible worlds.

One of these worlds is, indeed, "historical" and offers queer theory something that neither poststructuralist Marxisms nor even their eroticized manifestation in *K.I.P.* considers: the world of the working classes, or at least of laborers, whose own vulgar presence (not only embodied but erotic) we seem to have scrubbed from so much deconstructionist and Marxist criticism alike. In *A Midsummer Night's Dream*, Duke Theseus and his parallel in the fairy world, the fairy king Oberon, move in tandem with one another. With their entrances and exits exquisitely choreographed in counterpoint, Theseus and Oberon demonstrate how synchrony with one another and power over the timing of others intersect. Both have the power to control time literally, through their servants: Philostrate's disorderings are supposed to make time go by more quickly for Theseus as he awaits his wedding, and on behalf of Oberon, Puck disrupts Queen Titania's normative time for falling in love by making her fall in love with the first object she sees upon awakening. But the two noblemen also have power over time ideologically, through their control of women's reproductive and marital roles: Theseus both speeds up the time that passes all too slowly, delaying his nuptial consummation with Hippolyta and also insists that Hermia agree to her arranged marriage within four days; Oberon fast-forwards Titania's desire as well as object-choice because he wants her adopted Indian child.

The play's "rude mechanicals," on the other hand, are both "rude" and "mechanical" precisely insofar as their timing is off both with one another and with the temporal expectations of the aristocrats. "Here is a play fitted," intones Quince the Carpenter as he casts the characters in their play-within-a-play, punning on Snug the Joiner's trade.[46] But Snug is both the most and the least fitted to his part. He is the most apt for the part because, he and the players agree, all he has to do is roar, which any idiot can do. But Snug is also unfitted: Quince instructs him to speak "extempore" (1.2.64), literally out of time, making him the figure for a play that is simultaneously too short ("ten words," says Philostrate) and too long (by exactly those ten words, he adds) (5.1.61–63). In fact, the entire play-within-a-play is out of joint, with its clumsy literalizations and malapropisms, its botching of the heterosexual love plot that frames the rest of the play, its dragging on and on of some scenes. Furthermore, as Snug remarks, Bottom's wandering off into the forest delays their presence at the wedding, preventing them from becoming rich. In a pun suggesting not only financial success but also heterosexual consummation, Snug declares that "if our sport had gone forward," meaning if they had caught the wedding revelers earlier, "we had all been made men" (4.2.17–18).

The mechanicals are not "men": apparently unmarried, failed in their efforts to accumulate wealth, unsynchronized with one another and with dramatic conventions of pacing, they live in the slow time of delay and deferral. As Snug puts it, "I am slow of study" (2.2.63). The craftsmen's queerness, then, consists of a bodily difference that cannot be reduced to sexual orientation, a class relation that cannot be reduced to ownership of the means of production or the lack thereof—and they are not simply "premodern" in their slowness. What the artisans lack are the properties of temporal decorum and life-trajectory that distinguish their social superiors: as Marcel Mauss writes in his discussion of habitus, prestige accrues to those who can perfectly imitate "the ordered, authorized, tested action" of a given culture.[47] But as queerly classed subjects, the mechanicals are shadows of the "apprentice problem" in early modern Europe: not being allowed to marry, forced to delay forming families until they had accumulated something, apprentices and servants were viewed as sexual threats.[48] Their status as bound was at once economic, sexual, and temporal. *A Midsummer Night's Dream*, then, poses an important question for this project: how is class "timed"?

It's Class Time

Part of what I aim to do in this book is to restore a differently queer body to queer theory—the body erotic thought not only in terms of its possibilities for making sexual cultures but in terms of its capacities for labor—by which I mean both the social relations of production/reproduction and the expenditure of bodily energy. Thus far I have argued that the discipline of "timing" engenders a sense of being and belonging that feels natural: in fact, Bourdieu's description of the rhythms of habitus appears in his discussion of the differences between kinship under the law and what he calls practical kinship, or the actual patterns of interaction that form the social field as such. For Bourdieu, habitus organizes a form of belonging that subtends and supersedes kinship—and that is class. Where physical appearance and name fail to secure likeness, the hidden rhythms of gesture, giving and withholding, play and humor, courtship, and etiquette, among other things, establish similarities between strangers that seem to be inborn. These techniques, Mauss writes, are felt by the subject who performs them as "*actions of a mechanical, physical, or physico-chemical order*."[49] With Shakespeare's mechanicals, on the other hand, the gears stick.

Let me hazard that "queer" names a class relation of a different sort from the standard Marxist definition of a relationship between people who own the means of production and people whose biggest asset is their labor power — even as both of these forms of power also involve time. We might think of class as an embodied synchronic and diachronic organization. In its dominant forms, class enables its bearers what looks like "natural" control over their body and its effects, or the diachronic means of sexual and social reproduction. In turn, failures or refusals to inhabit middle- and upper-middle-class habitus appear as, precisely, asynchrony, or time out of joint. And as denizens of times out of joint, queers *are* a subjugated class in the sense I have described it, even as many of us occupy other positions of power including the economic.

With queers and/of the working class, too, the synchronic aspect of habitus out of joint meets the diachronic aspect of generationality. In other words, these two sometimes but not always overlapping subject-positions, queer and working class, also confront time longitudinally. In "Theses on the Philosophy of History," Walter Benjamin writes that "Social Democracy thought fit to assign to the working class the role of the redeemer of future generations, in this way cutting the sinews of its greatest strength. This training made the working class forget both its hatred and its spirit of sacrifice, for both are nourished by the image of enslaved ancestors rather than that of liberated grandchildren."[50] Anticipating Edelman's *No Future* by many decades, this passage suggests that the perils of reprofuturity bear upon a more traditionally Marxist class struggle. Unlike Edelman, Benjamin asks that the working class not only reject the future but also turn back toward the suffering of their forebears. Yet, as I have argued here, suffering need not be the only food the ancestors offer. *K.I.P.* turns back toward the elders (if not the ancestors, in the genealogical sense of the term) for a different form of nourishment. Nguyen's diaphanous, lusting queer archivalist gazes hungrily into a scene that excludes him, mouth agape to receive lineal bliss. And this turning back feeds not hatred but entitlement, not the spirit of sacrifice but a commitment to bodily potentiality that neither capitalism nor heterosexuality can fully contain.

one. Junk Inheritances, Bad Timing

Familial Arrhythmia in Three Working-Class Dyke Narratives

> We are verses out of rhythm,
> Couplets out of rhyme . . .
> — Simon and Garfunkel, "The Dangling Conversation"

In *K.I.P.*, the image of queer "ancestors" not only offers an alternative to reprofuturity by way of a blissful past but also gestures toward the history of visual technology's participation in the making of genealogies and intimacies. Even prior to modern nationalism, people have understood themselves as such and as part of a larger historical dynamic — usually an ascent based on rank, wealth, or other status — through imaging sequence and cumulation in familial terms. They have used narrative tools like pedigrees and legends of their forebears, and visual tools like painted portraits and heirlooms, to represent continuities with unseen others across temporal vistas. Ideas like a noble house, a chosen people, or a superior race, then, all connect microsocial forms like marriage and childbirth to grand narratives of continuity and change. In this production of a generational peoplehood, groups make legible not only themselves but also history thought of, in its simplest terms, as the passage of time beyond the span of a single life.

When visual technologies such as photography and film emerged, they certainly made time available to the senses in new ways: as Mary Ann Doane argues, they both participated in the newly rationalized time-sense of the industrial era and offered ways out of rationalized time by privileging the index, the archive, the gap between frames, and other devices that stopped or "lost" time.[1] Yet as these technologies became available to middling folk, they were often harnessed to and furthered the representation of collective longitude. Over the course of the nineteenth and twentieth centuries, families increasingly "mattered" or both appeared before themselves and came to seem consequential in and of themselves through the visual technologies marketed at ordinary people — daguerreotypes, snapshots, and eventually home movies.[2] Historically, the photographic media participated in the emergence of a highly heterogendered, middle-class discourse of family. The very earliest mass-marketed photographic technologies, as Shawn Michelle Smith demonstrates, turned away from the public iconicity associated with the painted portrait and toward depicting an elusive psychic interiority, coded as highly feminine. Generally portraying individual subjects and families posed in interior spaces surrounded by household items and furnishings, daguerreotypes celebrated privacy and yet teased the viewer with the voyeuristic pleasure of imagined access to both rooms and souls.[3] They evoked the "timeless" spaces of heart and hearth, the stillness of a domestic life imagined as a haven from rather than a necessary correlate of industrial time.

The technologies that followed may have dimmed the daguerreotype's aura of singularity insofar as they allowed for multiple prints, but their domestic users drew from the conventions of daguerreotypy by privileging homes and family groupings. As Marianne Hirsch writes, after the invention of the Kodak camera "photography quickly became the family's primary instrument of self-knowledge and representation — the means by which family memory would be continued and perpetuated."[4] Smith contends that by the end of the nineteenth century the photograph of the child, in particular, had become a means of visualizing not just time but the future, and not just any future but one congruent with middle-class aspirations illustrated by poses, settings, and props. Candid, infinitely reproducible pictures of live babies and children replaced the daguerreotype era's cult of dead children, figuring a new congruence between technological reproduction and the saving of the Anglo-American "race," now understood in terms of skin color as well as ancestry. In the hands of ordinary fathers and, increasingly, mothers, domestic photographs "trac[ed] the imaginative trajectory" of the family line toward continued racial purity, physical health, and prosperity.[5] In this way, they inserted the family into, and made the family into an image of, the nationalist march of "progress." In other words, domestic photography helped merge the secularized, quasi-sacred time of nature and family with the homogenous, empty time across which national destiny moved: representations of family made simple reproductive sequences look like historical consequence. The spatial conventions that attended domestic uses of the visual media also contributed to this effect. For instance, the family portrait is often recognizable as such because the subjects are usually posed with the elders at the back (and sometimes even portraits of ancestors on the wall behind them), the children in the front, and an adult male-female couple at the center, flanked by their own siblings or eldest children. Individual portraits of different family members or the same person are often shot or displayed in sequences that emphasize physical likenesses across time, as in the living room display of family members organized top-to-bottom and/or oldest-to-youngest, or of the child posed in front of the same tree once a year.

But as I suggested earlier, queer time emerged from within, alongside, and beyond this heterosexually gendered double-time of stasis and progress, intimacy and genealogy. While the antebellum nineteenth century was marked by a dialectic between sacred, static "women's" time and a secularized, progressive, nominally male national-historical time, the later nineteenth and twentieth centuries saw a dialectic between "primitive," slow, recalcitrant time and the time of speedy production, rapid distribution, and constant novelty. This ostensible division of mutually informing and co-constructed categories was not only gendered, as before, but now also explicitly racialized and sexualized. The discourses of racial degeneration in criminologists like Cesar Lombroso, and of neurotic repetition in Freud, made it possible to imagine and represent a certain stalling of any smooth movement from past to present, stillness to action, time to history. These discourses foregrounded compulsive returns, movements backward to reenter prior historical moments rather than inward or outward to circumvent historical time. As film technologies emerged in the late nineteenth century, they seemed to materialize the possibility of return that subtended modernity: as Mary Ann Doane demonstrates, the plots of early fictional films such as *Life of an American Fireman* (1903) contained scenes in which the same action was shown twice, shot from different vantage points, to emphasize spatial continuity. Some "actuality" films depicting real events were shown backward and forward, asking spectators to marvel in buildings that resurrected themselves, or glasses that knit their fragments back up. Some were shown in a continuous loop, encouraging viewers to notice different details in each showing. Some early directors enhanced the credibility of the historical reenactments they portrayed by beginning with establishing shots taken on the day of the historical event, returning spectators to the original time and place before launching a reconstruction of the events that took place there. Thus, though film seemed to highlight the irreversibility and linearity of time through the relentless forward motion of the apparatus, it also enabled a kind of mass repetition-compulsion, enabling spectators to stop time or see it run backward. Whether explicitly correlated with racial and sexual otherness or not, film's ability to manipulate time or to enable historical return resonated with the late nineteenth century's tendency to align blacks, homosexuals, and other deviants with threats to the forward movement of individual or civilizational development.

Cecilia Dougherty's independent video *Coal Miner's Granddaughter* (1991) queers family by bringing film's work on time to the level of acting and embodiment. At its outset, *Coal Miner's Granddaughter* promises a suture between family and collectivity, representation and reproduction, using the conventions of home video. At one point in this piece, a working-class family sits down to dinner at their home in Lancaster, Pennsylvania, the week before an election.[6] Among the family members is the protagonist, Jane Dobson (Leslie Singer), who has announced before the story begins, "My name is Jane Dobson and this is my damned story," and who will make her way up from the family dinner table and out of the closet by the narrative's end. But by invoking both the country singer Loretta Lynn's hit "Coal Miner's Daughter" (1970) and the film of the same name (1980), the title of Dougherty's video suggests Jane's complicated relationship to her family of origin. Ostensibly, it signals that her personal history includes a connection to not only extended family but also a collective form of labor and its representational history. In Popular Front, Depression-era portraits by Walker Evans, James Agee, and Dorothea Lange, for instance, coal miners' families have typically registered the progress or regress of an industry and the culture surrounding it; similarly, the lyrics to Lynn's song suggest that her memories of her home at Butcher Hollow preserve a lost way of life. Viewers of *Coal Miner's Granddaughter*, then, might expect something magisterial, a female "Up from Wage Slavery" that lends gravitas to an individual life by embedding it in a larger collective drama of gender, sexual, and/or class struggle.

But plain and lumpish Jane is a watered-down version of Lynn's earnestly gritty protagonist, half a century removed from the world of collective organizing that many now romanticize (see figure 2). Thus "granddaughter" ironically invokes a certain de-generation, of which homosexuality is only one aspect in the video. Jane's "damned story" involves not the rags-to-riches progress of a star but the movement from *the* Depression to just plain old depression, and the lesbian awakening of an ordinary young woman who ends up in San Francisco's early 1990s pro-sex queer subculture — neither of which, it might be noted, add up to something as grandiose as damnation in the religious sense of the word.

There is no grandparent with whom we might expect Jane to somehow identify, perhaps even as a source informing her lesbian identity. In fact, the actors are of more or less the same age, with only minimal costuming — the mother's obvious wig and dark lipstick, the father's ill-fitting suit — separating the parents from the "children" (see figure 3). The latter, with the exception of the hippie sister Rene (Amanda Hendricks), wear ordinary late 1980s/early 1990s clothing and haircuts. Though the narrative begins when Jane is a child, she is not played by a child actor but by Singer speaking in a childlike voice, and nobody visibly ages within the story's roughly two decades. It is as if this family cannot go anywhere in time; indeed, much of the camerawork consists of disorienting and claustrophobic close-ups shot inside a small interior, rather than of the action shots and exterior scenes that traditionally align the passage of time with motion and changes in setting. There are no coal mines visible either; and though the election results in the father getting a job as the postmaster of Lancaster, he spends much of his time sitting around a kitchen table with his family members.

Leftist Democrats and Catholics, the Dobsons seem vaguely lower middle class, which is mostly indicated by the few props in the kitchen and by the father's job. But they are visibly untouched by any particular community or industry. These absences lend a certain pathos to the title insofar as they mark the kind of vacuum left behind when mining and other heavy industries are outsourced. Indeed, as if to mark the shift from a manufacturing to a temp economy, Francis, the father (Kevin Killian), says, "I'm the only man in town with two jobs." The other job apparently involves work with the Democratic Party on behalf of prisoners, ironically enough, for Francis imprisons his own family in stereotypically heterogendered expectations justified by his hatred of communism. Given the loss of pater familias here, we might expect the family's women, at least, to display enduring patterns of working-class sociability; we might even wish these patterns into resembling queer bonds in Jane's present or the future. But *Coal Miner's Granddaughter* refuses to excavate the kind of past that might situate Jane and her family in a larger narrative encompassing and correlating both working-class and lesbian identity. As a reviewer writes, "Jane as a subject never really comes through. Perhaps this is the point: she is the absent center of her own life."[7] In this video, time stalls in the failure of a granddaughter to be either a grand representative of her class legacy or a proper daughter — or even, perhaps, a subject at all. Unmoored from the representational logic that sutures biological

2–3. Stills from *Coal Miner's Granddaughter*.
Copyright Cecilia Dougherty, 1991. Courtesy of the artist.

reproduction to social history through visual technologies, Jane's biography simply bobs along, inconsequentially.

In short, *Coal Miner's Granddaughter* presents a degenerated working-class solidarity, and this sense of loss and absence extends to the very materiality of the video. Repudiating both earnest documentary and Hollywood biopic, Dougherty shot her piece in PXL 2000, popularly known as PixelVision — an extremely cheap camera that records images onto audiotape, available primarily as a toy sold by Fisher-Price between 1987 and 1989. *Coal Miner's Granddaughter* also emerged within a fleeting moment of the late 1980s and 1990s, dubbed the New Queer Cinema, whose artists and critics were already self-consciously theorizing its own emergence and ephemerality.[8] The term "New Queer Cinema," apparently coined by the film critic B. Ruby Rich, encompassed films that eschewed gay identity as a point of departure or return and instead represented same-sex relations in terms of acts, situations, aesthetics, and unpredictable historical or social collisions.[9] To describe the New Queer Cinema somewhat overschematically, it generally avoided individual coming-out narratives, realistic depictions of urban gay social milieux, and other "expressive" narrative or filmic conventions that would stabilize or contain homoeroticism, correlate particular bodies to particular desires, or reduce erotic practice to sexual identity.[10] And crucially, the New Queer Cinema engaged in what Rich called "a reworking of history with social constructionism very much in mind . . . a new historiography," about which less has since been written than one might expect.[11] In keeping with the New Queer Cinema's emphasis on the constructed nature of both identity and history, Jane's life is memorialized on the nearly obsolete medium of a cassette tape, the original of which cannot even be played except on a discontinued machine. Portraying a granddaughter who is a bad copy of Lynn's famous daughter, in a medium that is itself considered a bad copy of film, and indeed in a low-quality version of even that medium intended for children, *Coal Miner's Granddaughter* is less about descent or legacy than it is about inferior derivations and the inheritance of qualities with no value to middle-class culture. Even in its physical aspect, the video incarnates the clichés that a lesbian is a bad copy of a man, that a queer life leaves nothing enduring, that a working-class subject has, in Rita Felski's words, "nothing to declare."[12]

Insofar as this video follows the generic conventions of a coming-out story, it certainly participates in an earlier identity politics on the level of content. But what is queer about it surfaces in the formal register: materially, a master tape that is destined to corrupt and fade, and structurally, a saga that fails to be anything but utterly ordinary. These elements clearly resonate with contemporary analyses of queerness as a force that distorts or undermines the logic of sequence — at one point in the film Jane says to her brother Jon (Glen Helfland), "I could just stay here, go to Temple, get married, get some kind of office job till I get pregnant . . . why don't I just blow my head off right now?"[13] But the video also refuses to disrupt narrative sequence per se and align dissident sexuality with a simple ateleological postmodernism: scene follows scene in relatively expected ways as Jane fights with her family, leaves home, arrives in a gay Mecca, comes back to visit Lancaster now and again. Here, queer does not merely oppose linearity. Dougherty herself has stated that she "wanted to make a narrative instead of an experimental piece . . . I'm really sick of artsy videos . . . It looked like film was going to be the vehicle for narrative and video was slated for documentary or experimental work. I thought video was underutilized."[14]

Dougherty's contribution to a queer politics of time is, then, more complicated than mere postmodernism: like Nguyen, she blocks the transformation of time itself into grand historical narrative, especially as this metamorphosis is effected through the progress of a people depicted visually. But she also blocks the transformation of class consciousness into Marxist History-with-a-capital-H, or the proletariat's eventual triumph. By explicitly referencing Loretta Lynn's *Coal Miner's Daughter*, Dougherty suggests how key the trope of heteronormative, ex-tensive kinship is to these two interlocking grand narratives of collective destiny. But her play with the time of heteronormative family life engages an axis of temporal power that cannot be reduced to the generationalized class saga, even if it functions alongside it: *Coal Miner's Granddaughter*, despite the diachronic overtones of its title, engages most deeply with the synchronic, or the power of *timing* to effect solidarity.

As with all legitimate groups, families depend on timing. Their choreographed displays of simultaneity effect a latitudinal, extensive set of belonging to one another: in popular rhetoric and imagery, for instance, the family that prays together supposedly stays together.[15] As Homi Bhabha points out in his work on nationhood, these performances of synchrony may seem to consolidate collective life, but the coherence they provide is fragile.[16] Dougherty's disruption of heterotemporality, likewise, appears less as a matter of narrative derangement or antiteleology than as a matter of theatrical and theatricalized decoordination, much like that of the bumbling artisans in *A Midsummer Night's Dream*. In *Coal Miner's Granddaughter*, the players are neither documentary subjects nor professional actors but amateurs from Dougherty's everyday life (Jane, for instance, is played by the video artist Leslie Singer). The production had no script, and Doughterty's players improvised from a minimal plot outline. Dougherty sketched out a set of sequential vignettes that added up to a story, then gave the players broad descriptions of each scene and index cards with key phrases that she wanted them to use as they acted them out in what appear to be single takes.[17] Much of the dialogue in the video is therefore marked by stutters, mismatches between the tone and content of sentences, and non sequiturs, as the untrained, unscripted players fumble their way through stilted conversations. In fact, *Coal Miner's Granddaughter* flaunts consciously off-kilter mimicry at perhaps the most celebrated, the most representationally charged, of what Ernest Renan called the "daily plebiscites" that both enact and renew American family life — the shared evening meal.[18] From the privileged vantage point of the voyeuristic dinner guest, we can see how the Dobsons' prosodic and gestural twitches are at odds with middle-class familial habitus.

In a way, the video *is* realistic, for who hasn't sat through family dinners as boring, awkward, and pointless as the ones *Coal Miner's Granddaughter* portrays? But the actors' verbal clumsiness, flat affect, and misfiring of dialogue and interactions constitute what I think of as this video's "queer accent." I mean this phrase to echo and to revise Voloshinov's theory of "multiaccentuality." Voloshinov argues that members of different classes, though they use the same ideologically loaded terms, inflect them differently, with subjugated classes deploying them toward ends that contradict or compete with dominant ones, or stressing subjugated or archaic meanings.[19] This definition departs from the usual spatio-temporal way of seeing accent as a vestige of location in a particular geographical place, as in a Southern accent, or even a discrete historical moment, as in an Elizabethan one. For it implies the *rhythmic* aspect of the word "accent" — its definition as *stress* or, in the *Oxford English Dictionary*, "a prominence given to one syllable in a word . . . over the adjacent syllables."[20] In terms of speech, to share an accent with someone is to have similar patterns of not only tone and phoneme but also meter. And accent, as the work of Bourdieu and Mauss makes clear, extends beyond the spoken rhythm of individual words and sentences to encompass kinetic tempos and the prosodics of interactions between people. Accent is part of habitus, that somatic effect primarily achieved in and through conventions of timing that feel like natural affinities. Those who can synch up their bodily hexes and linguistic patterns, who can inhabit a culture's particular tempos with enough mastery to improvise within them, feel as if they belong to that culture (this is why humor, which often depends on physical and/or verbal timing, is so culturally specific and such a marker of insiders and outsiders). Thus a class accent is not simply a matter of manners, as with television shows of the 1980s like *Married with Children*, which featured a family of perpetually broke, gum-cracking slobs yelling at one another. Instead, it is a matter of shared timing. The Dobsons of *Coal Miner's Granddaughter* seem unlike members of a united working class—and more jarringly, unlike even a family—because the timing of their interactions with one another is so imperfect. Their inadequate mastery over time and timing registers incompetence with and insufficiency to, or perhaps just refusal of, the forms of working-class solidarity and familial intimacy. If the actors quite literally don't know how to act together, the family gives off the impression of not wanting to act "together," even as the mother, Phyllis (Didi Dunphy), whines over and over again, "We'll always be together. We'll always be happy together."

The video's commitment to bad timing, then, queers what might otherwise be its univocally class-inflected accent: perhaps the Dobsons fail to enact class belonging because they fail in the first place to act as a "normal" family. And conversely, perhaps class complicates what would otherwise be a more recognizably lesbian accent. Singer's acting certainly gets better in the San Francisco scenes, which perhaps inadvertently suggests that queer life fits Jane, and she fits it, a bit better than life with her family of origin. But this too gets complicated by a wholly different subplot: on her arrival in San Francisco, Jane finds not pure bodily liberation but, tellingly, chronic pain in her joints. Her brother Jon has already said that the two of them should "blow this joint" and get out of Lancaster, but Jane finds instead that her own articular surfaces are covered with mysterious cysts. While the soundtrack plays a recurrent riff, "If you wanna move, then move over here," Jane learns from her doctor (Ramon Churruca) that her movement will always be limited. This bodily condition, in turn, metaphorizes her inability to become a fast-paced, sexually blasé urban dyke; for instance, in a later scene, Jane is forced to call her non-monogamous lover Victoria (Claire Trepanier) for help with food and chores, and Victoria impatiently scolds Jane for messing up her other dating plans by expecting her to come immediately. Later, when Jane's doctor asks after her chronic pain and she replies "I think I'm just getting used to it," he is pleased. "Ahhh . . . that's good progress," he intones. "You have to learn to live like that." Ironically, a commitment to stasis becomes the sign of Jane's progress.

Unbound from traditional working-class history, Jane finds herself equally unjoined to queer modernity. In the video's last scene, in which Jane is house-sitting and a neighbor (Amy Scholder) brings up some misdelivered mail, Singer reverts to the mistimed, babbling stiffness of the early dinner scenes. Several times, Jane offers up the lame joke that the postal carrier must be on drugs: his lunch hour, she says, must be "a burrito and a joint." And that is where the video ends: with a coincidental, promisingly flirtatious encounter facilitated by an inept mailman who seems to be a caricature of Jane's father, and with Jane, who is out of synch with both her working-class background and her newfound "community," and then set adrift into what may or may not be a new plot.

Coal Miner's Granddaughter suggests that familial timing implicates both class and sexual relations. Purportedly the fulcrum between the biological and the social, the cyclical and the historical, family is the form through which time supposedly becomes visible, predominantly as physical likeness extending over generations — but also, Dougherty suggests, as natural likeness in manner, or orchestrated simultaneities occurring in the present. Following these insights, this chapter excavates a model of simultaneously queer and class-accented "bad timing" in two other works of art by lesbians who were, like Dougherty and her protagonist, born to working-class mothers, though my two texts focus on the mother-daughter relationship as a distilled version of family. One of these texts is Diane Bonder's short video *The Physics of Love* (1998), which portrays a daughter so alienated from her housewife mother that she cannot grieve her mother's death and is therefore melancholically fixated on the Hollywood mother-daughter melodramas of the 1940s and 1950s.[21] The other is Bertha Harris's novel *Lover* (1976), which portrays five generations of women who loop back upon one another in time to touch in erotic ways.[22] Unlike Dougherty, for whom the temporality of "family" does not differentiate along gendered lines, Bonder and Harris depict characters who are unable either to comfortably occupy or to fully repudiate their mothers' legacies. These characters are also ambivalently situated vis-à-vis their mothers' modes of keeping time, which turns out to be a matter of both class and (gendered) sexualities.

These two texts emerged roughly twenty years apart and like *Coal Miner's Granddaughter* were the product of low-budget, independent, queerly collaborative scenes. *The Physics of Love* was funded, shot, edited, and distributed by the late Diane Bonder, who was part of the loose network of independent lesbian filmmakers emerging on the East Coast in the early 1990s; like Dougherty's work, Bonder's has had very few public showings, predominantly at festivals and curated shows. *Lover* was originally published by Daughters, Inc., a small feminist press specializing in avant-garde novels, and still has only a cult following and little scholarly attention despite its reissue by New York University Press in 1993. Though Harris's and Bonder's texts are in different media, they share a commitment to interrogating the temporal logic of family and, correspondingly, the familial logic of their own particular histori-cal moments. For Bonder, that moment is, though only implicitly, a queer "renaissance" that privileged an impossible-to-complete rebellion from the maternal figure, one predominantly available to middle-class les-bians.[23] For Harris, that moment is lesbian-feminism, with its roman-ticized, middle-class ideal of conflict-free relations between women, em-blematized by mother-daughter love. Like *Coal Miner's Granddaughter*, these two works are less about lesbian or queer "history" per se than about the timing of lesbian and queer lives. They are about exploring the ideology of familial intimacy (and its converse, the privileged subject's complete refusal of family) as class-marked temporal phenomena within which less privileged queers stumble, and departing from which they might find new ways of being.

Both *The Physics of Love* and *Lover* are more self-consciously anti-narrative than Dougherty's piece, and each features one or more non-sequential storylines as well as various misalignments of what is ordinarily synchronized in its particular medium. *The Physics of Love* (hereafter *Phys-ics*) uses the Newtonian laws of motion as the dominant visual and verbal motif for failed intimacy. *Physics* features an original musical score that is constantly interrupted by nondiegetic snippets of sound—a scratchy re-cording of Frank Sinatra singing "Something's Gotta Give," a fragment of dialogue from an old western, recitations of plot summaries, beeps, ticks, rattles. Its image track juxtaposes, repeats, and abruptly cuts between several kinds of footage, including snapshots, home movies, stills from motion studies, images on a television set, and title cards. Thematically, the film works by accreting the same few scenes and visual tropes: a wrecking ball hitting a building, water moving over cards imprinted with phrases, twirling three-dimensional miniatures of household appliances, hands performing domestic tasks, laundry blowing in the wind. Harris's novel *Lover* is as formally fragmented as *Physics*. This novel tracks the movement of an interrelated group of women toward the rarified status of "lover." *Lover*'s governing aesthetic principles come from the visual arts rather than from the tradition of the novel: "*Lover*," writes Harris, "should be absorbed as though it were a theatrical performance. Watch it. It is rife with the movie stars and movies of my childhood and adoles-cence . . . *Lover* has a vaudeville atmosphere."[24] Though the novel may be peppered with allusions to Hollywood and Wagnerian opera, vaudeville is the more apt metaphor for its arrangement: *Lover* features a cast of characters who do not so much develop as simply enter and exit, appear and reappear, telling stories and performing scenes set in different times. It has no overarching plot but instead cuts between several storylines in nonchronological order, stacking them atop one another and weaving in fragments from saints' lives and philosophical musings from various narrators. In both of these works, formal experimentation takes place against an exaggeratedly heteronormative temporalized discipline, figured by the mother-daughter relationship.

Reimagining Family, Reimaging Time

The Physics of Love exploits the recursive properties of film to refuse the logic whereby through the domestic media likeness, sequence, and historical consequence become mutual effects. One of Bonder's first "shots" in a montage that precedes the film's title credit is a snippet of found footage from a home movie, in which a woman walks toward the camera shaking her finger rapidly. Immediately thereafter comes a shot taken from within an automobile, of windshield wipers moving across the front windshield, as if to literalize the filmic "wipe" that classically signals a transition from one time to another. These wipes, though, move back and forth, suggesting a more see-sawing kind of time; even as the car clearly moves forward, they indicate the possibility of wiping and "unwiping" progressive time, filmic motion forward, or even memory. Bonder follows up on this suggestion by rapidly alternating two black-and-white photographs from a turn-of-the-century motion study in which a nude toddler-aged girl approaches a nude woman and hands the woman an object. Their age difference and familiarity suggest that they are mother and daughter. The original motion study presumably figured familial intimacy itself as movement and hence as a temporal phenomenon; the child's steps toward the mother not only indicated the presence of time in the way Doane describes but also figured the "timing" of love. Love, the motion study seems to have implied, is a matter of progress toward the other, of reciprocal gesture, of giving and taking; it elevates the synchronies of shared habitus experienced to the highest degree. But as Bonder's film toggles between these stills, what should be the child's progress toward the woman becomes instead a two-step dance toward and away from her: here, stop trumps motion. By alternating these stills, Bonder figures both the narrator's ambivalence toward her mother and the temporal switchbacks that the video itself will later perform as the narrator struggles to be moved, to feel any emotion whatsoever about her

4. Still from *The Physics of Love*.
Copyright Diane Bonder, 1998. Courtesy of Kathy High,
Mona Jimenez, Liss Platt, and Elizabeth Stephens.

mother's death, to enter either the sacred time of grief and epiphany, or the forward-flowing time of going on with her life.

Having turned photography toward film's possibilities for reversing temporal order, Bonder then addresses the relationship between domestic photography and heterosexual reproduction. Toward the end of this set of shots a narrator says, "They were cut from the same mold." Immediately thereafter comes a set of two gold frames, each encasing one of the two stills, as if to arrest both motion and time. The images within the frames rapidly shift to twin images of peas in pods (as the narrator says "like two peas in a pod"), a large fly ("the resemblance was uncanny"), DNA helixes ("she took after her in every way"), chromosomes ("they could have been twins"), and then back to the stills, but this time a viscous liquid spatters on the glass (see figure 4). As this liquid hits, the narrator says, "You could say she was her spitting image." This line, itself doubling possible pronominal referents (who is whose image?) sounds twice in rapid and overlapping succession. So not only does this series of shots eventually repudiate—literally spit upon—the likeness it seems at first to celebrate but the echolalic last line of the segment's soundtrack also disrupts forward movement, doubling the sentence back upon itself. Just as the child's back-and-forth stepping in the early motion-study stills figures a stuttering kind of time rather than progress toward the future, in this set of images genetic reproduction fails to produce enough difference and hence change.

5. Cover of the 1976 Daughters, Inc., edition of *Lover*. Copyright Loretta Li, 1976.

Bertha Harris's novel *Lover* also introduces domestic photography on the cover of its original edition and on its first page, only to disrupt immediately that medium's hetero- and chrononormative functions. The sole image on the cover of the 1976 edition is a black-and-white photograph, centered in a field of black, of a little girl standing in front of a house and holding a doll (see figure 5). The doll is practically as big as the child, who looks to be about two years old. The little girl has inadvertently hiked up the doll's dress, and the doll's sidelong glance, combined with the circular blush spots on her cheeks and the placement of her cloth hand over her heart, make the doll look embarrassed or scandalized. This cover clearly signals the novel's preoccupation with the erotics between mothers and daughters, and with some feminists' sanitizing reduction of lesbianism to a chaste mother-daughter or sororal relationship. It also visually redoubles the name of the publishing house, Daughters, Inc., as well as intimating the power struggles between Harris and her publishers that she narrates in her preface to the 1993 reissue published by New York University Press.

The cover photo reappears in somewhat different form in the opening paragraphs of *Lover*. After a dizzying couple of very short scenes that introduce the names of the novel's central characters — about which more below — the reader is presented with "a series of snapshots" depicted only in words.[25] These pictures, we are told, depict a preschool-aged child in the 1940s — Veronica, who will turn out to be the novel's artist and the one with the most multiple and shifting identities. The narrator reports that the photo of Veronica is shot from the back; two others apparently show her standing in a lake, wearing a wool bathing suit that is appliquéd with a duck. The photos initially seem to offer the reader help in situating *Lover*'s large and unwieldy collection of women into a historical moment and into generations of family: perhaps Veronica, described just before the introduction of the photographs as sitting on a swing sucking candy with her childhood "sweetheart" who is also named Veronica, is a descendant of some sort. Yet the name Veronica itself references the first picture of Christ — the vernicle made by the woman who held the Shroud of Turin to Jesus's face, which act signals Christianity's turn from the patriarchal blood family of Judaism to a scheme of proselytizing and conversion (reproduction by other means), and from an anti-imagistic theology to one that privileged the image.[26] Perhaps, then, Veronica the artist is *Lover*'s matriarch, its Mary. But the novel's first sentence about Veronica is that she "came out of nowhere," in contrast to the novel's other main characters, Samaria, Daisy, and Flynn, whom the opening sentences confirm are clearly born to one another in some order or another. Veronica seems completely unreproduced, a photo without a negative.

Veronica's photos reappear at the end of the novel, when Daisy appears and tells Veronica that either she (Daisy) or her mother, Samaria, has murdered a man. "But I say *Samaria* and you say *my mother*," says Veronica, "How do I know which is the mother and which is the daughter? How can I know that for sure?" (211). Daisy tells her to "find something to remind you of something else — perhaps a snapshot of *me* in a little woolen bathing suit, a bathing suit with a duck on it, and I'm standing at the edge of a lake with my feet in the water" (211, my emphasis). As with Bonder's mother-daughter snapshot, here domestic photography unhinges memory and sequence rather than facilitating it: Daisy, born to Samaria, who is Veronica's lover and contemporary, could not possibly be the child in the photo. Veronica retorts, "It could be Samaria in that picture, not you . . . I wonder who the real one is. It might be me. Like everything else, one is real, the other a forgery" (212). Daisy teases, "Which is the mother, which the forgery? My goodness, Veronica" (212). The implication here is that domestic photography produces, or "forges," familial relations rather than representing preexisting ones. *Lover*'s fictional photographs serve to emphasize technological reproduction over biological maternity, the simulated over the natural: mothers are not simply fakers but fake themselves.

More importantly for the project of theorizing family time, *Lover*'s pictures disorder sequence, revealing photography's central role in imaging time as familial by scrambling the logic of family lineage. For the photos make their first appearance just after the novel's aforementioned opening paragraphs, which detail some kind of birth scene or scenes:

> This one was lying strapped to a table. Covered in her juices, Samaria was being pulled through her vulva. This is how Samaria met her.
>
> She was being pulled, yelling already, through the lips of Daisy's vulva. This is how Flynn met Daisy. (5)

As with Bonder's "she was her spitting image," here the referential ambiguity of "this one," "her," and "She" makes it unclear here who is giving birth to whom, which is the mother and which is the daughter in this daisy-chain of women. They coil upon one another, each one's bodily boundaries apparently occupying not only two spaces, inside and outside, but also two distinct moments in time. The image is botanical, like a convolute leaf or flower bud.[27] And indeed, this opening confirms an even earlier, more literally vegetational image of a family unbound from linear time. For the novel opens with a frontispiece, a hand-drawn family tree of sorts: a leafy vine with the names Flynn and Bertha at the center. Rather than situating characters above and below one another to indicate generations, this tree shows six fronds shooting out centrifugally from its center. The names of all the characters in the novel perch on or hang from one frond or another, in no particular order. Furthermore, this genealogical kudzu ensnares *Lover*'s incidental characters, a few Catholic saints, pets mentioned in passing within the novel, and "A British bottle of vinegar" (1).

In a sense, this is an antikinship diagram. The anthropologist Mary Bouquet suggests that anthropology has relied on the conventions of the Euro-American family photograph to define what kinship looks like. In her analysis, the kinship diagram is the abstract version of a family portrait, with the lines of connection and transmission overtly symbolized rather than left implicit in pose and physical likeness. Anthropology "proves" kinship by representing those practices that can be best objectified by this symbol-system of genealogy.[28] Harris's is a kin diagram turned rhizomatic: collapsing the generational scaffolding, it prefigures the skip-hop movement of the childhood snapshot whose subject, it turns out, could be any one of several women supposedly situated in different historical moments.

The still images of mothers and daughters in *Physics* and *Lover* — photographed, filmed, drawn, and described — affirm two contradictory things. Certainly, they reiterate the fact that kin relations themselves are an important form through which time itself is comprehended as linear: the domestic photograph (along with the conventions of display that accompany it) and the conventionally genealogical kin diagram are two interdependent genres that materialize temporal difference and organize this difference into sequentiality. However, the still "shots" and static diagrams in *Physics* and *Lover* also affirm that lesbianism dangerously muddles generational time, albeit somewhat differently in these two works by queer women of two very different generations. Both Bonder and Harris seem well aware of the exhausted trope of lesbians as mother and daughter, a trope that figures lesbians as immature, asexual, and pathologically interdependent. As Kathryn Bond Stockton writes of Djuna Barnes's *Nightwood*, "Th[e] figurative mother-child relation . . . dooms [lesbian lovers] to a time that by definition can never arrive: the time when mother and child will inhabit the same generation."[29] Yet Bonder and Harris do not jettison this trope in favor of a more lateral, intragenerational, or peer-centered model in which (as *Coal Miner's Granddaughter* implies) the achievement of a lesbian present tense might necessitate distancing oneself from the past or refusing to age. Instead, their texts work by a filmic principle of temporal oscillation, the same gyroscopic movement I have claimed as queer. In *The Physics of Love* a little girl steps forward and back, a set of windshield wipers performs and then reverses the filmic "wipe," and the video tells its story by returning over and over again to specific still shots, snippets of home movie, segments of new footage, musical motifs, and fragments of monologue. Harris's plot (such as it is) swings back and forth between the stories of its main characters, abruptly abandoning one to take up another without transitional cues or even a shift in tense. *Lover*'s grandmothers, mothers, and daughters appear out of order, grow "down, then up" (7), and occasionally become lovers with one another across generations. In both works, mothers and daughters do collide in time and, in Harris, even inhabit the same generation.

The formal principles of these works, then, invoke different kinds of time than that of kin and generation. Certainly, their reiterative structures traffic in what Kristeva calls a maternalized "cyclical" time.[30] They also dabble in monumental time in the tropes of, respectively, 1950s Hollywood cinema and medieval saints — about which more below. But rather than privileging cyclical or monumental time and thus turning toward essentialist or mystical paradigms, both *Physics* and *Lover* struggle with domestic time, a particular heterogendered and class-inflected chrononormativity, an enforced synchronicity that seems at once to suffocate their female characters and to offer queer possibilities.

Tracking Domestic Time

What does it mean to say that domesticity is a particular tempo, a way of living time rather than merely a relationship to the space of the home? By the time industrial capitalism had decisively transformed the United States, women's work inside the home had also begun to take the form of a rationalized, coordinated, and synchronized labor process.[31] Domestic manuals such as Catharine Beecher's *A Treatise on Domestic Economy* (1841) stressed the need for order and efficiency in the home, at the same time that women's labor was naturalized into feminine influence through the figure of the angel in the house who magically kept things clean and people fed without seeming to lift a finger. In other words, middle-class femininity became a matter of synchronic attunement to factory rhythms, but with the machinery hidden. Moreover, the clash between task-based agricultural and household temporalities and the abstract and equal units of mechanized time was symbolically resolved in the home, through what the historian John Gillis calls the "ritualization of family life."[32] Gillis details the emergence of rituals associated with the family: by the 1850s, a newly commercialized, domesticated, and secularized Christmas had replaced the harvest ritual, and a decade later families were expected to have nightly dinners together rather than eating in shifts to accommodate farmworkers' hours. The word "weekend" entered the American lexicon in 1880; the early twentieth century saw communal Sabbaths increasingly replaced by nonreligious familial activities such as the Sunday drive.[33] The "family," in short, was no longer comprehensible through the rhythms of its labor and Sabbath-keeping but manifested itself through its own, separate hourly, daily, weekly, and yearly calendar of leisure activities. Once families began to be defined by clocked rituals and schedules, Gillis writes, "one could say that family was put into cultural production, representing itself to itself in a series of daily, weekly, and annual performances that substituted for the working relationships that had previously constituted the everyday experience of family life."[34] Here we can see how events coded as familial and photographic technologies of memory are practically coterminous. Family life was supposed to be like a moving watchworks, showcasing the precision of its routines and the synchronicity of its motions as evidence of intimacy, even as a kind of household habitus. And domestic photography became an integral part of this shift: as Hirsch writes, it "both chronicles family rituals and constitutes a prime objective of those rituals."[35] Family time, as it emerged, moved a formerly religious ritual time into women's domain, replaced sacred time with the secular rhythms of capital, feminized the temporalities considered to be outside of the linear, serial, end-directed time of history, and demanded and depended on visual technologies that required increasingly less physical effort from their users. While ritual self-representation required enormous amounts of work on the part of a household's women, who prepared holiday dinners, planned and executed family activities, and so on, the technologies for representing family time hid their own workings behind one-touch buttons.

This secularized cyclical time, in turn, offered a new version of monumental time. Within the ideology of normative domesticity, the proper maintenance of cyclical schedules and routines produces the effect of timelessness. But only with its routines seeming to manage themselves could the domestic sphere shelter this form of time: the work of the household took place within a protective casing, a temporal stasis that kept history at bay. By the mid-twentieth century, bourgeois mothers and their behind-the-scenes servants were responsible for what Thomas Elsaesser has described as the aesthetics of the still life, a tranquil household marked by not only visual order but also smooth transitions, recurrent rituals, and safety from accidents and untimely intrusions from the outside world.[36] That is, the middle-class household not only effaced the conditions of its own production (the housewifely and servant labor necessary to produce such order and stasis) but also appeared as pure temporal plenitude — as a surplus of what the late twentieth century would call "quality time." Again, popular visual culture both represented and partook in this temporal mode. Elsassaer claims that the aesthetics of quality time, of the household as still life, reached their apotheosis in the so-called women's films produced by Hollywood studios in the 1940s and 1950s. The careful mises-en-scène of these films, their tendency to linger on household decor and objects, and their dilatory rhythms of repressed emotional excess at once stop narrative time and hyperbolize the timeless, seamless, ideal middle-class household. Time literally becomes quality; the "woman's film" dissolves action into the elements of texture, color, meticulous placement, telling gesture.

Physics and *Lover* invoke and displace this mystified form of time. As if to hearken back to Beecher's ethos of streamlined domesticity, for instance, *The Physics of Love* both portrays and formally reiterates this pseudo-domechanical synching of the household. At one point on the video's soundtrack we hear factory noises — sanding, grinding, whirring, metallic whining, against which background a slow tick-tick-tick becomes audible. Over this we see an optically printed shot of a hand on an iron, moving back and forth on an ironing board, the juxtaposition of sound and image suggesting a possible congruence of household and factory time. But as the factory sounds and ticks continue, a narrator reads a series of dates and weights, from "January 14th, 1982: Weight: 164½ pounds," through successively later dates and smaller numbers, to "February 12th, 1982: Weight: 156 pounds." Layered with the previous sounds, we hear another, muffled female voice reading: "linoleum crumbling . . . ceiling cracked . . . window glass cracked," the occasional pauses in the voice-over filled with the ticking of a clock. Clearly, one message here is that housework consumes the female body, as the crumbling house of the working-class mother becomes a metaphor for what we later learn is her declining health. This linear temporality of decrease and bodily diminishment is complicated by the repetition-compulsion that is housework, as the image track flashes forth shots of various domestic routines and of miniature household appliances, and the factory sounds fade into the rattling sounds of a kitchen: the voice-over says, "She has taken thousands of footsteps, back and forth across the same patch of linoleum . . . the same movements, over the same spaces, over the same length of time. Why didn't she go mad? Thousands of others did. Too busy, too poor, too tired to have time to consider it." The soundtrack, a rattling fugue whose parts are clock-time, the slowly ebbing time of the dying body, and the hyper-regulated time of factory and kitchen, highlights the exhausting labor required to maintain a routinized household. Yet insofar as the parts of this segment of *Physics* don't fit, as sound fails to match with image and voice-overs overlap and interrupt, the video here suggests a class-accented form of maternality similar to the Dobsons' familial life. Just as the Dobsons fail to synch up their dialogue, the narrator's mother fails to produce a restorative and soothing symphony of household sounds.

In *Lover*, Harris invokes the synchronic time of domesticity more iron-ically. We learn from Flynn that as a child she accidentally unfastened her mother's watch and the timepiece was lost. A present from the boy who was Flynn's father, Daisy's lost watch signals *Lover*'s refusal of a hetero-sexualized chronometrics. Instead, the novel offers a lesbianized — but not domestically feminine — temporal scheme. Halfway through the novel, Veronica and Samaria have become lovers, after having been estab-lished as long-lost cousins who were once simultaneously married to a bigamist. Veronica, Samaria, Flynn, and Flynn's twin sisters Rose and Rose-lima all seem to be living together: the narrator reports that "there seems to be more women than usual in the house" (87). As the love affair progresses, Veronica amplifies "the erotic volume between herself and Samaria until the entire household begins involuntarily to twin her every move; to act identically" (86). This action recalls Veronica's job as an artist of sorts: she earns her living as a forger of paintings and so produces sameness as a matter of course. Here, as she becomes lovers with Samaria, eros "forges," that is, copies, as the references to twinning and identicality suggest. But eros also "forges" — welds by a certain heat — concurrent movements rather than images or objects. The members of this house-hold move and act in tandem, rather than being or looking the same. And unlike the households in *Coal Miner's Granddaugher* or *The Physics of Love*, whatever harmony Veronica achieves here comes from her *sexual* desire rather than her status as a mother, her ability to orchestrate an *erotics* rather than a family dinner. Veronica's skill as a choreographer of domes-tic time may be parodic, but it captures how the novel hyperbolizes and queers the cyclical and synchronous times associated with women, par-ticularly mothers.

Both *The Physics of Love* and *Lover* also lay bare the terms of mater-nalized, secularized "eternity," the monumental time of the angel in the house. *The Physics of Love* engages directly with the domestic melodrama that Elsaesser calls the bourgeois still life. Among the video's many re-turns is its obsession with Hollywood tales of overinvested and self-sacrificing mothers. Every so often, a scratchy female voice with a thick New England accent interrupts the layered soundtrack of *Physics*, reciting the plot summary of a Hollywood "weepie." One summary seems to be of *The Bad Seed* (1956), though the speaker's synopsis ends with "she de-cides the only way to save her daughter is to kill her" and omits the daughter's convenient death by lightning. Another recounts the story of *Mildred Pierce* (1945) and ends with the mother's "final sacrifice as her daughter begs her not to turn her in" for killing the man they both love. In the manner of Nguyen's work with the original tape of *Kip Noll, Superstar*, Bonder also presents a segment of George Cukor's *The Women* (1939) playing across a flickering black-and-white television set, a scene in which Joan Crawford as Crystal Allen and Virginia Weidler as her stepdaughter argue bitterly. With these synopses and snippets Bonder further compresses the already cramped time of the maternal melodrama. Nothing remains even of the films' own historical moment, and the summaries take up so little narrative space that their events seem to happen simultaneously. It is as if these melodramas are playing all at once, intersecting with and departing from the story Bonder's narrator tells in bits and pieces, of her mother dying piecemeal of cancer and her own growing addiction to narcotics. Both of these times — of cancer and of addiction — are indexes of not only the mind-numbing repetition of domestic life, akin to being dead or doped up, but also that most privatized and abbreviated genre, the case history. Yet eventually, as I will go on to argue, they offer up other ways to calibrate time in promisingly ahistorical ways.

Lover too trades on the plot summary to invoke and perform monumental time. Its inscrutable "preface" appears after the family diagram and consists only of a synopsis of Richard Strauss's *Der Rosenkavalier*, later revealed to have been authored by Veronica. Thereafter, the novel is divided into short sections somewhat like chapters, each of which is prefaced by a tale of a female saint's life, printed in italics. The first one appears atop the opening birth scenes and descriptions of photographs I have described and portrays an encounter between two virgin martyrs: *To save herself from marriage, Lucy gouged out her own eyes; but Agatha appeared to her and declared, "Thou art light"* (5). Lucy is one of dozens of female mystics whose lives and grisly deaths *Lover* periodically recounts: we might call them case studies of female resistance, or, more simply, of female intensity. The typical tale of a female saint recounts her refusal to marry, her violent punishment at the hands of angry men, and the miracles that take place at or shortly after the time of her death.[37] Each saint is released from ordinary time into the eternity represented and granted by sainthood. In particular, though, Agatha's pronouncement "Thou art light" effects the apogee of quality time, time as a sensory but here utterly disembodied quality—much like the bourgeois woman's diaphanous household (non)presence.

Moreover, "Thou art light" recalls the importance of photography and film to the production of feminized interiority, generational sequence, and familial performativity. Yet by contrast to this aesthetic, *Lover* is insistently "vaudeville" and bawdy: referencing a jumbled history of popular performance genres, its characters variously act out scenes from *Hamlet* in drag, build a blow-up sex doll, go down Niagara Falls in a barrel, tightrope walk, flaunt their status as Siamese twins, and perform random vignettes for one another: "Then, a sudden charge of energy through Maryann manifests itself . . . in the appearance of a derby hat on her head and a plastic machine gun in her hand. She disappears; then as suddenly reappears in the doorway to drop two brown eggs on the floor; which is hilarious" (47). The novel commits not only to lesbianism but also to performance traditions — most of them not narrative — in a way that suggests a repudiation of home photographic technologies' heterosexist history.

Taken together, *The Physics of Love* and *Lover* track the ways domestic time — a gendered form of and a contributor to class habitus — is produced. They understand that a displaced form of industrial labor, household work, disappears into timeless and naturalized affect through chrononormative timings of bodies, and through dominant uses of visual media. And they understand failures in this process as both class-inflected and queer. The mother-daughter relationship, in the hands of Bonder and Harris, becomes a problem not of physical differentiation but of intimacy and inheritance, troped as rhythm and sequence: will the lesbian daughters repeat their mothers' gestures ad infinitum, disappearing into the vortex of maternalized timelessness? Equally problematic, will the lesbian daughters leave behind their mothers' heterogendered ways of being and in doing so evacuate their own working-class pasts? The arrhythmia of *Physics* and *Lover*, the ways they shift between past and present, between the stillness of photography and the motion of television, cinema, and live performance, suggest an alternative relation to time. These new temporalities, though, are anchored to the body in ways that both risk and resist essentialism: for Bonder and Harris, "queer" is a differential meeting of eros and time, body and timing.

The Physics of Queer

Thus far, I have argued that domestic time emerged as a disembodied, secularized, and hypervisualized version of Kristevian "women's time": disembodied insofar as the biological rhythms that anchor Kristevian "cyclical" time get subsumed into patterns of household labor and ritual, secularized insofar as the stasis of the eternal gets replaced with the bourgeois mise-en-scène, and hypervisualized insofar as home photography and video secure the status of family as such and make domesticity visible *as* a form of temporality. Kristeva's own essay, interestingly, offers up its own possibility for a dissident, gendered, embodied temporal "otherwise." "Women's Time" ends by privileging the bodily experience of reproduction, arguing that pregnancy is an ethics insofar as it offers the "radical ordeal of the splitting of the subject: redoubling up of the body, separation and coexistence of the self and of an other."[38] In Kristeva's analysis, mother-love has the potential to be a form of postmodern, poststructural *askesis* of the sort celebrated by queer male critics like Bersani and Edelman, wherein the function of queer sex and queer being is to breach the borders of the ego. Kristeva's model, though, celebrates a certain languor: "the slow, difficult and delightful apprenticeship in attentiveness, gentleness, forgetting oneself."[39] Slow time, she suggests, is the time of the other, the time, we might say, of an ongoing breach of selfhood that both resonates with Bersani and Edelman's model of self-shattering sex practice and departs from those critics' privileging of phallic sexuality and modernist short, sharp shocks.

Kristeva, however, jettisons her own suggestions about the transformative possibilities of slow time and turns to space. She presciently relocates the pregnant woman's split embodiment in the project of dissolving "personal and sexual identity itself, so as to make it disintegrate in its very nucleus," a formulation that characterizes much of the anti-identitarian thinking of queer theory thus far.[40] She argues that the truly radical (non)subject must interiorize "*the founding separation of the socio-symbolic contract*," or somehow internalize as a form of consciousness the split between Real and Symbolic that accompanies the entrance into language.[41] This is certainly a more palatable and plausible way to characterize a queer insurgency than her initial metaphor of pregnancy, especially for those who choose not to reproduce or parent or who become parents without reproducing. Yet Kristeva's reformulation not only evacuates the force of the temporal for a spatial model but also recontains the messy and recalcitrant body: the radical possibilities suggested by a corporeal event are relocated to the realm of pure signs. It is as if she is advocating some kind of poststructural, Lacanian pregnancy, though how the space of that "interior" could survive such a split is left unexamined. In *The Physics of Love* and *Lover*, on the other hand, the corporeal event itself returns outside of heteronormative timing: Bonder's and Harris's characters are daughters but in Bonder's case never mothers, and in Harris's never depicted as pregnant. Yet both texts certainly bank on the body's persistent refusal to cohere with or as a singular identity. Furthermore, like Kristeva they locate that stubbornness in the fact that the body is a temporal rather than a spatial phenomenon. In fact, in these texts the body itself epitomizes the bad timing that can counteract the forms of time on which both a patriarchal generationality and a maternalized middle-class domesticity lean for their meaning.

Initially, *Physics* and *Lover* wrench the body from both visual economies and heteronormative timings by seizing the discourse of blood. For Bonder and Harris alike, blood indicates a body that refuses to disappear and temporalities that are irreducible either to genetics or to postmodern freeplay with chronos and history. In the mother-daughter relationship marked by differences in class and object of desire, it seems, blood neither flows down genealogical lines nor gets displaced into warm fuzzy sentiment but spurts, surges, coagulates, as in a wound. "My mother associated me with blood, discomfort, and sacrifice," says the narrator of *Physics*. She describes her mother dragging her back to the scene of her own birth by displaying a Caesarean scar: "She would show it to me occasionally, as a reminder of my ingratitude for the physical manifestation of her unconditional love. I kept waiting for it to talk, to say something, to tell me who had done this to her. I knew it couldn't have been me. I could remember nothing." The mother is pure, silent body; she possesses nothing of value to pass on to her daughter, nothing to say, nothing that allows closure and continuation — again, nothing to declare.[42] But though the daughter in *Physics* refuses memory, she is transfixed by her mother's wound, attached by the gaze to the scene of her own birth. Later in *Physics*, we see a close-up of a finger, blood bubbling up out of a pinprick, with another finger touching it. We don't know if the finger that touches belongs to the body of the finger that is bleeding or to someone else: here, blood has ceased to figure consanguinity. In fact, in most of *Physics*, blood is pure anatomy, disarticulated from familial destiny. It appears in segments or stills showing a translucent medical mannequin, a stain of platelets seen through a microscope, a snippet of video showing a surging vein, an anatomical slide with labels for the major arteries.

In *Lover*, blood initially marks sacrifice, but the sacrifice is that of personhood rather than of body. Flynn's grandmother compares her first menstruation to men's blood in battle: "They can only die. But we are never the same again, and *that is worse* . . . They said, Now you are a woman. *I* had been exchanged for a *woman*" (102, emphasis in original).

Flynn intends no such sacrifice of her humanity for womanhood: having witnessed her mother, Daisy, bleeding through a dishtowel stuffed into her underwear, Flynn wants to "stop blood" (111) and to encase her brain in a glass case that will keep it alive forever, independent of the body. But the body reappears in bloody scene after scene: the female saints who punctuate the text are variously stabbed, beheaded, garroted, eaten alive, and removed of body parts like eyes and breasts. These woundings signal both the body's necessity as the grounds for transformational sufferings, and its transience, its this-worldiness. They mark the sacrifices of personhood necessary for new forms of embodiment and power.

Queered by these two texts, blood departs from its heterogendered functions and begins to look suspiciously like sexuality. Rather than representing the biologized "before" to a postmodernistically queer "after" of mechanical reproduction, blood instigates alternative, and alternatively binding, temporal flows. On the one hand, like sex practice, blood gets aligned with discipline and stigma in Bonder's Caesarean show-and-tell and Harris's gallery of maimed saints. On the other, blood also eventually correlates with perversion, with proliferating forms of bodily pleasure that exceed the discourses from whence they came. In other words, in these texts blood enters a different bodily economy that is, in turn, a temporal economy binding mothers and daughters (if, in this logic, they can still be called these names) through means *other* than synchronous intimacy or genealogical sequence.

In *Physics*, intravenous drug use—the slow drip of the morphine bag, and the quick rush of the heroin high—is the predominant motif for the mother/daughter tie, rethought as a radically "junk" inheritance. Bonder's narrator alternates between descriptions of her mother's chemotherapy and pain management and descriptions of her own addiction to heroin: "The cure ate away at her body, replacing those fluids we shared with fluids that brought a bitter taste to her mouth. I tasted the bitter flavor of guilt as I watched her shrink, daily," she says, and later, referring to her own drug use, she states that "the cure renewed my body daily, adding those fluids which tasted like mother's milk." This commentary invokes the pre-Oedipal stage of nondifferentiation, but with a twist, for chemo and heroin are processed substances injected into the body, not "natural" secretions developed within it. In an unlikely scenario, the mother and daughter end up hospitalized in the same room, dying and detoxing respectively: "We lie side by side in matching hospital beds, each with our own IV drip pumping the life back into us. We share the soft glow of a narcotic haze. We feel comforted, and loved, although not by each other. Never by each other . . . It is the first thing we have shared in years."

This opiate fusion of women in an institutional setting looks like not only a repudiation of biological kinship but also a savagely ironic counterpoint to the sacred, monumental time of the pre-Oedipal, and to the film's earlier retellings of melodramatic plots in which a mother merges her identity into that of the daughter. In fact, the scene utterly mocks synchrony. Here, only in the distorted time and space of the drug trip can mother and daughter truly meet one another, the "bad blood" (as the film puts it in an intertitle) that has failed to bind them replaced by human-made liquids that succeed. The narrator goes on to disrupt the pre-Oedipal scene by describing herself and her mother taking photos of one another: "And I am caught, laughing. And guilty, full of her fluids." "Her fluids" are neither milk nor blood; in fact, it is quite possible that the addict daughter has stolen from her mother's stash of morphine. Here too, photos conceal as much as they reveal, index difference and antagonism as much as they foreground likeness and love. Recalling the figure with which *Coal Miner's Granddaughter* ends, that of the drugged-out postman lunching on a "burrito and a joint" who inadvertently creates[38] the conditions under which Jane meets a potential lover, this scene suggests something important about queer affinities, class, and the politics of time. I have argued that when industrialization synched up not only wage-based production but also household labor, it created new bodily hexes cued to the needs of profit but experienced as modes of enjoyment: work "force" and house-bound "family" were social relations borne of historical change that felt like natural and eternal affinities. We might read the kinds of jointures created by drugs, by contrast, as a figure for a class-conscious queer politics: one in which we understand ourselves as embedded in social relations — temporal as well as spatial — that may be generated *by* capital and thus illusory, but that also take on aspects and functions not fully serviceable *for* capital, just as narcotics can bind people to one another as well as to the drug trade.

Lover's ties between women resonate with Bonder's way of thinking about relationality in terms of alternative temporalities, and sexual dissidence in terms of temporal dissonance. Consider, again, the saint's tale that opens the novel: *To save herself from marriage, Lucy gouged out her own eyes; but Agatha appeared to her and declared, "Thou art light."* Earlier,

I argued that this scene ended with a disembodied, eternal time. But Agatha also affiliates with Lucy through nonconsanguinous blood, insofar as both women bear gaping wounds: in Catholic iconography, Saint Agatha is usually represented holding her own chopped-off breasts on a platter. Agatha's appearance before a female saint-to-be who has gouged out her own eyes suggests the power of blood to conjoin bodies in ways that go beyond the logic of genetic inheritance so often buttressed by the conventions of family photography, and even the puncturing of the hymen or the gushy fluids of pregnancy and childbirth. Indeed, as the medievalist Karma Lochrie writes, the eroticized mystical transports associated with medieval virgin-saints and holy women included fantasies of being "invite[d] to touch, kiss, suck, and enter the wound of Christ."[43] This trope invokes a feminized and punctured Christ whose wound is open to penetration like a vagina, and the simultaneous possibility of a hymen kept all the more intact by these vulval and oral, nonpenetrative "sealings" between Christ and his female followers. Following Kristeva, we might say that in the passage above and in Lochrie's account blood confounds the boundary between inside and outside to figure a subject split and made holy by *temporal* difference, by encountering the "slow time" of the eternal. And this binding of profane to sacred time is emphatically corporeal.

Lover's traffic in saints offers a model of the wound as a mode of affiliation rather than of poststructuralism's eternally deferred relationality, of transformation rather than of shared victimhood, and of breaching the boundaries of time rather than those of ego or identity. This wounded mode also goes beyond kinship as the dominant model for conceiving cross-temporal binding. It seems akin to Luce Irigaray's call for a rethinking of generativity "without reducing fecundity to the reproduction of bodies and flesh" and without the sacrifice of bodies, or even bodily pleasures. In Irigaray's view, the temporality of the body itself could usher in "a new age of thought, art, poetry, and language: the creation of a new *poetics*."[44] In "Questions to Emmanuel Levinas," she declares — somewhat cryptically — that pleasure itself is time.[45] Perhaps she means that in contrast to a male bodily economy where the sacrifice signaled by orgasmic expenditure produces momentary bliss, pleasure in the female bodily economy engenders more pleasure and thus more time. In this typically French feminist economy, then, pleasure figures multiplication and, crucially, change. Whether or not this bodily metaphor for a new temporality is essentialist, it is surely heteronormative in the way it ignores the potential of, say, anal eroticism or sadomasochism to multiply pleasure on male and female bodies alike. Yet Irigaray does offer the radical suggestion that bodily pleasure and temporality have something to do with one another (though the copulative "is" seems too simple). In suggesting a relationship between pleasure and time, she implicitly critiques the temporalities associated with heteronormative family: against generational and domestic time, she posits a time of the erotic encounter—but one that is also different from the ephemeral, urban, quickie encounters celebrated by the antisocial thesis and (alas) available so much more often to men than to women.

The Physics of Love has both a visual and a verbal lexicon for encounters between mother and daughter that exceed or eschew the familial forms of time I have described. Its image track figures the relationship between mother and daughter as a plate smashing on the floor, a wrecking ball hitting a building. The narrator speaks of the pair in terms of force and object, action and reaction, hand and striking surface, citing Newton's laws of inertia, acceleration, and reciprocal actions. But the final words of the video, spoken by the narrator, suggest that these encounters do not add up, either to a relationship or to history: "In this story, everyone suffers amnesia." Here she refers back to an earlier synopsis of an apparently made-up film:

> [Voice-over:] In this story a woman gets into an accident and becomes an amnesiac. After wandering like a vagabond for many years, she arrives and gets waitressing work in a small town. As she becomes friendly with the daughter of the restaurateur, she begins to have strange and violent memories. Convinced she has done something terrible to her own family, and has lost her memory to cover it, she attempts suicide. The young girl comes to her rescue and with this act her faith and memory are both restored.

Here, the amnesia trope serves to literalize the time of the maternal melodrama and of domesticity in general, for as several critics have argued, amnesia is popular culture's symptomatic trope for a loss of historical memory.[46] At the same time, though, the synopsis above suggests that amnesia also offers an escape from the burden of family. As the narrator puts it in another summary that seems to refer self-reflexively to *The Physics of Love* itself: "In this story characters bounce off of one another like atoms following independent trajectories. No action has irreparable consequences. No behavior has moral value . . . In this story there is no beginning, middle, or end."

In other words, under the spell of amnesia, all encounters are as contingent as those between brute matter. By the end of Bonder's video, the domain of physics, which is not dependent on memory or time and for the most part not subject to a visual economy, has trumped the logic of genetics and likeness. *The Physics of Love* leaves it at that. There are no rescues, no daughter figures rushing to restore maternal memory, no mothers capable of implanting lasting impressions. And the narrator has also fully replaced both the mother and the temporal regime of family with drugs: "I lived for those moments, those seventy seconds a day I was truly alive . . . Then the seventy seconds shrank down to nanoseconds, and those irreplaceable moments became electrons."

These atomic metaphors invoke the idea of unbound, pure energy, available for physical pleasure, for creative thought, and for self-directed action. In *Physics*, the mother's bodily energy, her capacity for eros and creation, has been expropriated for heterosexual reproduction and for unpaid work in the home. And as the images of whirling miniature appliances that punctuate the film suggest, capitalism has expropriated her bodily energy not only for profit in the workplace but also toward wanting and purchasing the commodities that promise domestic efficiency and order. In the first, more straightforward kind of expropriation, the homogeneous and segmented time necessary for wage work parallels and in some sense determines the mechanized domestic time through which the middle class articulates itself, and allows for the quantification of whatever else the body could do, as expropriable surplus labor or as leisure. In the second, more insidious kind of expropriation, the monumental and pseudo-progressive time of the commodity parallels and in some sense determines the temporal plenitude that depends on the effacement of household labor. This form of "time" actually annuls time, promising on the one hand release from work and death, and on the other a recurrent newness and vigor, both of which are continually deferred into the next product, and the next. Capitalism synchs up these times to direct the paltry amount of bodily energy left over after the extraction of surplus labor toward the consumption of ever more objects that seem to supplement that "lost" bodily energy. This theft of the body's capacities is achieved through a manipulation of time that Bonder's opiate seconds, nanoseconds, and moments refuse: thought literally as time available neither for work nor for shopping, the vitality signaled by Bonder's microtemporal reappropriations could, at least theoretically, be used for a new physics, for the making of new life-worlds beyond the shared drug trip (though not necessarily excluding it).

Lover takes that project of world making to the nth degree, beyond any recognizable social form: its women float in and out of several houses such that setting is almost impossible to nail down, and their relations exceed the categories not only of family but also of political movement or subculture. Interestingly, Harris traces her astonishing novel back to her mother's differential seizure of perhaps the quintessential commodity-experience marketed to poorer women. "I was a child aesthete . . . a lonely, anxious, skinny child," she writes in her preface to the reissue of *Lover*. "On a daily basis my mother compellingly described to me how worthless I was. I had early on elected to love beauty rather than love or hate my mother" (xvi–xvii). It turns out that this is what mother and daughter have in common. Shortly after Harris is born, her mother moves in with a beautician and becomes a hardcore fan of beauty pageants:

> My mother told me why she'd moved in with the beauty parlor operator: "Because I worship beauty."
>
> Rather than love or hate me, my mother elected to become a confirmed aesthete; I became acquainted at Mother's knee, so to speak, with a way to overwhelm reality that has come to be called the gay sensibility. (xxii)

In an echo of Plato's *Symposium*, Harris's mother rejects heterofamilial love or hate for an infinite potential to attach to objects, people, and ideas in ways that "overwhelm reality," passing on her love of a déclassé aesthetic production as yet another junk inheritance.

But Harris's gay (or at least camp) sensibility, though indebted in part to her mother, involves thinking sex itself in the broadest terms, as the taking back of a corporeal energy otherwise devoted to work and family, as the unsynching of the normative habitus for which "beauty" is a mere placeholder. This is what Harris means when she writes of her characters becoming "lovers," which is something more than, and yet depends on, sex between women. As she writes in the preface, "I am no longer as certain as I used to be about the constituents of attraction and desire; the less certain I become, the more interesting, the more like art-making, the practice of love and lust seems to me" (xxi). Becoming-lover, then, is a way to "overwhelm" the heterosexualized elements or "constituents" of attraction and desire: not only the supposedly natural continuum from female anatomy to feminine self-identification to desire for the opposite sex to pregnancy and childbirth but also the sequential, irreversible, teleological time that orders and gives meaning to this continuum.

Harris's becoming-lover seems akin to what Audre Lorde describes in "The Uses of the Erotic"; it is an eroticized joy in a form of creation that supersedes reproduction but is still anchored in the body.[47] It is also akin to the Deleuzean body-without-organs, whose connections across multiple surfaces catalyze new becomings.[48] For instance, dreaming of herself as "lover," Flynn fantasizes that "all she must do to maintain paradise is to fuck women . . . Flynn gives them all they need; and they do not burst but multiply and Flynn increases" (123). Her "increase" consists of herself, her multiplications engendering more pleasure rather than children, expanding the potential for encounter rather than sealing off the household. The novel also formally enacts the dynamic between encounter and increase on several registers: at the very least I would include the shifting first-person narrative voice that seems to multiply points of view; the untagged dialogue that allows speech to attach to more than one speaker; and the simultaneously centrifugal and centripetal force suggested by the kinship diagram, which seems at once to draw potentially everything into the family circle and to push major characters to its edges. In short, this is a novel based on the idea that accidental encounters — the very same ones figured as random in *Coal Miner's Granddaughter* and as violent in *The Physics of Love* — produce pleasure and affiliation, which then produce more encounters that produce more pleasures, and so on. As it turns out, this has implications for rethinking *class* as well as sexuality in temporal terms that go beyond *Coal Miner's Granddaughter*'s theatricalized arrhythmia, or *The Physics of Love*'s attention to and interventions into the tempo of domesticity. *Lover*'s structure of complex and contingent transgenerational affiliation gives form to a revolutionary theory of time, one that binds class and sexuality.

In a complex argument to which I cannot do justice in this space, Cesare Casarino links the enchainment and amplification of noncommodified bodily pleasures to class struggle through just such a theory.[49] Gesturing at something like a physics of love, Casarino cites the long history of Marxist thinkers, beginning with Marx himself, who engage with Lucretius's *clinamen*. This term names the arbitrary and unaccounted-for element of chance that causes an atom to deviate from what would otherwise be a straight fall downward, to touch another atom and thereby to create new matter. The atomic collision inaugurates a temporality similar to Irigaray's time of *poesis* — and indeed Harold Bloom identified it in his famous *The Anxiety of Influence* as one particular temporal logic that poesis can take: a turning back to literary ancestors that is also, both deliberately and inevitably, a misreading.[50]

For Casarino as for Bloom, the clinamen is a time of creation, of material and semiotic transformation and extension; in Casarino this comes without self-denial or exploitable surplus. Following Negri, Casarino writes that "time *is* the turbulent and intractable becoming of substance, time *is* productivity — and nothing else."[51] As productivity, the time of the clinamen does not defer fulfillment; it is at once means and end (and thus sounds a great deal like Irigaray's conception of pleasure). But tracking the term back to Harold Bloom's appropriation of it, the time of the clinamen also names a form of productivity that allows the atom's original path, which we might call, for our purposes, *history*, to be viewed anew: in the sparks that fly when atoms collide, "it is the continuum, the stationing context, that is reseen."[52] That Bloom Oedipalized the clinamen by figuring the collision as one between anxious poets and their mighty precursors should not blind us to its figurative power. For it heeds the call to make, of the sufferings and pleasures of one's predecessors, something new.

It is this form of temporality — one might call it simply the capacity to effect change in ways informed by but not die-cast by the past — that capitalism both liberates in the form of collectivized labor and then attempts to lock in for itself in the forms of both abstract labor and the commodity, which depend on quantifiable and expropriable segments emptied of historical time. Or, to put it differently, time can be money only when it is turned into space, quantity, and/or measure. Outside of a capitalist and heterosexist economy, though, time can be described as the potential for a domain of nonwork dedicated to the production of new subject-positions and new figurations of personhood, whose "newness" is not without historical insight, though it does not follow in any precipitated way from the past.[53]

In *Physics*, the possibility for new figurations of the sort I have suggested appears only in passing, in the languid sequence of images that ends the film. An old man, played by Bonder's father, slowly twirls a white dress glowing in the sunlight as it hangs from the ceiling of his porch. Shot in close-up black-and-white, a pair of lace curtains flutters. With only her torso showing, a woman wearing a long skirt whirls in circles and the skirt

6. Still from *The Physics of Love*.
Copyright Diane Bonder, 1998. Courtesy of Kathy High,
Mona Jimenez, Liss Platt, and Elizabeth Stephens.

dips and sways. Caught in the barbed wire atop a chain-link fence, strips of cloth and pieces of plastic bag flap unevenly in the wind. The narrator utters the film's last line, "In this story, everyone suffers amnesia," over a shot of a clothesline on which hangs a white chemise, lit from behind, waving gently in the breeze (see figure 6). The laundry returns us to the history that hurts, to the drudgery of the domestic sphere, and indeed, on the left-hand side of the screen, a small loop of clothesline hangs down like a noose: both this and the aforementioned barbed wire suggest that the daughter cannot fully escape domesticity. But the motion of fabric in these last few shots suggests a certain openness and play, a temporal multidirectionality, as things move back and forth and around and around. The motif of the fold certainly suggests something about the way memory works — that it is more tactile than visual, more about brief and achronological touches of one moment to another than about the magisterial sequence of generations in history.[54] The undulating fabrics, stand-ins for the earlier atomic encounters, also suggest something about pleasure. Casarino writes: "The fulfilled moment of pleasure would constitute the point at which desire folds back upon itself so as to go on producing other such points, other such moments. Pleasure is the fold of desire: it is the immanent point of *tangency* between our bodies and the force of desire . . . It is only deep from within the folds of such a temporality that one can begin to ask — as Spinoza does ask in the *Ethics* — what the body can do, what a revolutionary and liberated body might be."[55]

Textiles are an apt metaphor for the tactile meeting of body and desire, even for skin itself as the body's most delicate and voluminous surface of tangency. And *Physics* offers up the body as just such an absent presence, or missing possibility, within its folds upon folds: its dresses and skirts and chemises are like skins, empty of bodies, ready for them, yet also material in and of themselves, encountering only themselves as they move.

Lover offers a bit less on the level of imagery, though Harris grants at least a few of her characters the possibility of a bodily time released from both heteronormativity and, somewhat more obliquely, capitalist discipline. Samaria, having fallen in love with her granddaughter Flynn, escapes by boat to an island across from the home the women all share and stumbles across a severed head: "Gazing on a severed head was ease; it was rest. It took on the light of her working concentration: watching, she sighed. Something had happened, then she — like work — had begun to happen to the first thing" (206). Here, Samaria moves from the object of happening ("something had happened [to Samaria]"), to its co-agent, along with work ("she . . . had begun to happen to [the something]"). Work makes the worker "happen" rather than depleting her. The head Samaria gazes on belongs to a shadowy character, the male murderer of a nameless nine-year-old, and Daisy or Samaria have murdered him in revenge. But it also refracts an earlier image of Flynn, who in the novel's beginning had attempted to separate her head from her body, harnessing it to a machine so that she could be all brain and not subject to the vagaries of sexual desire. The return of the severed head represents, oddly enough, a certain restoration of Flynn to herself. For "Flynn," thinks Samaria, "was no longer recognizable except as lover" (206). As lover, Flynn now has some of the artistic capacities Veronica possessed all along; these are made concrete in Flynn's decision to become a rope-dancer: "[Flynn] goes back up, ready, nerveless, her arms her only balancing pole. She puts one foot out, readies the second. Beneath her is lamplight and space; and smells of old wood, turpentine, colors. Before she moves, she breathes. It is as if she breathes the colors — yellow to blue, brown to green to purple. Then she is into the light and gone, nearly across before she has even begun, Veronica wrote, the end" (213–14).

Flynn's synesthetic breathing of colors and movement "into the light" recall Saint Agatha saying to Saint Lucy "Thou art light." Each scene suggests a body both restored and transformed, but Flynn disappears rather than reentering the visual economy of the family photograph with which the novel began. That Flynn can be "nearly across before she has even begun" also points toward a looped rope, a folded temporal order, a convoluted history in which beginnings and endings touch.

As the consummate lover, though, Veronica has the last word, for the final sentence bleeds right into "Veronica wrote, the end," establishing that she has been both a character in and a writer of *Lover*. Throughout the novel, she has been producing new forms of subjectivity and new types of human beings, not only seducing women into lesbianism but also forging the new spatiotemporal representational orders that her "lovers" both emblematize and require. One of these is indeed the by now familiarly postmodern order of the simulacrum: Veronica is a forger of paintings for which there are no originals, and a time-traveler who "at any moment . . . can render herself again into all the creatures she started as" (7). Indeed, the novel is filled with fakes; to give only a few examples, Flynn has "become interchangeable with her fake . . . [and] no-one, not even Flynn, can tell them apart" (9); the novel's only two male characters, Bogart and Boatwright, spend most of their time making a gigantic foam-rubber doll; and of course there is the passage I cited earlier in which Daisy mockingly asks Veronica "Which is the mother, which the forgery?" (212). Thus *Lover* certainly privileges "unnatural" reproduction, at once denaturalizing motherhood, linking it to women's other creative, culture-making activities, and suggesting webs of caretaking and exchange for which the normative kinship diagram and generational logic seem entirely inadequate. And the forgeries can be read as a postmodern reworking of monumental time insofar as they do seem to evacuate history, not into a timeless domestic order but into a kind of cubist space, with times touching one another at odd angles. But what makes the process of "forging" so interesting in this novel is that it is so tightly linked to sexual pleasure. Being "lover" ultimately seems to mean being able to engage erotically, corporeally, with the fake: "When I did become a "lover—" Flynn says, "Veronica stopped painting me—because my face did not seem real anymore" (155). And here, of course, we see yet again Veronica's link to St. Veronica, whose imprint of Christ's "real" face in death —a touch with a textile—helped facilitate a religion based on an economy of imitation, replication, and metamorphosis.

This bodily contact with and enactment of forgery is where, I want to suggest, we can perceive this novel's most counterintuitive class accent, and the meeting or syncopated simultaneity of its queer and class accents. In 1983, Fredric Jameson offered the provocative suggestion that multinational capitalism (the emergence of which he famously dates at 1973) offers a different sort of pleasure from the Barthesian *jouissance* of the 1960s, a new experience that Jameson calls "the pleasure of the simulacrum."[56] This pleasure is a historically specific version of the Burkean Sublime, or the experience of encountering something so awesome, of such force or magnitude, as to endanger, shrink, or question the very autonomy and sanctity of the individual body and psyche — and perhaps a more collectivized version of the sexualized self-shattering that Bersani and others link to queer epistemology.[57] Jameson contends that the culture of simulation, its routine dissolutions of body and ego, may represent "so many unconscious points of contact with that equally unfigurable and unimaginable thing, the multinational apparatus, the great suprapersonal system of a late capitalist technology."[58] In other words, the copy-without-an-original, the whole matrix of mediation under which we live, is both a product of capitalism's ability to penetrate human consciousness *and also* a means by which we may see "behind" that matrix, if only momentarily. Jameson goes on to admonish his readers that any genuinely political demand for sexual pleasure must be both concrete and abstract: concrete in terms of a demand for pleasure in the here and now, and abstract in the way that a particular pleasure must be read as a figure for (rather than, and here I would concur with him, the means of) transforming society as a whole. Thus *Lover*'s traffic in simulacra, its sexualization of the simulacrum whose power lies in its stubborn claim to bodily sensation, becomes in this analysis a mode of apprehending and figuring the *economic* horizon under which Harris herself, along with her own mother, are just so much exploitable flesh. In other words, it is the simulacrum, the figure itself, and not the real that paradoxically enables and enacts a bodily form of apprehending history — both the past and the collectivized potential for change.

In very different ways in the three texts I have discussed, the temporal orders on which heteronormativity depends for its meanings and power, themselves imbricated with the whole system of production and consumption, can be contested only with an equally forceful commitment to thinking queer pleasures. These works suggest that queer pleasures are at once matters of the body, matters of timing, and tropes for encountering, witnessing, and transforming history, with a capital H and otherwise. It is to these reimaginings of specific queer pleasures as modes of historical apprehension — specifically, drag performance, sexual "bottoming," and sadomasochism — that I turn in the next few chapters.

two. Deep Lez

Temporal Drag and the Specters of Feminism

Every wave has its undertow.
— Meryl Altman, "Teaching 70s Feminism"

Thus far, I have argued that photographic media reveal, even as in their dominant uses they also coordinate, the diachronic time of repro-generationality and, more surprisingly, the synchronic, sychronized time of middle-class domesticity. I have also suggested that in several works by lesbian artists the microtemporalities of the queer female body — figured as a matter of chronic pain, violent wounding, addiction, and even atomic collision — counter these dominant uses. Rethinking such postmodern pieties as the similacrum, the works discussed in the previous chapter imagine eroticized modes of sensory contact that have the potential for apprehending horizons of oppression and change. Yet the time implied by their physiological and atomic metaphors is not necessarily *social*; that is, it does not necessarily correlate with the movements of human beings whose bodies are inscribed with contingent and often limiting meanings, and whose collisions take place not in "pure" space but in scenes of differential privilege and on sites already sedimented with import.

In her ongoing project *In the Near Future*, the New York performance artist Sharon Hayes performs yet another series of collisions between bodies past and present, but this time in spaces ghosted by bygone political moments. The project began when, once a day from November 1 to November 9, 2005, Hayes stood in the street at a different location in which an important activist scene or public speaking event had taken place.[1] Each day, she held a simple black-and-white lettered placard with a slogan, a new one every day: "Actions Speak Louder than Words." "We Are Innocent." "Strike Today." "Who Approved the War in Viet Nam?" "Abolish H.U.A.C." "The American President Might Have to Call in the National Guard to Put This Revolt Down." "Nothing Will Be as Before." "I AM A MAN." "Ratify E.R.A. NOW."

The slogans Hayes used did not merely reiterate what had been said in that place on some significant date. Instead, some were invented by Hayes herself and seem proleptic as well as anachronistic: "The American President Might Have to Call in the National Guard to Put This Revolt Down" invokes Kent State, the L.A. riots, and the worldwide rallies against the war on Iraq, but it also seems to incite as well as to cite mass action. The more generic "Strike Today" and "Actions Speak Louder than Words" (the latter held up in Manhattan's Union Square) remind us of the labor movement gutted by Reaganism and of silent protests from lunchroom sit-ins in the civil rights era to ACT UP's die-ins, even as they call for a response to current economic problems. "We Are Innocent" transforms what once might have been the slogan for prisoners' rights or the unfairly convicted into a sinister vision of Americans' post–9/11 victim mentality and naiveté about our place in a global economy—especially given that Hayes held this particular placard in Times Square. Some of Hayes's signs hearken back to specific historical moments, asking viewers to make connections to the present political situation: "Nothing Will Be as Before" echoes both the sloganeering of May 1968 and the governmental and media rhetoric after 9/11; "Abolish H.U.A.C.," suggests ties between McCarthyism and the era of the Patriot Act; "Who Approved the War in Viet Nam?" links two shady executive decisions on Viet Nam and Iraq; "I AM A MAN" sutures the 1968 Memphis transportation strike to contemporary lesbian and transgender activism.

Among all these incitements to action, all these gestures toward the past's unrealized futures, only one looks to be a completely infelicitous performance.[2] The sight of Hayes standing alone, holding a sign that says "Ratify E.R.A. NOW" (see figure 7) seems simply pathetic, even in contrast to the similarly anachronistic "Abolish H.U.A.C." For while HUAC was indeed abolished, the Equal Rights Amendment has a painful history of failure.[3] And according to some critics, it was fairly toothless, offering equal treatment under the law and in government but not in the private sector, abstract equality not substantive changes in gender roles.[4] While certainly Hayes's invocation of that battle reminds us that equal rights for women are far from secured, her own reiteration fails in two directions. Backward-looking, it seems naive in the face of numerous critiques of so-called equality feminism. Looking forward, the phrase "Ratify E.R.A. NOW" is not portable; it does not shed new light on contemporary situations, and were a reinvigorated, mass-popular feminism to appear again

1. Sharon Hayes performing *In the Near Future*,
New York City, November 2005.
Copyright Sharon Hayes, 2005. Courtesy of the artist.

on a national level, it would be unlikely to simply continue that particular battle. In short, Hayes's "Ratify E.R.A. NOW" lacks the hauntological call to action of the others.

All of Hayes's appearances in *In the Near Future* manifest the power of anachronism to unsituate viewers from the present tense they think they know, and to illuminate or even prophetically ignite possible futures in light of powerful historical moments. In "Ratify E.R.A. NOW," though, not only the slogan but also Hayes's very body turn into a vintage display. Dressed in drab but contemporary clothing and sporting an androgynous hairstyle, standing with legs planted firmly and slightly apart, expression grim and vaguely sad, Hayes looks a bit like the archetypal humorless lesbian feminist. Yet, born in 1970, Hayes would likely have come of age as a queer activist not within the lesbian feminism of the mid-1970s to the mid-1980s but rather within the late 1980s emergence of the gender-coalitional ACT UP, Queer Nation, and Women's Health Action Mobilization (WHAM), or within the butch/femme, S/M, pro-sex lesbian subcultures of the late 1980s and 1990s. Were Hayes to appear dressed in ACT UP/Queer Nation/WHAM's uniform of black-and-white sloganed T-shirt, jeans, and Doc Martens, or in campily masculine or high-femme gear, her ERA placard might read as a dated but ironic commentary on the failure of lobbyist politics and perhaps as an invitation to consider direct action again. As it is, in this moment of the performance her body looks less like a historicizing *detournement* than corporeal and sartorial recalcitrance.

I'd like to call this "temporal drag," with all the associations that the word "drag" has with retrogression, delay, and the pull of the past on the present. This kind of drag, an underdiscussed corollary to the queenier kind celebrated in an early 1990s queer studies influenced by deconstruction, suggests a bind for lesbians committed to feminism: the gravitational pull that "lesbian," and even more so "lesbian feminist," sometimes seems to exert on "queer." This deadweight effect may be felt even more strongly twenty years after the inauguration of queer theory and politics, in the wake of *Queer Eye for the Straight Guy*, legalized same-sex unions, and *The L Word*. In many classroom, popular, and activist discussions of the relationship between lesbian feminism and queer politics, and sometimes in academic scholarship too, the lesbian feminist seems cast as the big drag. Even to entertain lesbian feminist ideas seems to somehow inexorably hearken back to essentialized bodies, normative visions of women's sexuality, and single-issue identity politics that exclude people of color, the working class, and the transgendered.[5]

Queer theory has privileged transformative differences not only across gender, which is why Hayes's "I *AM A MAN*" looks so timely, but also, until recently, in the name of a radical future: this is why feminism on a lesbian can look politically anachronistic. Lesbianism and feminism are certainly not redundant with one another, but there are those of us for whom queer politics and theory necessarily involve not disavowing, or even having a commitment to, feminism and its histories. The bind I describe — and here I use this word to suggest both a problem and an attachment — is less about group identity than about time. How can we know for certain that something is securely done with?[6] How can we attend to feminism as, as Robyn Wiegman puts it, "our most challenging other" whose otherness is more than simply the state of being dead and gone?[7] Finally, what happens if we take Sharon Hayes's lead and reconsider "drag," so central to theorizing the mobility of gender identification and the visible excess that calls the gender binary into question, as a *temporal* phenomenon? As an excess, that is, of the signifier "history" rather than of "woman" or "man"?

These questions might reenvision the meaning of drag for queer theory, asking: what is the *time* of queer performativity? In her landmark theory of performative drag, *Gender Trouble*, Judith Butler's implicit answer to this question seems to be that time is basically progressive, insofar as repetitions with a difference hold the most promises. In her analysis, an identity-sign such as "lesbian" is most powerful for the unpredictable ways it may be taken up later. Repetitions with any backward-looking force are "citational," but Butler tends to read these as consolidating the authority of a fantasized original, even if citationality itself unsettles the idea of an origin: in *Gender Trouble*'s "repetition with a difference," the crucial difference seems to be novelty, not anachronism. Ordinary masculine and feminine performativity are retroactive, of course, but not in a way that intersects with any actual past, for the "original" sexed body that seems to guarantee the gendered subject's authenticity is in fact a back-formation, a kind of hologram projected onto earlier moments. To put it another way, *Gender Trouble* disregards citations of pasts that actually signal the presence of life lived otherwise than in the present. This particular version of Butlerian performativity, of course, has a historical context of its own. Just as late-nineteenth-century European and American sexologists proliferated and reified models of sexual nonnormativity in ways that followed the emergent logic of the commodity fetish, so does early Butler privilege futures in ways that are symptomatic of late finance capitalism before the crashes of the early twenty-first century. But the results of these temporal formulations can be that whatever looks newer or more-radical-than-thou has more purchase over prior signs, that parodically "signifying" on a sign is more powerful than taking it up earnestly, and that whatever seems to generate continuity seems better left behind. And as other critics have pointed out, theoretical work on "queer performativity" sometimes (though not always) undermines not just the essentialized body that haunts some gay, lesbian, and feminist identity-based politics but also political history itself—the expending of physical energy in less spectacular or theatrical forms of activist labor done in response to specific crises.[8] This may be one way that drag, as thought by queer performativity theory, actually occults the social rather than creating it.

Moreover, to reduce all embodied performances to the status of copies without originals may be to ignore the interesting threat that the genuine *past*-ness of the past—its opacity and illegibility, its stonewalling in the face of our most cherished theoretical paradigms—sometimes makes to the political present. Might some bodies, by registering on their very surface the co-presence of several historically contingent events, social movements, and/or collective pleasures, complicate or displace the centrality of *gender*-transitive drag to queer performativity theory? Might they articulate instead a kind of *temporal* transitivity that does not leave feminism, femininity, or other so-called anachronisms behind? I ask this not to dismiss Butler's early work—which has facilitated all kinds of fruitful decouplings of identities and practices — but rather to use it to think specifically about the history of feminism. In doing so, I intend to bring out the temporal aspect of Butler's important turn from a theory of performativity based on the play of surfaces to what she calls "the psychic life of power," where the subject inevitably "turns back" on itself and its pasts, and the psyche necessarily traffics in the deep time of the prior.[9]

The turn backward is always a constitutive part of subjectivity, at least in the Freudian scheme: *Nachträglichkeit*, or "deferred action," refers to the way that the Freudian subject reenacts, in displaced form, events that she could not give meaning to at the time they occurred. The Freudian symptom is the paradigmatic form of *Nachträglichkeit*, especially when the memory trace is acted out physically rather than worked through narratively, cognitively, or in dreams: in the hysterical gesture, the subject literally relives a past she could not "live" at the time. Robyn Wiegman captures the shift toward Freudian time in Butler's work most succinctly, writing that Butler's "psychic life" involves our ambivalent or failed subjection to these temporal and structural norms I have called chrononormativity: causality, sequence, forward-moving agency, and so on.[10] Butler's own backward turn reflects yet another moment in late capitalism, when the government and medical industries' slow response to the AIDS crisis shortened life spans, and the ensuing losses demanded a queering of mourning itself — a way of conversing with so many dead whose projects were incomplete and with the all-too-brief culture of exuberant sexual experimentation that Nguyen's video *K.I.P.* also longs to revivify.[11] As I will go on to argue, Butler's commitment to psychic life, to the temporal differential that constitutes subjectivity in general and that marked the early years of the AIDS crisis in particular, provides a way of thinking about identity and social change relationally across time — about "drag" as a *productive* obstacle to progress, a usefully distorting pull backward, and a necessary pressure on the present tense.

But the form of drag I would like to extrapolate from Butler's work moves beyond the parent-child relation that has structured psychoanalysis and structures her account of subjectivity, and might therefore usefully transform feminism's tendency to view politics in terms of generations or waves. Some feminists have advocated abandoning the generational model because it relies on family as its dominant metaphor and tropes feminist identity as a property passed on through inheritance.[12] Yet the concept of generations linked by political work or even mass entertainment also acknowledges the ability of various technologies and culture industries to produce shared subjectivities that go beyond the family. "Generation," a word for both biological and technological forms of replication, cannot necessarily be tossed out with the bathwater of reproductive thinking. Even the "waves" that periodize feminism are not the still, enveloping waters dear to maternalist rhetoric but are rather forces affected by gravity, which pull backward even as they seem to follow on one another. As Meryl Altman remarks in the epigraph to this chapter, the undertow is a constitutive part of the wave; its forward movement is also a drag back. It may be crucial, then, to complicate the idea of horizontal political generations or waves succeeding each other in progressive time with a notion of "temporal drag" thought less in the psychic time of the individual than in the movement time of collective political fantasy. Exteriorized as a mode of bodily adornment or even habitus, temporal drag may offer a way of connecting queer performativity to disavowed political histories.

Packing History

Elisabeth Subrin's *Shulie* (1997), a short, experimental video meditation about the radical feminist Shulamith Firestone, presents a vision of the queer embodiment I have described, one that explicitly intersects with feminist concerns about generationality, continuity, and historicity.[13] *Shulie* is a shot-by-shot video remake of an unreleased 1967 documentary film with the same title. The earlier film examined Firestone as a not yet famous twenty-two-year-old student at the Art Institute of Chicago, just before she went to New York to organize the New York Radical Women in 1967, the Redstockings in early 1969, and the New York Radical Feminists in the fall of 1969, and eventually to publish the groundbreaking feminist manifesto *The Dialectic of Sex* in 1970.[14] Rather than working the 1967 *Shulie* into a documentary that would link the post-adolescent art student to the pioneering radical feminist she became, Subrin restaged the original film's scenes and meticulously duplicated its camerawork, adding only a montage sequence at the beginning followed by a title card reading "Shulie, ©1967" and a few explanatory titles at the end. From Subrin's final titles we learn that in 1967, four male Art Institute students were commissioned to film portraits of the "Now generation" of the late 1960s, including one of Firestone. Subrin's text reveals that the 1997 *Shulie* is a remake of the 1967 film, credits the original artists, and announces that Firestone moved to New York shortly after the filming to found the radical feminist movement and write *The Dialectic of Sex*. These final titles put Firestone into a feminist genealogy, for they also claim that her ideas about cybernetic reproduction anticipated many postmodern analyses of the relationship between technology and gender. And the 1997 *Shulie* honors the way that Firestone herself paid homage to her predecessors: *The Dialectic of Sex* is dedicated to "Simone de Beauvoir, who endured," while Subrin's credits end with a dedication to "Shulamith Firestone, who has endured," perhaps more in the contemporary feminist political unconscious than on women's studies syllabi. But despite this invocation of a feminist legacy, the 1997 *Shulie* consistently undermines the idea than an intact political program has been handed down from older women to younger ones. Further complicating its work as a feminist historical document, Subrin's video — like Hayes's street performance — is also infused with the vicariousness and self-conscious theatricality that are so often the hallmarks of queer cultural texts.

The first sequence of the 1997 *Shulie* begins with a sign that condenses the eroticism of 1990s lesbian-queer revivals of earlier butch/femme styles, and the historiographic energies that are often unacknowledged as a constitutive part of queer performance. In the foreground of Subrin's first shot of mid-1990s Chicago, we see a shabby warehouse, itself iconic of an industrial capitalism that Americans are encouraged to think is located in the past rather than offshore. The side of this warehouse reads "New Packing Co.," acknowledging that the video itself is a reshoot, an old film in a new technological container (see figure 8). The phrase also alludes to the repackaging of collective feminist activism into individualizing consumerist styles in the 1980s and beyond: it might momentarily remind Subrin's contemporaries of the central role that "packing" — the wearing of dildos — had as radical separatist feminism met the feminist sex wars of the 1980s and the transgender movement of the 1990s and beyond. Finally, the warehouse sign is the sign of a historical ellipse: Subrin has reshot a film that was literally warehoused because Shulamith Firestone apparently asked its makers never to show it.[15] What the contemporary audience can see, instead, is a repackaging of feminist history's outtakes, which turns out to pack a punch.

The opening sequence goes on to juxtapose video clips of the empty streets and still buildings of 1990s Chicago with a montage of audio clips that invoke the late 1960s: an announcer describing "thousands of young people . . . being beaten in the streets of Chicago," crowds shouting "Peace now!," a warbling tenor singing the Miss America theme, and

8. Detail from *Shulie*.
Copyright Elisabeth Subrin, 1997. Courtesy
of the artist and Video Data Bank.

voices demanding "Am I under arrest?" Over this, sirens shriek, as if to
come from the past to sound an alarm, as if to jolt the current moment
out of its passivity. The title and copyright then mark the beginning of the
video's diegetic time and its merger with the prior film. But for the character Shulie, played by Firestone in the original and Kim Soss in the reshoot, 1967 seems just as politically empty as the streets of 1997. Though
Subrin's camerawork and action exactly follow the 1967 original, we see
little evidence of the earlier period's activism. Instead of a documentary
history of radical feminism, a biopic of Firestone's entire life, or an explicit
comparison of feminisms "now" and "then," Subrin redelivers a series of
throwaway observations and minor incidents in the life of a somewhat
depressed-sounding, very smart young Jewish woman in her final year at
the Art Institute. Listening to Shulie's commentary, which is startlingly
apropos of Subrin's 1997 present and of the present from which I write,
audience members are forced to confront the fact that the prehistory of
radical feminism is very much like its aftermath, that we have a certain
postmodern problem that no longer has a name — or rather, whose names
are under increasing erasure as today's women improvise individual solutions to lower wages, housework, childcare, unwanted pregnancy, and
other "personal" problems. And Shulie is clearly a point of retrospective
identification for Subrin herself, also a very smart, middle-class Jewish
female artist who had just graduated from the Art Institute when she

began shooting. History reappears neither as monument nor as farce but as the angel face of a twenty-two-year-old ("so young!" moans Shulie's art teacher at one point in the film), as promises not yet redeemed for the videomaker thirty years later.

Subrin's video, though, engages a much different aesthetic than that of a classic drag performance. *Shulie* isn't campy but, like Sharon Hayes's performance, entirely deadpan. There are no inside jokes or arch witticisms, only a stream of seemingly random comments. And as with Hayes and the ERA placard, *Shulie* privileges the political subject-position that has seemed, at least in queer theory, most at odds with the drag queen — the purportedly humorless radical feminist. But in its chronotopic disjunctiveness, Subrin's work does partake in a temporal economy crucial to queer performance and harnesses it to movements that go beyond the shimmyings of individual bodies and into the problematic relationship between feminist history and queer theory. Moving from an opening landscape that features the evacuated warehouses of 1990s Chicago, to follow Shulie through junkyards similar to those Firestone photographed in the 1960s, and ultimately toward the question of what 1970s radical feminism might mean to those who did not live through it except possibly as children, the video partakes in the love of failure, the rescue of ephemera, that constitutes the most angst-ridden side of queer camp performance. As Andrew Ross and Richard Dyer have both argued, the camp effect depends not only on inverting binaries such as male/female, high/low, and so on but also on resuscitating obsolete cultural signs.[16] Camp is a mode of archiving, in that it lovingly, sadistically, even masochistically brings back dominant culture's junk and displays the performer's fierce attachment to it. This temporally hybrid aspect of camp seems to inform Subrin's use of what she calls Shulie's "minor, flawed, and nonheroic" experience at the Art Institute, and even the video's willingness to redeploy radical feminism as a failed and yet also incomplete political project.[17]

Shulie's investment in cultural castoffs and potentially embarrassing prehistories also resonates with the crucial turn in Butler's work that I briefly mention above: the change from a nonnarrative, future-oriented model of "iteration" to a more narrative, past-oriented model of "allegorization," in which the material by-products of past failures write the poetry of a different future. As Butler suggests at the end of her essay "Imitation and Gender Insubordination" (1991) and amplifies in *The Psychic Life of*

Power, normative gender identity may be melancholic, emerging when a subject is forced to renounce her desire for her same-sex parent and then compensates by assuming as her own bodily gestalt the one she has been forced to give up wanting sexually. Preserving the lost object of improper desire in the form of a properly gendered identity, the manly man or womanly woman is, as Butler eloquently puts it, "the archaeological remainder . . . of unresolved grief."[18] And that ringing phrase is as true of any contemporary, gender-normative straight person as it is of Shakespeare's Hamlet, whose grief for his father unmans him (or mans him up) into paralysis. As Butler goes on to suggest: "[Drag performance] allegorizes *heterosexual melancholy*, the melancholy by which a masculine gender is formed from the refusal to grieve the masculine as a possibility of love; a feminine gender is formed (taken on, assumed) through the incorporative fantasy by which the feminine is excluded as a possible object of love, an exclusion never grieved, but 'preserved' through heightened feminine identification."[19] In this revision of the Oedipus complex, the lover's gendered identity takes shape not only as it does in Freud—through the melancholic preservation of the same-sex beloved as an object of identification—but also through her outward inscription of the beloved onto her own body, *as* her own body. Butler's parenthetical phrase "taken on, assumed" suggests that out of the depths of loss might emerge such exterior displays as gendered clothing, gesture, and so on.

Butler italicizes the term "melancholy," and that term has generated important rethinkings of queer politics and subjectivity.[20] But the term "allegorize" also restores a certain syncopated narrative energy to the discussion of drag. Allegory, a strongly narrative mode, has an affinity with ritual, a mode of performance—in that allegory often personifies abstractions, turning notions like beauty or love into bodies that interact on stage or page.[21] In another version of the term, allegory involves a telling of an older story through a new one (as, say, C. S. Lewis's *The Lion, the Witch, and the Wardrobe* retells the Passion of Christ), suturing two times but leaving both times visible as such. If drag turns bodies into emblems and vice versa, and if it tells a personal story that is also a story about a bygone form of gender, then it is, indeed, allegorical in the traditional literary-critical sense of the term. Normative heterogenders, on the other hand, turn identification *with* the same-sex parent into identity *as* that parent, perforce erasing the passage of years. The correlating literary-critical term for ordinary masculinity and femininity would be not allegory but symbol, which fuses incommensurate temporal moments into something singular and coherent, supposedly lifting a thing or idea out of history and into eternity.

And in fact, normative masculinity and femininity can only preserve the lost object of homosexual desire in the form of the lawfully gendered subject by evacuating the historical specificity of that prior object. For instance, if I renounce my mother and wear her body as my "own" gender, I certainly don't wear it as *she* did at the moment of my supposed Oedipal renunciation of her, circa 1969. But if I disseminate my mother's body in all its former glory onto the surface of my own in clothing, hairstyle, gesture, or speech patterns, I don't look or sound normative at all. As "Mom, circa 1969," my appearance writes onto my body not only the history of my love for my mother (or even the spending of her youthful body on the making of my own) but also and crucially *at least two historically distinct forms and meanings of "womanhood."* Occupying the temporal structure of allegory, as a femme in vintage wear I tell the contemporary story of my own gender by telling a prior story of gender — her gender. One comments on the other, using disruptive anachronisms to pivot what would otherwise be simple parody into a more earnest montage of publicly intelligible subject-positions lost and gained. As with *The Physics of Love* and *Lover* in the previous chapter, this story is neither one of continuity nor one of complete repudiation but instead a story of disjunctive, sticky entanglements and dissociations. For many committed to, say, both butch-femme and feminism, this kind of play on the flesh with "tired" models of gender performs just the kind of temporal crossing that registers a certain queerness irreducible to simple cross-dressing. And crucially, dressing circa some other decade, flaunting outdated feminine norms, has been one important way to signal femme identity.

Butler's momentary reference to allegory also goes beyond psychoanalysis to commit to the culture-making work of queer performativity. For allegory might be seen as the form of *collective* melancholia. Melancholia connotes inward movement, for it preserves the lost object as an aspect of one grieving person's subjectivity, interior, unconscious. Allegory, on the other hand, traffics in collectively held meanings and experiences, pushing the melancholic's rather solipsistic incorporation back outward in order to remake the world in a mock-imperialist gesture. Allegory's narrative "cure" can never be merely personal, or the allegory itself would not make sense: the prior story that gets retold must already be in the public domain. Thus the primary work of queer performativity,

9. Still from *Shulie*.
Copyright Elisabeth Subrin, 1997.
Courtesy of the artist and Video Data Bank.

rethought as complexly allegorical, might be to construct and circulate something like an embodied temporal map, a fleshly warehouse for contingent forms of being and belonging, a closet full of gendered possibilities. In fact, the performance theorist Diana Taylor's term for this "non-archival system of transfer" is "repertoire"—in her analysis, embodied practices and knowledges that we might also call, simply, habitus, except that the term "repertoire" suggests a more willful play with materials from the past.[22] Repertoire is a corporeal mnemonic, whose work is to reincarnate the lost, nondominant past in the present and to pass it on with a difference.

This ethic deeply informs Subrin's casting and costuming in the 1997 *Shulie*, which insists on the presence of a feminist repertoire in the 1990s queergirl.[23] Kim Soss's performance of Shulie, and Subrin's direction of that performance, neither pass as perfect reconstructions nor explode into campily hyperbolic deconstructions. Instead, they make use of anachronisms that disrupt what might otherwise be a seamless simulacrum of the prior text. For instance, Soss wears a rather obvious wig and glasses that look contemporary (see figure 9). Some of the video's critics have also commented that the main difference between Soss and the Firestone of the 1967 *Shulie* is affect. Jonathan Rosenbaum focuses on the contrast between Firestone's rather tortured emotional intensity and Soss's "colorless . . . guarded . . . vacan[t]" delivery of her lines.[24] Soss's Shulie seems to epitomize the "Whatever" generation rather than the Now generation. There are also several historically anomalous objects in the 1997 video, including a sexual harassment policy statement in the post office that Subrin used to remake the scenes of Shulie at her day job, a Starbuck's coffee cup, and a cameo appearance by Subrin herself.

These anachronisms of costuming, affect, props, and character break the 1960s frame, but none of them functions as parody, for they are neither excessive nor particularly funny. The 1990s touches are simultaneously minor failures of historical authenticity and the sudden *punctum* of the present. The idea that Shulie's wacky glasses, mini-dresses, and weary tone looked somehow cool in the moment of the reshoot, and might also be all that is left of the movement she founded, is a sobering reminder that politics can be defanged into commodified subcultures. Or perhaps it is inspiring, insofar as she looks a bit like a 1990s Riot Grrrl, and this latter movement initially reinvigorated some important precepts of radical feminism. But the subtle 1990s touches work against our own neoconservative tendency to consign to the irretrievable past anything that challenges a dominant vision of the future — and also remind us that social progressives have a tendency to be too easily embarrassed by earlier political moments. Shulie's seemingly formless "now" clearly resonates with our own, and since hers was about to detonate into a transformative future, the video implicitly asks, why not ours? In short, the 1997 *Shulie*, like the ERA moment of Hayes's *In the Near Future*, suggests that there are iterations, repetitions, and citations which are not strictly parodic, in that they do not necessarily aim to reveal the original as always already a copy. Nor do these performances simply consolidate authority, in that they leave the very authority they cite visible as a ruin. Instead, they cannily engage with the uncanny, with both the alterity and the familiarity of prior times, and tap into a mode of longing that is as fundamental to queer performance as laughter. Reanimating cultural corpses, *Shulie*'s iterations suggest, might make the social coordinates that accompanied these signs — rather than just the signs — available in a new way.

This strategy both extends and modifies an earlier tradition of the feminist reshoot pioneered by artists such as Sherrie Levine, Cindy Sherman, and Barbara Kruger, who imitated high cultural masterworks or the codes of popular genres, forcing viewers to speculate on what female (re)authorship or the insertion of an unidealized female body into these frameworks might reveal about their ostensibly universal representational stakes.[25] Both Subrin and Firestone herself do this kind of work for the documentary genre. The anachronistic touches that remind us that the 1997 *Shulie* is *not* documentary footage also temporally reframe Fire-

10. Still from *Shulie*.
Copyright Elisabeth Subrin, 1997.
Courtesy of the artist and Video Data Bank.

stone's struggle to resist her position as a woman in the arts, putting her into proleptic dialogue with the feminist artists who would follow her, including not only Levine, Sherman, and Kruger but also Sharon Hayes. This time-warp effect is most evident in a scene where Art Institute instructors critique Shulie's work (see figure 10). In *The Dialectic of Sex*, Firestone wryly describes how "liberated" women turned to the arts in order to seem like groovily occupied chicks rather than clinging, uptight wives: "Women couldn't register fast enough: ceramics, weaving, leather talents, painting classes . . . anything to get off his back. They sat in front of their various easels in tears."[26] Here she seems to be hearkening back to her time at the Art Institute, where her own art suggested that turnabout is fair play: little boys and male nudes, seated figures, construction workers, and civil servants crowd her canvases, all painted in a somewhat abstract expressionist manner. Assuming that the paintings that Subrin used in 1997 mimic Firestone's actual style, Firestone was clearly exploring the fragilities and cultural distortions of male embodiment long before masculinity studies hit the academy. Or perhaps she was declaring "I AM A MAN" before either the sanitation strike a year later or the transgender movement decades later. Yet her teachers genericize and feminize her work, claiming that her paintings "are what they are," and that "the theme behind" her photographs is "the same . . . your interest in people, and the[ir] lives," as if she is merely giving form to a natural womanly concern with others. If Subrin has indeed duplicated their camerawork, even the four male documentarians of 1967 seem to have caught the irony: they apparently shot Shulie painting a male figure so that she seems to return the male gaze, for Soss looks back and forth at the cameraman himself as if he were her model. Her five male teachers do not seem to have been so bright. Dismissing her work with the male body and the male social subject as "grotesque," "a little on the dreary side," and "very indecisive," the art faculty pushes her toward filmmaking, claiming that cinema is a more direct treatment of reality. The irony of this is palpable too, since in the original film Firestone is clearly already working with and in the postrealist techniques made available through this medium by performing the part of the "documentary" subject Shulie, just as Soss performs Firestone performing the part of Shulie in the 1997 video.

Despite Firestone's play with what would later be recognized as the postmodern representational strategies of returning the gaze and performing the self, Subrin refuses to reinstall her into a linear feminist art history. In a complicated and confusing scene that follows the art critique, Shulie herself goes on to explicitly repudiate the cultural logic of reproduction whereby "generation" is a secure figure for either continuity or for complete rupture — and by repeating this scene, the 1997 *Shulie* complicates the relationship between Shulie and her reanimator, younger and older, prefeminist and postfeminist. In the reshoot, Subrin (who plays the on- and off-camera part of the original documentarians) asks Shulie if her feelings of connection to outsiders relates "to this question of being a generation." Coming from a man as it originally did, this question seems narrow-minded, for it misrecognizes as a generation gap what Shulie's artwork has already clearly rendered as a gender gap. But because Subrin herself takes over the role of a somewhat authoritarian, misguided interlocutor, gender does not simply trump generation, linking the two women across time. For the scene also captures the failure of two *women* to constitute a meaningful political cohort, of Second Wave and Generation x to merge smoothly into some eternal Generation xx. Shulie, sounding surprised, repeats the question about "being a generation." The documentarian replies, "I mean, this is something that's very strong among so many people of your age, that they see themselves to be part, very importantly, a part of an important generation." Because Subrin's impatient voice comes from the 1990s, "your age" becomes ironic, suggesting her own slight irritation with 1960s radicals as perhaps the most self-consciously "generational" cohort, and paying wry homage to the fact that women from the "important generation" of the 1960s now often make major decisions about the careers of women like Subrin herself.

But Shulie retorts, "Well, I wouldn't say that there are so many who feel alienated from it," apparently shifting the topic from the Now generation to mainstream society, and thereby dismissing even shared outsiderhood as a form of groupthink. The documentarian reiterates, "I'm saying that there are many who feel part of it, not alienated, but who feel very much a part of it," reorienting the "it" back to the Now generation. "Oh," says Shulie, "You said that they feel part of it, and I said I didn't." The documentarian assents. Here, Shulie seems to hold out for a feeling of alienation that might register something besides a simply chronological generation gap, a feeling that the subsequent departure of many feminists from the traditional left would make explicit in gendered terms. "Well," Shulie says, apparently giving up on pursuing her discomfort with the idea of a collectivity whose main claim to politics is being born within a few years of one another or witnessing the same events together, "Yes, you know. That's true." But she does not seem to mean this any more than she does when she gives up and agrees with the cruel dismissals of her work in her art critique.

This conversation about generations adds another layer of irony: though the historical Firestone could not possibly feel herself literally a part of Subrin's generation, Subrin's address to the past suggests that Firestone might have done better "here." For Firestone's later interest in cyborg reproduction outside the womb as the key to feminist liberation is more in keeping with the antiessentialist theories in which Subrin was trained in the 1980s and 1990s than with what critics have associated with second-wave feminism. Subrin, on the other hand, seems to feel herself more part of Shulie's "pre"-feminist moment than her own "post"-feminist one: Shulie's commentary and experiences reveal that the prehistory of 1970s radical feminism is very like its aftermath. B. Ruby Rich insists that Subrin's version of *Shulie* "completes a certain cycle: the first generation of feminist theory as revisited, fetishized, and worshipped by the new generation."[27] But I am not sure that the language of worship does complete justice to the profound ambivalence of the video, which is as accusatory as it is reverential, as much about the lack of a genuinely transformed context for women born into the 1970s and beyond as it is about an admiration for ideas that came earlier. The cycle of social justice for women is, Subrin's presence in the film suggests, far from complete, and the video is a way of "being in time with feminism," as Wiegman puts it, which "is more a problem of desire than of history or politics."[28] In that latter sense, *Shulie* is a queerly lesbian-feminist film, for Subrin's desire for an unreferenced "something" is palpable.

If anything, Subrin *refuses* to solve the problem of desire for feminism through the fetish, to disavow what is not present in her primal encounter with Shulie (at the very least, the "real" Firestone, a fully available past, a coherent origin for radical feminism, and an intelligibly political doctrine issuing from her documentary subject), to cover that lack with the false totality of interviews with Firestone's friends or successors, or to provide explanatory voice-overs suturing the scenes to Firestone's biography as a whole. Similarly, Shulie refuses to dismiss her own feelings of lack just because she cannot name them in the available political terms of her moment: speaking of her own alienation from the Now generation, she says, "Well, I know that's not very hip. I'm sorry, it just happens to be true." The documentarian asks urgently, "Why, what's hip? What's your definition of hip?," as if this will finally locate Shulie in her "own" generation. Shulie replies, "To live in the now." "To live in the *now?*" the documentarian reiterates, "Where's that?"

Where, indeed? If *Shulie* demonstrates the impossibility of fixing something securely in the past, it recognizes the same unlocatability of the present, for where is the feminist, lesbian, or even queer "now" in 1967, in 1997, or whenever you are reading this sentence? In the video's only moment of genuine parody, Shulie signals the uselessness of "now" by rattling off the mantras of live-and-let-live hippiedom: "Don't worry about tomorrow, live in the now . . . Life is fun, life is pleasant, we enjoy friends and drinking and smoking pot . . . Why should we worry about anything?" In the same breath, she emphatically rejects this outlook: "Sure, that's fine, good for them. I don't care. I want to give it some form." Here and in other parts of the video, she seems to be speaking only of art as a form of cognitive mapping: "Reality is a little chaotic and meaningless, and unless I give it some form, it's just out of control." She declares, "I hate any date that goes by that I haven't made some kind of landmark . . . I hate the shapelessness of it . . . It's not enough for me to just live and die; I don't like it enough."

But it turns out that she was also forging ways of giving the present a collective, political, and historical form, rather than the individualist and aesthetic one her comments imply. For the documentarians of 1967 picked the wrong locale for "Now," and the "Shulie" character does not clue them in as to what Firestone was apparently doing during the original film's production. She seems to have hidden from them her activities with Chicago's Westside group, the first radical feminist group in the country.[29] These activities appear only in her vague statements that sexual involvements with men who agree with her on "these sorts of things" have not been a problem, but that men "don't agree with this, still." In both the 1967 and the 1997 versions, the question remains open whether the "things" in these statements were, at the moment of the filming, her individual pursuit of artistic or intellectual work, her private views about gender roles, or her activities in a fledgling movement. Even in the *original* film, the crucial political referent is missing.

Though Shulie seems to be speaking the language of the alienated, resolutely anticommunal, formalist artist, she also gives a clue to the historical method she herself employed a short time later and that Subrin herself reworks: she says she would like to "catch time short, and not just drift along in it." She doesn't mean she wants to freeze time into period tableaux: rather, she wants to seize it for the kind of historical rupture that would make "progress" and "regress" obsolete measures, to use a caesura or time lag to show how her own "now" has already been staged as a desirably hip and modern destination.[30] By the time Firestone wrote *The Dialectic of Sex* in 1970 she would flesh out her relationship to the generational logic she resisted in the 1967 *Shulie*. The epitaph for that book comes from Engels, and is worth quoting in full:

> When we consider and reflect upon Nature at large or the history of mankind or our intellectual activity at first we see the picture of an endless entanglement of relations and reactions, permutations and com-

binations, in which nothing remains what, where, and as it was, but everything moves, changes, comes into being and passes away. We see therefore at first the picture as a whole with its individual parts still more or less kept in the background; we observe the movements, transitions, connections, rather than the things that move, combine, and are connected. This primitive, naive, but intrinsically correct conception of the world is that of ancient Greek philosophy, and was first clearly formulated by Heraclitus: everything is and is not, for everything is fluid, is constantly changing, constantly coming to being and passing away.[31]

Here Firestone claims allegiance with Marx's and Engels's dialectical materialism, a direct descendant of the Heraclitean notion of flux precisely insofar as it demanded attention to the relations between things rather than to their essences. "Because they were able to perceive history as movie rather than as snapshot," Firestone writes, "they attempted to avoid falling into the stagnant 'metaphysical' view that had trapped so many other great minds": for her the Marxist vision of history is cinematic *avant la lettre*, insofar as both are capable of revealing new connections between things and apprehending time through change.[32] Firestone also claims that the metaphysical error "may be a product of the sex division" — implicitly, this suggests that any genuinely historical analysis would necessitate a reorganization of gendered labor.[33] To motivate a transformative politics, Firestone argues, we need a vision of capital that sees labor as a gendered social relation, that understands how the "natural" progression toward capital begins with the appropriation of women's biological capacity to raise children.[34]

The Dialectic of Sex also disrupts the ostensibly revolutionary presentism of her own feminist peers: to "catch time short" does not mean to celebrate a break with the past but something closer to what I mean by temporal drag. By "historical analysis" Firestone sometimes seems to mean, if her own method and commentary in *Shulie* and in parts of *The Dialectic of Sex* are any indication, a way of forcing the present to touch its own disavowed past or seemingly outlandish possible future. For Firestone claims that "feminism, in truth, has a cyclical momentum all its own."[35] She insists that science will free women from biology, allowing women the time and optimism to develop political ideas, and that "cyclical momentum" involves the inevitable backlashes that have reduced those political ideas to a demand for equal rights rather than a remaking of social relations. While her focus on biology as the core of women's oppression and her faith in technology seem less tenable today, her use of feminist history is more promisingly complex. She states that the radical feminist position of the late 1960s and early 1970s is "the direct descendant of the radical feminist line in the old movement," and despite the genealogical language, rehabilitates the very activists whom her own feminist peers rejected.[36] She describes the nineteenth-century American Women's Rights Movement (which she calls the WRM) as a radical grassroots agenda bent on transforming family, church, and state, and eventually overwhelmed by the "frenzied feminine organizational activity of the Progressive Era" and the single-issue suffragists.[37] Of course this rehabilitation was in many ways no different from any back-to-the-roots resurrection of earlier political moments; Firestone merely asked her fellow activists to think in terms of radical and conservative versions of the politics that travel under the sign of feminism, rather than in terms of horizontal breaks with a homogeneous past.

But in their cross-temporal identifications, Firestone, "Shulie," and Subrin all avoid both sentimental and sadistic/masochistic fantasies of intergenerational contact between feminists, where older women become the objects of reverence or the targets of outlawism.[38] While this model was clearly informing Firestone's peers' rejection of the WRM (at least as she narrates it), Firestone introduced a different politics of the gap: rather than the inevitable "generation gap" that supposedly aligns members of a chronological cohort with one another as they move away from their predecessors, she concentrated on the amnesic gaps in consciousness that resulted from the backlash to the first WRM.[39] Elliptically attaching the earliest WRM to her own movement just as Subrin elliptically attaches the moment preceding radical feminism to her own, Firestone let a former feminism flare up to illuminate the Second Wave's moment of danger, which was indeed played out — as Hayes also suggests — in the reduction of radical feminism to the ERA movement.

In an important contrast to Firestone, though, Subrin resists the rehabilitative gesture that would position the former as a heroic figure on whom a better future feminism might simply cathect. First, the film's most jarring anachronism appears in a scene that Subrin admits she almost cut from the film and that in an earlier, published version of this chapter I myself failed to address. Shulie works at a post office, where her fellow employees are all black women. As Subrin points out in her own essay about the piece, one scene at the post office looks at first like the historical turning point of the video, which finally locates its topic firmly in the past and its genre as a true-to-life documentary. Over shots of the women's daily routine, Shulie suggests that the high percentage of "Negroes" working at the post office is because "Negroes can't get anything except for a federal job." She might mean that she thinks they aren't qualified, or she might be referring to racial discrimination: the 1997 video refuses to clarify the 1967 film's ambiguity. Shulie goes on to say that "if you meet a Negro and you want a subject of conversation, the first thing you ask them is: how long have you worked at the post office? And then you have something to talk about!" She describes her "fraternity," a "brotherhood" of post office workers and the solidarity she feels with them, equating that feeling with having "gone to jail with them" in civil disobedience. Her patronizing, naive, cringe-inducing attitude and the outdated term "Negro" do feel, at first, like an anachronism of a different sort from the sly 1990s touches — one that comforts today's audiences by signaling the progress made since the supposedly white-dominated, racist, exclusive women's liberation movement that the video's Shulie seems on the surface to proleptically represent. But the terminology and Shulie's accompanying attitude are what Subrin calls "coded vintage discourse," which is to say that by refusing to change the script words to "African American," Subrin eschews either a decorative difference of language that would signal a progress narrative, or a humorously untimely insertion of today's language into yesterday.[40] Instead, *Shulie*'s "Negroes" and fantasized solidarities register the ways that many white feminists jettisoned the antiracist causes that first animated both the suffrage movement and women's liberation even as they appropriated the language and tactics of those causes. Shulie's monologue on race also reminds us that in modernity's various self-representations, racial difference has operated as the sign of anachronism *tout court*: however proto-postmodern Shulie herself might be, she sees "Negroes" as stuck in that bastion of state-sponsored inefficiency, the post office. As anachronism's emblem, racialized blackness seems to secure the present's modernity, its difference from rather than interpenetration with earlier moments: wherever "race" is, there modernity supposedly cannot be, *yet*.[41] Sadly, Shulie denies to African American activism and history the disjunctive mode of historicizing that Firestone advocated for feminism. Both the filmic character and the historical author confine African Americans to the waiting room, or perhaps locked post office box, of history.[42]

(Getting) Down with Children

Perhaps because children are others who have no prior activist history to rescuscitate or disavow, Firestone held more radical views of them than she did of "Negroes": in her view, the sexual liberation was incomplete if children were still property or, indeed, still marked off as physically and cognitively inferior. Subrin hearkens to this aspect of Firestone's radicalism by deploying the figure of a woman younger than herself, complicating that figure's location in an earlier time and availability for identification: in the 1997 *Shulie*, the elder is also a younger, much as in Toni Morrison's *Beloved* the return of the repressed history of slavery takes the form of the teenaged "ancestor" Sethe, who babbles and drools like a baby. There is something about Shulie's rawness of expression, the lack of terms with which she can think about her own experience, the meanderings of her thought-trains, that the video captures as a mode of political possibility. Neither political foremother, nor peer, nor wayward daughter, Shulie, like "Now," is multiply elsewhere.

One of these elsewheres is particular to Subrin's own moment and to the political context in which the 1997 *Shulie* was produced, when the figure of the young girl illuminated so many zines, manifestos, and other cultural productions coming out of or extending the Riot Grrrl movement.[43] According to Subrin, the middle-aged Firestone refused to cooperate with and thus far will not comment on *Shulie* — but Subrin's insistence on taking the young Firestone seriously as a political thinker and an object of obsession represents less a compromise than a commitment to the "girl" icon of Subrin's own feminist environs.[44] For in fact, feminist temporal drag itself had already emerged in the early to mid-1990s as a self-reflexive tactic of personal style, of performance, and of collective identification among young women who flaunted nonhegemonic femininities in misogynist urban hardcore scenes. Whether "girl" bands and collectives traveled under the sign of Riot Grrrl or not, they shared an aesthetic. Mixing punk and vintage clothing with such childlike accessories as lunch boxes, barrettes, and ankle socks, and overlaying jangly chord progressions with high, shrill voices, the look — like the sound — was something like Patti Smith meeting the Brady Bunch.[45]

When these 1990s artists and activists deployed the sign of the girl in their videos, zines, song lyrics, and eventually websites, they implicitly critiqued some radical feminists' repudiation of their own 1950s girlhoods as a time of false consciousness, allowing the politicized adult a more empathetic, indeed erotic relationship to her former vulnerabilities and pleasures. In zine titles such as "Riot Grrrls," "Girl Germs," and "Baby Fat," in band names like "Bratmobile," in songs like "Rebel Girl," "girl" embraced an embarrassing past as the crucial augur of a critical yet also contingent future. This revolution of "little girls" willingly exposed the fantasies, desires, and sexual experiments of childhood, and in retrospect seem to have epitomized Eve Sedgwick's suggestion that queer politics must refuse to abject even the most stigmatized child-figure from formulations of adult political subjectivity. As Steven M. Barber and David L. Clark elucidate, Sedgwick's work was in the first instance concerned with temporality: the hauntings of the gothic genre, the return of repressed homosexual desire within the homosocial, and eventually, via Henry James, the relation between "the queer adult that one *is* and the queer child that one *was*."[46] This latter relation, figured in Sedgwick's work as a promise, necessarily entails a dialectic between a protean sense of "queer" as polymorphous, as alienated, as somatically and psychologically estranged from adulthood in unpredictable ways, and a more pointed sense of the term as interventionist, as transformational, as antinormative. Such a dynamic between not only adult- and child-selves but also kinds of queerness entails a certain cleaving — that is, a simultaneous rupture and fusion. Correspondingly, the "girl" movement also refused to locate the girl as the beginning of either identity or politics; she represented what Elspeth Probyn calls "a political tactic . . . used to turn identity inside out."[47] The girl-sign acknowledged an uncontrollable past, the uncontrollability of the past, its inability to explain the present — and the promising distortions effected when the past suddenly, unpredictably erupted into the then-present forms of sexual and gendered personhood.

Refusing distance from the child-self also became, in the queer/ feminist culture of that moment, a means of critiquing contemporary public culture. In *Shulie*, in Subrin's prior videotape *Swallow*, in *The Judy Spots*, produced with Sadie Benning, and in other women's cultural productions of the 1990s, "girl" was a gendered sign of the cultural reorientation that Firestone advocated in *The Dialectic of Sex*: the constitution of children as members of a distinct public, whose socialization and demands might be thought collectively.[48] Early to mid-1990s references to *Free to Be You and Me*, *Schoolhouse Rock*, Amy Carter, and so on became the traces of a culture that was, for at least a while, genuinely hopeful about the relationship between children and the mass media. These 1990s reappropriations of 1970s culture were more than mere nostalgia on the part of a cohort born after 1965. The dissemination of "girl" as an ironic political identity implied that the liberal feminist turn toward equalizing parental roles in the service of producing more flexibly gendered children might have been a turn away from the broader social contexts in which parenting occurs[49] — the social contexts that Firestone attended to in *The Dialectic of Sex* when she wrote that "we need to start talking now not about sparing children for a few years from the horrors of adult life, but about eliminating those horrors."[50] Echoing Firestone's critique of the segregation of children into schools, parks and playgrounds, and for-kids-only culture, 1990s texts operating under the sign of "girl" spoke insistently of a feminized, eroticized children's public sphere *beyond* even the most progressive productions made by adults for children. In a sense, the girl icon seized the symbology of missing children and lost childhoods, which Marilyn Ivy has persuasively read as a sign of the privatization of culture, but used it to disseminate children's and adolescents' *public* spheres untethered from commercial profit and parental guidance: high school bands, all-ages shows, zine networks, video diaries, and the like.[51] The queered girl icon demanded the transformation of sentimental love for the "inner child" and for the child-as-future into both an acknowledgment of children as sexual subjects and a collective reorganization of the conditions of childhood itself. The slogan for this movement might have been "regress for redress": adults in kidwear, tantrums and rants as forms of political expressivity, juvenilia as manifesto.

Shulie is not a child, yet her odd hesitations and outbursts do contribute to a childlike aspect that the original Firestone apparently lacked. Subrin's revivification of her elder in the form of a younger self registers some hope that a revolution *for* as well as *of* little girls might be in the works — that Firestone's call for the political and sexual liberation of children might have been answered in the 1990s cultural politics evoked by Soss's costuming and gestures. Subrin's illicit recreation of Shulie also resonates with the sadistically loving culture of queer fandom, in which stars' most vulnerable younger (or aging) selves become the nodal points for shared feelings of shame, defiance, and survival. And Shulie's status as not-yet-identified (as "adult woman," as "feminist," as "lesbian," as the representative of a completed movement) allows Subrin a point of entry into the contemporary moment of the reshoot in terms other than "post." In fact, *Shulie* forces us to reimagine our historical categories, to rethink our own position in relation to the "prehistorical" rather than in relation to the relentlessly "post." Subrin's intervention offers a corrective to the idea that we can ever be genuinely postfeminist — unless "post" signifies an unlocking of Shulie's post office box, an endless dispatch between past and present social and subjective formations including those that seem to have been disjoined somewhere along the way, as with various antiracist and feminist movements.

Shulie's promise lies in what the language of feminist "waves" and queer "generations" sometimes effaces: the mutually disruptive energy of moments that are not yet past and yet are not entirely present either. She is a figure who has not yet entered her own history, her own official biography. The messy, transitional status of her thinking asks us to imagine the future in terms of experiences that discourse has not yet caught up with, rather than as a legacy passed on between generations. Reflecting on her own relationship to Marxism in *The Dialectic of Sex*, Firestone writes, "If there were another word more all-embracing than revolution, I would use it."[52] As in Bikini Kill's first album title, *Revolution Girl-Style Now*, Firestone claims the word "revolution" not as an inheritance from American and other national histories but rather as a placeholder for possibilities that have yet to be articulated.[53]

Yet almost twenty years after the Riot Grrrl movement, the purchase of the little girl icon and the idea of a revolution of little girls seems much more problematic. It is certainly possible to argue that the sign of the child, girl or boy, has limited political valence in a culture obsessed with fetishizing childhood as a state of innocence and vulnerability, and/or mobilizing that sign as a generic index of an apolitical progressive future.[54] Furthermore, "Girl Power" now signals increasing state and market penetration of children's sexualities. In the public sector since 2001, this phrase has been the name of a government-sponsored initiative to keep girls between the ages of nine and thirteen from taking drugs, getting pregnant, or becoming anorexic (all of which threaten, of course, to burden the social welfare system as well as to compromise the health of individual girls), to develop a "personal style" of dressing, to cook, to celebrate solemn and wacky national holidays.[55] As the *Oxford English Dictionary* defines it, Girl Power names a "self-reliant attitude among girls and young women manifested in ambition, assertiveness and individualism," a series of all-American personal traits reminiscent of Emerson and Horatio Alger rather than of Riot Grrrl's commitment to sexual and political freedom.[56] And in the private sector since at least the mid-1990s Spice Girls advertising campaign, the phrase has become a way to sell clothes, records, TV shows, online games, dolls, and pink and purple plastic things to young females. Finally, Riot Grrrl's earliest members themselves now reflect that they lacked "the knowledge to situate [their] own agenda in the history of the Women's Movement, and especially radical feminist organizing."[57] In other words, by identifying with past personal histories and selves, rather than with movement time — including the ACT UP strategies available at the moment of Riot Grrrl's inception — at least some Riot Grrrl chapters foundered on a "self-referential insularity."[58]

Shulie, like the work of Sharon Hayes, points us toward the identities and desires that are foreclosed within *social* movements, illuminating the often unexpected effects of such deferred identifications. Both artists suggest that there may also be a productive afterlife to the subject-positions that seem foreclosed within these artists' differing present tenses: second-wave feminist, girlchild of the 1970s. Most recently, "Deep Lez" has arrived to explicitly reclaim the politics of regression and of what I have called the prehistorical. Deep Lez, a catchphrase *cum* artistic vision *cum* political movement, works temporal drag toward a different kind of time — not the time of childhood but geologic time, the time of feminism and other dinosaurs, of fossilized icons and sedimented layers of meaning.

Feminism, or, When Dinosaurs Walked the Earth

In an interview in 2004, the Canadian artist Allyson Mitchell describes the genesis of a project that she frankly admits is an attempt to "will a movement into happening with art and ideas." She and a gay male friend were in a Value Village and chanced upon an old macramé wall-hanging in the shape of an owl, decorated with wooden beads and dried nuts. "Oh my god," said her friend, "That's so deep lez." Mitchell remarks, "The discarded handicraft from another era became a metaphor and a warning sign, or more Deeply Lez, an omen."[59] Here Hegel's owl of Minerva, in jute-and-nut drag, takes flight in the falling dust of a thrift store.[60] Yet rather than acknowledging that reality can be apprehended only in retrospection — as Hegel does in his avian figure for what is certainly one version of temporal drag, the ability to comprehend a historical situation only as it becomes obsolete — Mitchell's macramé owl figures what Lucas Hilderbrand has called "retroactivism." This is a mode of regeneration that aims to awaken the dissident and minor future once hoped for in the past.[61] Judith Halberstam has adroitly examined recent subcultural productions that rely on aurality for this kind of temporal binding of past and present lesbian cultures, specifically "wimmin's music" and contemporary dyke/feminist hardcore.[62] The musical works of mutual homage and interrogation that Halberstam examines are queer, activist, self-aware bindings not to a child-self or a children's public sphere but to disjunctive moments in feminist history, much in the way Firestone cathects onto the nineteenth-century women's rights movement. Mitchell's Deep Lez art extends the performance historiography that Halberstam describes to the media of visual and tactile art.[63] For quite a bit of Mitchell's oeuvre comprises a retrospective of discarded feminisms as well as junked craft objects. She often works with the literally prehistorical: in several recent pieces, the uncontrollability of the past and its ability to endanger the present, appear in the motifs of taxidermy, diorama, endangered species, and primeval monsters.

For example, in the installation *Lady Sasquatch* (2005), described by one reviewer as a meeting of "natural history displays, roadside sculptures and 70s rec rooms," Mitchell presents sculptures of large, hairy, female beasts made of yarn and polyester "fun fur" in various shades and textures, with accessories such as vampire teeth, dog noses, and wigs styled into high updos.[64] Lady Sasquatch is Mitchell's female counterpart to the mythical Pacific Northwest version of Bigfoot: Sasquatch and Bigfoot have long figured the racialized threat of the aboriginal inhabitants of North America. In Mitchell's installation, this she-beast appears in two giant sculptures at a campfire, situated in front of a brown living room set; above the couch is a fun-fur wall hanging that depicts two long-haired women of different races holding hands with their backs to the camera. A lamp with a Lady Sasquatch base, numerous hairy throw pillows, crocheted plants, and a shag rug complete the ensemble (see figure 11). At the installation sites, Mitchell adds a soundtrack that mixes the sounds of jungle animals and retro dance rhythms.[65]

Mitchell's "primitives" and "prepoliticals" are not polymorphous kids but suggest how fantasies of atavism manage the threat of *adult* female libidinality as well as of racial difference. The sculptures in particular, with arms outstretched upward and fangs bared, hearken back to and literalize, in loving homage, Helen Reddy's famous song "I Am Woman [Hear Me Roar]" (1972). Though these objects nod to North American racial fantasy, other aspects of the installation present fantasies of interracial contact differently. Since the inception of *Lady Sasquatch*, the installation has also included panels such as *Barb and Barb* (2006), a wall of faux-wood paneling into which Mitchell has inlaid the figures of two shaggy cave-women holding hands; in this and other wood veneer pieces, different

11. Allyson Mitchell, *Lady Sasquatch* (installation view), 2005.
Copyright Allyson Mitchell, 2005. Photo by Cat O'Neill. Courtesy of the artist.

grains and colors of wood suggest shadows, skin tones, and texture. It has also included latch-hooked wall hangings such as *Shebacca* (2005), featuring the Star Wars character as a reclining and masturbating female nude; *In a Wiccan Way* (2005), depicting Lady Sasquatch squatting to reveal her vagina; and *It Ain't Gonna Lick Itself* (2005), which consists of Lady Sasquatch and a faceless blond performing oral sex on her, worked into a conventional floral rug. In these and other latch-hooked pieces, the female bodies consist of a patchwork of yarn and fun-fur textures and tone-on-tone colors ranging from brown to orange to red. In counterpoint to the sculpture's invocations of sexualized racial difference, the veneers and latch-hooks suggest that epidermal differences might invite visual and tactile enjoyment. If this is exuberantly naive, it is no less so than the primitive fantasies, and Mitchell highlights by reproducing, in fabric, the excess of both fantasies of racial difference.

The latch-hooked nudes, with their long hair, flowing curves, soft textures, and gleefully abundant body hair, also evoke the goddesses celebrated in feminist projects to reclaim nature, female deities, and safe spaces. This resurrection of the goddess culminates with *Big Trouble*, a separate installation first shown at a Canadian Art Foundation gala dinner in 2004. Its centerpiece was a thirteen-foot-tall orange plush-covered woman named "Big Trubs," sporting a triangular patch of fun-fur pubic

12. Allyson Mitchell, "Big Trubs," 2004, fun fur with found shag, 125″ × 83″ × 36″. Copyright Allyson Mitchell, 2004. Courtesy of the artist.

13. Allyson Mitchell, "Tiny Trubs #1," 2004, cement and glass, 18″ × 12″ × 12″. Copyright Allyson Mitchell, 2004. Photo by Nina Levitt. Courtesy of the artist.

hair, ample breasts and thighs, and macramé and crochet baubles dangling from her hands (see figure 12). In the center of each dinner table Mitchell set a cement "Tiny Trubs," a similarly buxom miniature nude with wide black eyes modeled after both the putty-colored plastic Russ Berrie "Sillisculpt" figurines of 1960s and 1970s and Margaret Keane's big-eyed waif paintings (see figure 13). In this installation as in *Lady Sasquatch*, these female bodies and the staging of their environments reclaim the degraded crafts of sewing, woodwork, latch-hook, crochet, amateur collecting, and other "folk" hobbies popular in the 1970s. The effect is to reanimate all kinds of cultural dinosaurs: the legend of Sasquatch, the sexually excessive racial primitive, the hairy radical feminist, the Wiccan icon, the home arts.

Yet the Trubs and Sasquatches are objects of longing as well as of amusement. They suggest the thrill and power that a discounted past—indeed, a literally "discount" past cobbled together from cheap textiles and anonymous strangers' jettisoned home craft projects—can bring to a much more slick contemporary moment. They recast feminism's political temporal heterogeneity in a tactile mode, as differences in "feeling." And feeling is crucial to Mitchell's work, where castoff pasts also offer a differential way of experiencing one's own bodily stigma. Mitchell's project, that is, uses temporal drag to interrogate not only feminist history but also the fat body: she is a feminist fat activist and holds a Ph.D. from York University, having written a dissertation on "a feminist theory of body geography" that examines how women's body images change in different contexts.[66] While the emphasis on geography in Mitchell's scholarship suggests spatial differences, her thrift-shop aesthetic suggests a more temporal analysis. Her artwork suggests that the planned obsolescence built into commodity-time actually provides multiple historical contexts for the experience of one's own size—that cultural dumps might mitigate a certain dumpiness. For example, the installations in *The Fluff Stands Alone* include latch-hooked figures quite different from the ones in *Lady Sasquatch*, for they reference the cartoons from early issues of *Playboy*. Importantly, the women in the original cartoons were far more voluptuous and curvy than today's supermodels. Mitchell's description of her early experiences with these images suggests that in them she found not only an object of desire but also a way of feeling the desirability of her own body.[67] With titles like *Rugburn #1* (2003), *Fluffer Nutter* (2003, see figure 14), and *Venus of Nudiesque* (2003), Mitchell's two-dimensional pieces reclaim *Playboy*'s big-rumped and top-heavy women, their pigtails,

14. Allyson Mitchell, *Fluffer Nutter*, 2003, found textile, plywood, vintage wallpaper, 66″ × 48″ × 3″.
Copyright Allyson Mitchell, 2003. Photo credit: *Canadian Art Magazine*. Courtesy of the artist.

wide eyes, hot pants, and bright pink lips, albeit with more ethnic variety than the originals had.

Mitchell also enhances most of these women's physiques with even meatier thighs and big rolls of belly fat. To reupholster the female form in this way is itself to relish yet another anachronism, flaunting a body whose social status in Anglo-American cultures has fallen dramatically since the days in which portraits of bourgeois European merchants and their wives, and even of nobility, emphasized the portly physiques that signified wealth.[68] Within lesbian milieus, Mitchell's reclamations also embrace the icon of the fat feminist, whose despised pull backward on the politics of sexuality is supposedly equaled by the downward movement of her own body parts: her breasts sagging from not wearing a bra, her rear spreading as she sits in endless grassroots meetings, her belly descending from the weight of so much navel-gazing. Mitchell's technique of putting *Playboy* models in fat drag recalls Michael Moon's and Eve Sedgwick's moving collaborative piece about the intersection of queerness and obe-

sity. Moon and Sedgwick use their own friendship (technically, one between a gay man and a "straight" fat woman) as a relay toward theorizing
the mock-celebrity actor Divine's figuration of "interlocking histories of
stigma, self-constitution, and epistemological complication proper to fat
women and gay men in this century."[69] The term "Divinity," which Moon
and Sedgwick name after John Waters's performance character Divine,
condenses the "emotional and identity linkages" between gay men and fat
women, that is, the dynamic common to both, between shame and pro-
test, abjection and daring, humiliation and gleeful flaunting.[70] Interestingly, the authors do not mention the fact that the stigmatic histories of
female fatness and lesbianism interlock on a single body rather than in a
friendship or a drag performance: the taunt "fat dyke" is hurled at many a
large-sized straight woman as well as at ordinary-sized lesbians. If, as I
have contended, contemporary queer theory has generally treated lesbian
stigma as if it were coded primarily by transgender embodiment, we have
overlooked how in recent history it has also been coded, unlike that of gay
men, as a problem of sizable bodily proportions. Thus while the effect of
"Divinity" can be "a compelling belief that one is a god," the effect of —
what shall we call it? Roseannity? — is considerably less glamorous.[71]

In *The Fluff Stands Alone*, one piece epitomizes Mitchell's view of
supposedly obsolete feminisms as, also, discredited modes of embodiment. *The Michigan Three* (2003) is a latch-hooked wall hanging that
depicts three naked fat women of various skin tones, with *Playboy* cartoon
lips and hair, posed together in a woodsy setting reminiscent of the annual Michigan Womyn's Music Festival site (see figure 15). If the reference to Michigan suggests a relic of the lesbian-feminist past, these plus-
sized ladies suggest the Three Fates, who were themselves dedicated to
the textile arts that Mitchell reclaims: in Hesiod's *Theogony*, one sister
cuts, one spins, one measures. If the original Fates control the future,
then the "Michigan Three" seem poised to take charge of the fate of the
feminist past, to make it sexy again or perhaps even as sexy as it actually
was, as their lipstick and wild manes of fun-fur hair suggest. Their exuberant interracial contact also reanimates a necessary future out of white
feminisms' failed concatenation with antiracist organizing. And they recall the place of women's music festivals, often left out of traditional
accounts of lesbian and gay political organizing, in the history of the
lesbian-feminist movement.

But what temporalities, if not the sacred one invoked by Divinity, do
these women's fatness animate? Through the concept of temporal drag,

15. Allyson Mitchell, *The Michigan Three*, 2003, found textile and plywood, 66″ × 48″ × 3″.
Copyright Allyson Mitchell, 2003. Photo credit: *Canadian Art Magazine*. Courtesy of the artist.

I have implied thus far that in the lexicon of lesbian epithets, "dowdy" might signal a certain transtemporality, or an embarrassingly belated quality of the lesbian feminist in the queer world that is nevertheless constitutive of subjectivity in general and of movement politics in particular. "Fat," on the other hand, generally signals a transgression of spatial norms (taking up too much space), and emotional ones (failing to control the will). But as Lauren Berlant argues, "fat" also suggests the failure of a subject to be chrononormative. Obesity—especially when coded as part of an epidemic, as it has been in the early twenty-first century—connotes a mode of living in which a subject continuously deteriorates, as opposed to suffering an event-centered trauma or achieving event-centered goals.[72] In other words, while the epithet "dowdy" names the temporal recalcitrance I have been discussing thus far as a mode of queer historiography, "fat" connotes a refusal of agency onward and upward (or perhaps, as in the far more respectable case of neurosis, inward and downward). Fat signals an embrace of what Berlant has described as lateral agency, a movement outward that is often figured as slow, childish, or pointless, like a hippo doing an arabesque.

Yet motions do not always go forward. If identity is always in temporal drag, constituted and haunted by the failed love-project that precedes it, then perhaps the shared culture making we call "movements" might do well to feel the tug backward as a potentially transformative part of movement itself. And the verb "feel" I use here aims to recapture something about the "Michigan Three's" lateral form of potential agency. Though they are confined to a wall-hanging, their long fun-fur hair wafts beyond the two dimensional, floating laterally, outward, toward the body of the viewer, taking up more space than high art would allow it. In addition to appearing on wall-hangings, paneling, and rugs, the hairy dykes of *Lady Sasquatch* and *The Fluff Stands Alone* also decorate bedspreads smoothed over the large round beds found in honeymoon suites, beckoning audiences to sleep, make out, have sex, rub their faces in so-called second-wave feminism. As one reviewer remarks of *The Fluff Stands Alone*, "I resisted the temptation to rub my face on the art, but it was a struggle."[73] In this sense, textile art really is the fat art I described earlier in this book: refusing an anorexic relationship to meaning, it goes *beyond* the linguistic and even pictorial, overpacking the "language" of high art with other sensations. And like Hayes's street performances and Subrin's videography, Mitchell's textile art also overpacks the discourse of history. But Mitchell's work opens up a tactile relationship to a collective past, one not simply performative or citational but physical and even erotic. This erotic technique, this method of literally *feeling* the historical, is not only a queer historiographic method but also one with a history of its own — a history that, as the next chapter will show, remains a repressed element of scholarly inquiry into the past.

three. Time Binds, or, Erotohistoriography

From the vantage point of temporal drag, what would a genealogy of history itself look like? Any search for the origins of queer historiographical pleasure, it seems, would resurrect the very impulses that the texts that I have explored thus far resist. But in the texts that follow, pleasure — instead of appearing as foundational to a discipline or identity — flashes up from the past as the loser in bygone battles over what the discipline of history itself should become. As the winners of a battle between sensory and cognitive modes of apprehending history declared it, history should be understood rather than felt, and written in a genre as clearly separable from fiction (if not from narrative) as possible.[1] Yet from at least the 1800s, fiction has offered traces not only of unrealized pasts but also of the unrealized past of history itself.

The conflict between rational and emotional understanding, reportage and fiction, is visible in a rather old chestnut of both literary and queer theory, Mary Shelley's *Frankenstein, or, The Modern Prometheus*. Shelley's novel is in many ways critical of both the genealogical logic and domestic-sentimental chrononormativities that Dougherty, Bonder, and Harris would undermine over a century and a half later, as I detailed in chapter 1. And *Frankenstein*, as I will show, is also committed to the performance of anachrony I called "temporal drag" in chapter 2. But most important, *Frankenstein* allows us access to a counterhistory of history itself — an antisystematic method that informs other, much later artistic productions traveling more explicitly under the sign of queer.

I call this method *erotohistoriography*. Erotohistoriography is distinct from the desire for a fully present past, a restoration of bygone times. Erotohistoriography does not write the lost object into the present so much as encounter it already in the present, by treating the present itself as hybrid. And it uses the body as a tool to effect, figure, or perform that encounter. Erotohistoriography admits that contact with historical materials can be precipitated by particular bodily dispositions, and that these connections may elicit bodily responses, even pleasurable ones, that are themselves a form of understanding. It sees the body as a method, and historical consciousness as something intimately involved with corporeal sensations. And if erotohistoriography does not begin with *Frankenstein*, that novel at least offers us figures for witnessing the history of a discredited form of knowledge and for tracking its afterlife.

Frankenstein: Bodying Forth History

As many critics have recognized, *Frankenstein* is fiercely antigenealogical. Judith Halberstam writes that in the novel, the family is "as fragmented and incoherent as the monster himself" and seems most authentic and normative when its members are apart.[2] Certainly the novel's kin groups — the fictionalized Byrons and Shelleys who meet near Lac Leman, Switzerland, to tell ghost stories in Mary Shelley's 1831 "Author's Introduction"; Robert Walton and his sister Mrs. Saville, whose letters frame the novel; its main narrator Victor Frankenstein; and the De Laceys, who are at the center of the tale the monster tells — are marked by the same "unnatural" suture and disaggregation that mark the monster's body. For instance, the historical Byrons and Shelleys were entangled in all kinds of adulterous liaisons, out-of-wedlock children, bisexual affairs, and custody disputes, which histories are at least partially visible in the rivalry of their fictionalized counterparts as they compete to tell the best horror tale. Then, too, the ostensibly devoted Walton never appears in the same diegetic space as his supposedly beloved sister. The Frankenstein family of whom Victor Frankenstein speaks to Walton is a mix of adopted and biological kin eventually torn asunder by murders and accusations of betrayal. And the De Laceys, whom the monster describes to Victor Frankenstein, shelter their son's Turkish / Arabian fiancée from her vengeful father, in a hut that the monster eventually destroys.

But at least two of these families are also *temporally* out of joint in ways that parallel the monster's composition out of bits and pieces of dead flesh. For the Waltons' and Frankensteins' attempts and failures to achieve domestic synchronicity occur in the process of sending one another letters. Walton's narration is entirely epistolary; within the tale Victor Frankenstein tells him, letters between family members and friends constantly circulate. On the one hand, these letters forge a sense of immediacy and intimacy: these families know their members and recognize their status as kin through being addressed and represented in letter form. The letters also construct and perform familial status to an extra-domestic audience: as Jürgen Habermas reminds us, eighteenth- and early-nineteenth-century letters were often written not only to their addressees but also implicitly to larger publics within and beyond the extended family.[3] The structure of *Frankenstein* captures this process of "publishing the family," for the monster's self-narrated autobiography and tale of the De Laceys appear within a story that Victor Frankenstein, his creator, tells to the sympathetic stranger Robert Walton, whose record of it in letters to his sister Margaret Saville constitutes the novel as a whole, whose audience is both the group at Lac Leman and Shelley's eventual readers.[4] The result is a kind of closed circuit of writing and telling in which the monster is simultaneously the center (for he is the innermost narrator, framed first by Victor's narrative which in turn is framed by Walton's letters) and the margin (for though he speaks, he never writes, and this, I would argue, symptomizes his lack of familial connection).

Even as letter writing for a familial audience produces a kind of virtual coherence, though, it also opens up temporal fissures that undermine that very coherence. Most works of epistolary fiction play on the gap between the moment of writing a letter and the moment of receiving and reading one: among other things, this conceit allows the reader of an epistolary novel to know things before characters do, and for a plot element to be obsolete (that is, already undone by another event) even as it is revealed. Like the monster's body, then, many letters are dead on arrival. If the family form gains coherence through the virtual *space* or "worlding" enacted by writing letters, it is made dangerously incoherent by the *time* lags that this spacing depends on: this is most evident in the juxtaposition between Elizabeth's cheery and incongruous letter to Victor, relating the history of Justine Moritz's arrival into the family (which Victor presumably already knows), and the subsequent letter from Victor's father telling of young William Frankenstein's murder, eventually blamed on that same Justine. And of course, Victor's own role in the novel is also to arrive too late to prevent the deaths of his family members by the monster's hands. *Frankenstein* is nothing if not a novel of the *après-coup*.

Just as the Frankenstein family (and to a lesser extent the Walton family) is temporally dispersed by the very letters that spatially bind them, the body parts that supposedly make the monster a synchronized whole are ineluctably unjoined, insofar as they belong to different moments in history. Thus while Halberstam and others have read the monster as gothically and queerly hybrid because he collapses and interchanges any number of social structures (class, race, gender), I'd like to consider him queerly hybrid in a temporal sense. First, the monster embodies the wrinkled time that marks both the gothic and, as I have argued up to this point, the queer. As a genre, the gothic traffics in alternate temporalities or a-rhythms that present themselves in concretely historical terms, as dead bodies coming back to life in the form of vampires, ghosts, and monsters. These undead bodies, in turn, catalyze bodily sensations such as skipped heartbeats, screams, shudders, tears, and swoons in gothic characters, and presumably in some readers (who may also laugh, admittedly, but this is simply another physiological effect). Just as the monster's body is composed of dead flesh touching more dead flesh, the gothic character often experiences both a fleshly touch from the dead and an unpredictable fleshly response to it: the monster is, in many ways, a double for both the genre he inhabits and for the disaggregated sensorium of the gothic character and reader. Indeed, the literary critic Mike Goode speculates that gothic novels themselves enacted a kind of "ecstatic history."[5] That is, the genre transduced religious experiences — which always appeared at the boundaries of what could be encompassed by earthly knowledge — into terror, hallucinations, or sexual transport, themselves alternative or subjugated knowledge practices. In this sense, the gothic was a kind of historical novel *in extremis*, a register for encountering the past felt precisely at the boundaries of what could be encompassed by secular, disciplinary, and even "scientific" notions of history. And as the sociologist Avery Gordon argues, ghosts are the paradigmatic figure for these historical limit-cases, often appearing in gothic novels as tactile experiences not only of dead people but also of repressed events and social formations.[6] While Frankenstein's monster is not a ghost, precisely, his striated and heterogeneous anatomy can certainly be read similarly, as a figure for both the social conflicts of which history consists and the genre in which history announced itself in other terms. The monster, like Goode's and Gordon's undead, figures the outside of not only the human but also — crucially — of what can count as history and as its proper mode of apprehension.

On the face of it, this reading of *Frankenstein* as a novel about the writing and experiencing of history seems implausible. The knowledge that Victor seeks is not historical knowledge per se but scientific knowledge — specifically, the secret of life, and the ability to create new life, which he wishes to wrest from God and/or women. But interestingly, before he ever touches a cadaver, Victor begins his quest for knowledge through contact with the dead, for his early studies consist of reading obsolete, outmoded scientific works. Even once he discovers the fundamental error of this approach in college and joins the world of modern science, he eventually turns back to past ideas and methods for imparting life to dead matter. As he begins to raid charnel-houses in order to create his monster, he transfers his allegiance from dead authors to dead bodies. It might be argued that Victor cannot be characterized as a historian precisely insofar as he reads primary documents as if they inform him about the present, as if they were "live." But he is certainly what some Romantic-era historians condemned as an "antiquarian," someone whose obsession with the past threatened to become an end in itself.[7] In fact, Victor has not only the wrong method but also the wrong relationship to knowledge. His learning distracts him from attending to his family, as critics generally agree, but this is not benign neglect; indeed, his love for old texts takes a perverse turn. His passion for ancient science slides into literal contact with the dead when he begins robbing graves, and his obsession with his project of bringing this dead flesh to life substitutes for his romance with Elizabeth and his manly friendship with Henry Clerval. Eventually Victor's own body dessicates because of both his misguided intellectual program and his ghastly creation: Victor's studies and the monster's body are allegories for one another insofar as the monster is not only flesh but text, a body condensing Victor's, Shelley's, and a generation of critics' *knowledge*.

Indeed, *Frankenstein* is preoccupied with the relationship between cognition and the body, and specifically, as I will demonstrate, between historical understanding and the male body. In this sense, the novel reflects discussion among historians in the long nineteenth century, who were keenly interested in the question of how feelings and sensations in the present could illuminate past events.[8] The idea of apprehending and representing collective experiences from the past in avowedly embodied, not always painful ways might seem repugnant both to traditionalist historicist methods that rely on the principle of objective and disinterested analysis, and to Marxist understandings that genuine historical consciousness is precipitated by oppression. But this idea was absolutely viable in the Anglo-American eighteenth and nineteenth centuries. Goode writes that Enlightenment and Romantic-era discussions about historical method — specifically, a debate in 1790–91 between Edmund Burke and Thomas Paine — centered on how the male capacity for sensibility, figured in terms of bodily constitution, was crucial to historical understanding.[9] In Burke's account, manly somatic responses were considered a legitimate relay to historical knowledge. The era's "man of feeling" properly encountered history through sympathetic identifications with its personae and modes of living. This transferential relationship took place not only in the mind but also through more visceral attachments, identifications, and attempts to reinhabit past worldviews, all of which in turn reconstituted the historian's body as a finer instrument of sensibility. In other words, history was a use of physical sensation that, in a dialectical turn, *made* the very bodies capable of properly receiving those sensations. This process, as Goode describes it, was a sort of Foucauldian *ars erotica* of historical inquiry.[10]

But this relationship between the historian and his object always threatened to become carnal, a mismanaged encounter that could variously dehumanize, dry up, or even kill off the properly masculine body. Thus, argues Goode, the discipline of history arose in conjunction with, and partook in, a crisis about masculinity. Pamphlets and published cartoons from the 1790s figure antiquarians' obsessive interest in the archives as a sort of sexual perversion. The era's term "bibliomania" did not correlate directly with modern homosexuality, but it certainly included a morbid disinterest in women and, at times, a homoerotic interest in the lives of great men. Goode provides the hilarious example of a satirical cartoon from 1811, Thomas Rowlandson's *Modern Antiques*, in which a wizened and lecherous old man fondles the genitals of an ancient Greek statue in a museum storehouse, while a robust young heterosexual couple have sex in an empty Egyptian sarcophagus.[11] In this light, we can see Victor's obsession with building his monster from dead bodies as a turn from a vaguely perverse and homoerotic bibliomania to a deeply perverse necrophilia, in which physical contact with the dead substitutes for healthy sex between the living. Victor's morbid disinterest in women, or at least in Elizabeth, is part and parcel of his obsession with the dead. And his encounter with the past in the form of corpses, rather than textbooks or even marble statues, becomes more horrifyingly carnal than the old man's fondlings in the cartoon.

But beyond this analogy between dead bodies and the archive, it is also possible to read *Frankenstein*'s much-discussed emphasis on sympathy as a plea for a particular relationship to historical knowledge. In the moment Shelley wrote, "sympathy" was the key term for a liberal notion that justice, polity, and freedom rest on the capacity of human beings first to respond to the plight of others, and then to abstract and redistribute this capacity into a general, reciprocal political obligation among members of a group.[12] This response to others extended to the dead. For Edmund Burke, writing *Reflections on the Revolution in France* (1790), both jurisprudence and historical method involved a certain amount of sympathy, manifest in the ability to imaginatively inhabit and reenact the behavior codes of prior times, even if those codes were, in Goode's words, "malformed" and potentially unsuitable for the present.[13] Crucially, though, the Burkean historian must use this identificatory process to apprehend *differences* between his feelings and those of the past, in order to grasp the larger historical differences that would make precedent more or less applicable.[14] In other words, the man of feeling must first feel the feelings of the past and then feel their disruptive contact with the present. Seen in Burkean terms, then, Frankenstein's monster, deformed though he may be, is a much better historian than his creator. Victor applies his passion for knowledge to the wrong textual corpus, learning codes of scientific conduct from Paracelsus and Agrippa that are absolutely inappropriate for the present. He does not compare them with modern-day methods and interests until he is forced to do so at college, at which point he turns to dead bodies.

By contrast, the monster may wear and perform anachronistic behaviors in the literal form of mismatched body parts, but he actually learns virtue from precedent. He also "civilizes" himself by choosing rationally among thoughts and behaviors of long-past eras and fitting them to his present situation. For crucially, the monster learns about human culture and sympathy through books, including history books. Overhearing the cottagers reading Volney's *Ruins of Empires* to one another gives him "a cursory knowledge of history," but he also imitates their weeping "over the hapless fate of [America's] original inhabitants."[15] Here, historical events engender the proper feeling of compassion for others. Having learned to read, the monster also finds a copy of *Plutarch's Lives*, from which he learns "to admire peaceable lawgivers, Numa, Solon, and Lycurgus, in preference to Romulus and Theseus" (170). He remarks that "if my first introduction to humanity had been made by a young soldier, burning for glory and slaughter, I should have been imbued with different sensations" (170), suggesting that his character and sensory apparatus are malleable in exact proportion to the kind of history he reads. Through imaginatively projecting himself into the lives of history's oppressed and into the mindsets of the right heroes from the past, the monster develops virtue, much as Burke advocated the mimetic transmission of established manners and ethics.

Shelley clearly elevates the monster's sympathetic relationship to the past (including the life-histories of the cottagers) over Victor Frankenstein's combination of perverse antiquarianism, obsessive fixation, and eventually, cold, hard science. Indeed, what critics have generally seen as Shelley's commitment to the *feminine* sphere of the domestic affections may equally well represent her commitment to properly *manly* Romantic-era historical sensibilities. For she figures Victor Frankenstein in much the same terms as Thomas Paine figured Burke's affective historicism. As Goode explains, Paine reviled Burkean historicism because it animated and depended on feelings that were historically derived rather than spontaneous, on codes of conduct that were appropriated from the past rather than inborn. Paine accused Burke's approach to history of bringing the living too close to the dead, and so ruining the living body's constitution.[16] As if to embody Paine's fears, in *Frankenstein* the scientist himself becomes at least as hideous as the monster, degenerating into the withered, dried-up, sickly scholar caricatured in the popular presses of the 1790s. Indeed, popular rhetoric of the era cast those with an unnatural interest in the past as enslaved, their devotion to precedent diminishing their capacity for self-government in the present. We see a hint of this in a scene in which Victor tours an aspect of British history:

> We passed a considerable period at Oxford, rambling among its environs, and endeavouring to identify every spot which might relate to the most animating epoch of English history. Our little voyages of discovery were often prolonged by the successive objects that presented themselves. We visited the tomb of the illustrious Hampden, and the field on which that patriot fell. For a moment my soul was elevated from its debasing and miserable fears, to contemplate the divine ideas of liberty and self-sacrifice, of which these sights were the monuments and the remembrancers. For an instant I dared to shake off my chains, and look around me with a free and lofty spirit; but the iron had eaten into my flesh, and I sank again, trembling and hopeless, into my miserable self. (215)[17]

Here, "animating" recalls Victor's project of bringing the dead to life, yet it refers to history's proper effect on bodily constitution: Hampden's grave "elevates" its viewers from what is "debasing and miserable" and inculcates a revivifying notion of liberal freedom. Official national history seems to free Victor of his body and his particular past, to offer him a truly republican release from both. But Victor is, at the end of their outing, bound like a slave by chains of obligation to another past, fetters that have scourged his very body. The monster, too, refers to Victor as "Slave" in his long soliloquy at the novel's center. And the figure of the living body shackled to dead matter also appears more pointedly near the end of the novel, when Victor chases the monster over the Arctic ice in a dogsled: "Once, after the poor animals that conveyed me had with incredible toil gained the summit of a sloping ice-mountain, . . . one, sinking under his fatigue, died . . . I disencumbered the dogs of their dead companion" (281–82). The dogs, at least momentarily harnessed to a corpse, double Victor's enslavement not only to the monster but also to the dead.

For Paine, then, the Burkean body was just that—an artificial lump of matter tantamount to a corpse, composed as it was of other people's values and ideas, rather than a natural body whose sense of liberty and self-governance was innate. In this sense, Paine championed an ahistorical relationship to knowledge, and by extension the ahistorical body constituted by such a relation: the Paineite subject would just "feel right," as Harriet Beecher Stowe would later put it in *Uncle Tom's Cabin* (1852), knowing how to act and what to do rather than being constituted by forces that preceded him. As Goode's work clarifies, in the Paineite formulation bodily feeling, including feeling historical, doesn't *have* a cultural history, and any inherited codes, including those for gendered or sexual behavior, repress the body's natural inclinations. Frankenstein's monster, by contrast, is a body that contains a history of bodies and of bodiliness and thus figures a gender and a sexuality that themselves write a history of genders and sexualities. After Foucault, the monster suggests, we are all Frankensteinian monsters: or, after *Frankenstein*, the Foucauldian body emerges.

At the end of *Frankenstein*, the Victorian era of "hard" historical science that would succeed Romantic historiography glimmers out proleptically for a moment. Victor corrects Walton's transcription of his narrative in the Arctic: "Frankenstein discovered that I [Walton] made notes concerning his history: he asked to see them, and then himself corrected and augmented them in many places; but principally *in giving life and spirit* to the conversations he held with his enemy. 'Since you have preserved my narration,' said he, '*I would not that a mutilated one should go down to posterity*'" (285, both emphases mine). It is as if, here, Victor aims to bring the dead to life but is afraid of yet another monstrous creation, this time in the form of a historical narrative. Putting together a proper history in the frigid Arctic, he literalizes the Victorian turn to a colder, more objective, scientific relationship to the past. He intends that this history, unlike the one he constructed from dead bodies, will not engender such a frenzy, instead seeking one that, unlike his creature, will persevere as the unified corpus of knowledge sought by academic historians. The later Romantic era had already subordinated the monster's stigmatized passionate attachments to the past to a larger, decorporealizing project: while privileging a Burkean sensitivity to the past, the Romantics demanded that the archivist connect or coordinate small details to what they called "the spirit of the age" in which those details dwelt.[18] And the Victorians, in the name of science, would altogether distance themselves from Romantic historiography. Victor the mad chemist, then, is out of time in more than one direction. Not only does he revivify the stereotype of the scholar as pervert but he also prefigures the Victorian movement toward a disinterested, unsentimental, avowedly scientific approach to history. That the monster finally arranges and lights his own funeral pyre suggests how unbearable the weight of a more self-reflexively historical being, and the burden of visceral apprehension, must be in a culture that will increasingly demote these ways of knowing.

In sum, Frankenstein's monster is monstrous because he lets history too far in, going so far as to embody it instead of merely feeling it, even to embody the historicity of the body revealed when erotic contact with the past produces sensations that are unintelligible by present sexual and gender codes. He certainly emblematizes the passionate attachments to archival materials that were increasingly barred from historicist methodology as the nineteenth century progressed. But he also figures history's ability to effect shifts in bodily constitution in ways that were increasingly demonized, problematized, or disavowed.

In *Frankenstein*, we can also see the erotic relation to history that would suture contemporary affective historiography, which in its attachment to melancholia seems so pleasure-shy, to the model of *jouissance*, from whose ahistoricism queer theory has turned away. By locating the scene of gothic encounter in the hymeneal bed itself where Elizabeth sees the monster for the first time, *Frankenstein* suggests that Elizabeth's response to the dead, to Victor's secret history as the monster's creator, and to the presence of another historical moment in embodied form is directly sexual. In the famous wedding night scene, the return of history (in the form of the monster's retribution for Victor's murder of his beloved) ravishes Elizabeth far more completely than anything her new husband could offer. Or perhaps it ravishes Victor, who declares, "As I heard [Elizabeth's scream] . . . my arms dropped, the motion of every muscle and fibre was suspended; I could feel the blood trickling in my veins and tingling in the extremities of my limbs" (264). In light of the way this scene hints at a literally, even genitally ecstatic relation to the past, I would argue that *Frankenstein* is a novel explicitly concerned with the erotics of historical consciousness. Over and over, the novel codes contact with the past as a meeting of sensate body, historical understanding, and representation. In the erotohistoriographic mode, *Frankenstein* stages the very queer possibility that encounters with history are bodily encounters, and even that they have a revivifying and pleasurable effect.

In figuring both a threatening nearness to the materials of the past and the effect of that nearness on the body, the monster is a precursor to Virginia Woolf's famous Orlando, who chases his lovers across the timeline even as he is chased by his biographer, and, in a hilarious parody of the Romantic "spirit of the age," whose body morphs from male to female under the pressures of historical change. What distinguishes *Orlando* from *Frankenstein*, though, is the lesbian possibility that historical knowledge might depend not only on sympathetic feelings but also on sexual pleasure directly administered, and that the body might pleasure itself with the past. In the history of erotohistoriography that I am sketching out here, *Orlando* may stand as the first lesbian work in the genre.

Orlando: Fingering History

In the early 1800s, the London *Morning Chronicle* published a daily fashion column that was always prefaced by the epitaph "To shew / The very age and body of the time, / Its form and pressure."[19] In *Orlando*, Woolf seems intent on literalizing that body of "the time." Like Victor Frankenstein, Orlando is the historian as pervert figured by Burke's detractors. He/she also loses a self and what would otherwise be a normal and natural body by too much contact with the dead — yet he/she claims this loss exuberantly. Unlike Victor Frankenstein, Orlando's body does not wither, nor does he/she lose interest in women; Orlando simply changes genders. And if anything, contact with the past and the forces of historical change make him/her more robust, for he/she ages only about fifteen years in three hundred.

Woolf figures this departure from what by the Edwardian era were the norms of historical inquiry not as a contest between forms of masculinity but as a struggle among masculinity, femininity, and queerness. She rejects both a masculine national progress narrative and the dilettantish and anhedonic hobbies left to female antiquarians, embracing a juicily queer mode of seeing and writing the past. Woolf is merciless in her skewering of disciplinary history: her acknowledgments facetiously thank her husband, Leonard Woolf, "for the profound historical knowledge to which these pages owe whatever degree of accuracy they may attain" and laud "Miss M. K. Snowdon's indefatigable researches in the archives of Harrogate and Cheltenham [which] were none the less arduous for being vain."[20] Later in the novel, the narrator counterposes two fictional diary accounts of Orlando's coronation as Duke, in Constantinople: a bombastic and self-congratulatory report from one naval officer John Fenner Brigge on how the ceremony impresses the natives, and a gushing letter from one General Hartoppe's daughter Penelope, full of exclamation points and comments about fashion and good-looking men. But Woolf's predominant figure for the academic historian is the unnamed, ostensibly gender-neutral narrator, a professional biographer. The narrator claims to "enjoy the immunity of all biographers and historians from any sex whatever" (220) and declares that "the biographer who records the life of such a one [need never] . . . invoke the help of novelist or poet. From deed to deed, from glory to glory, from office to office he must go, his scribe following after, till they reach what ever seat it may be that is the height of their desire" (14–15). Here, even as Woolf satirizes supposedly objective and passionless history, she deconstructs its disavowed sexual basis, jokingly implying a sodomitical relationship between biographer and subject with her reference to their shared "seat" of desire.

In Woolf's own biography, this relationship was not sodomitical but Sapphic. As critics from Nigel Nicolson onward have recognized, the eroticized chase between Orlando and his/her biographer mirrors Woolf's attempt to textually seduce Vita Sackville-West.[21] If we read *Orlando*'s biographer as historiographer, and his object Orlando as a figure for the past itself, then the writing of history is also figured as a seduction of the past and, correspondingly, as the past's erotic impact on the body itself. Historiography even has the ability (if the narrator's obsession with Orlando's legs is any example) to seduce the seducer. Woolf's methodology, then, centers on an avowedly erotic pleasure: an *ars erotica* of historical inquiry that takes place not between the hearts of emoting men, as in Burke, but between and across the bodies of lusting women.

Woolf's novel tells the story of young Orlando's excursion through English literary and cultural history, an experience of history not only *on* but *as* a body. Our hero(ine) lives three hundred years, waking up one morning to find her sex changed from male to female midway through his/her journey. Of course, this is in part a story about the constructedness of gender: for instance, prose styles and costumes that are resoundingly masculine in Elizabethan England become foppishly feminine by the Restoration. But *Orlando*'s more interesting conceit, for my purposes, is that the protagonist him/herself experiences historical change as a set of directly corporeal and often sexual sensations. In a parody of the kind of historiography that speaks knowingly of a given era's zeitgeist, Woolf literalizes political or cultural climate as weather. The end of the Elizabethan period announces itself by thawing the frozen River Thames; the nineteenth century is ushered in with a damp that increases the birthrate and the vegetation; the twentieth century dries everything up. Orlando feels these various centuries not only as fluctuations in weather but also as reorganizations of his/her body, succinctly captured by the narrator's observation that "one might see the spirit of the age blowing, now hot, now cold, upon [Orlando's] cheeks" (236).

Not surprisingly for a feminist who had read Freud, Woolf also plays hard and fast with the motif of castration, describing three muses who, on encountering Orlando's change from man to woman during the Restoration era, "peeped in at the door and threw a garment like a towel at the naked form which, unfortunately, fell short by several inches" (138), the ambiguous "which" here referring not only to the towel but to the "naked form" and its suddenly missing inches. But Woolf also *historicizes* castration, figuring Orlando's morphing body in terms of the parts that become salient at different historical moments: the castration complex becomes a more generally somatic trauma in which the relation of particular body parts to the whole body shifts from era to era. In Orlando's Elizabethan incarnation as a man, for instance, his legs take center stage. As the scene with the three muses suggests, the Restoration era has a rather dramatic effect on his penis. By the nineteenth century, the now-female Orlando feels historical change as finger trouble:

> The nerve which controls the pen winds itself about every fibre of our being, threads the heart, pierces the liver. Though the seat of her trouble seemed to be the left finger, she could feel herself poisoned through and through, and was forced at length to consider the most desperate of remedies, which was to yield completely and submissively to the spirit of the age, and take a husband. (243)

Here, Woolf hints that not only gender but also the anatomical basis for "sex" itself may be historically contingent. The two-sex system in which Orlando finds herself trapped, Woolf seems to argue, is a product of rather than the precursor to the heterosexual-marital imperative. Castration, then, centers not only on the penis but also on the left ring finger: here, we might say, the Oedipal narrative meets the annular one.

Orlando is possessed of a radically metahistoricized body, a body like that of Shelley's monster insofar as it incarnates the history of sexuality. But during the male period of his life, he is also an antiquarian of sorts, obsessed with artifacts of the past in ways that echo Victor Frankenstein. Indeed, *Orlando* opens with a living person disturbing a fragment of dead flesh: we first see our hero/ine slicing at the rafters, trying to strike the head of an African "pagan" killed by one of his ancestors. In this contretemps, "Africa" represents both Orlando's place in an imperial venture and a racialized, racist trope for the past itself. Yet it also immediately establishes that Orlando is, temporally speaking, as out of joint as the desiccated head with which he parries. And as the novel progresses, Orlando becomes increasingly compelled by dead body parts and then relics in general. Several times, he visits the tomb of his noble ancestors, fondling their possessions and skeletal remains:

> [Orlando] would take a skeleton hand in his and bend the joints this way and that. "Whose hand was it?" he went on to ask. "The right or the left? The hand of man or woman, of age or youth? Had it urged the war horse, or plied the needle? Had it plucked the rose, or grasped cold steel? Had it —— " but here either his invention failed him or, what is more likely, provided him with so many instances of what a hand can do that he shrank, as his wont was, from the cardinal labour of composition, which is excision. (71)

The passage stages a conflict between a labile historiography and the selective principles of "disinterested" academic writing evidenced by Victor Frankenstein's editorial work on Walton's manuscript: in *Orlando*, proper scholarship appears as "excision" or castration of the hand. Orlando's problem as a historian, foreshadowed by his antics with the "pagan" head and appearing more overtly in his struggles to end his long poem "The Oak Tree," is that he can't cut anything out. Or off. Here, his surfeit of responses to the dead part-object in the tomb suggest what Carla Freccero refers to as "an alternate path to the Western melancholic's incorporation of the lost other and its permanent, if uneasy, entombment

within the crypt of history." Freccero suggests that this alternate relationship to the past might take the form of "a penetrative reciprocity, a
becoming-object for an other subject and a resultant joy or ecstasy."[22] This
suggests a kind of bottomy historiography: the potential for collective
queer time — even queer history — to be structured as an uneven transmission of receptivity rather than authority or custom, of a certain enjoyably
porous relation to unpredictable futures or to new configurations of the
past.[23] Woolf's inside reference to "what a hand can do" alludes to this
sort of flexible erotics between women as, also, a historiographic method.

Later, Orlando begins to practice erotohistoriography more methodi-
cally than his tomb fondlings suggest, for he becomes obsessed with
official history's cast-offs. Lovingly fondling Queen Mary's prayer book,
Orlando adds a flake of tobacco to the hair, bloodstain, and crumb of
pastry already stuck to its pages. These marks of use are all connected to
the body, which seems to variously shed, bleed, eat, and smoke a sedimented history that interests Orlando far more than the textual materials
enclosing it. Woolf here seems to gesture toward the late-eighteenth-cen-
tury Burkean ideal of the historian as a man of feeling. But she also
releases the erotic energies that this ideal, in its appeal to virtuous manhood, ultimately disavows.

Her trope for such a method is the hand, which redeems that aforementioned aching left-hand finger. Early in the novel, Orlando is presented to Queen Elizabeth, whom he encounters by way of her royal
hand; from this appendage he infers her ancient, decayed body buried
underneath its brocade and jewels. That night, the queen seduces him,
insisting that he bury his head in her skirts. "'This,' she breathed, 'is my
victory!' — even as a rocket roared up and dyed her cheeks scarlet" (25).
This militarized orgasm, following from what looks like oral sex with a
person so old she might as well be dead, prefigures what will later develop
into an explicitly desirous relationship between the individual historian
and the materials of a collective past. For at another point the narrator,
struggling to piece together the facts of Orlando's life, apotheosizes the
joking possibility of a lesbian historiography: "Just when we thought to
elucidate a secret that has puzzled historians for a hundred years, there
was a hole in the manuscript big enough to put your finger through"
(119). Here again, history is a hole to penetrate, but not with the usual
instruments.

That Sapphic finger, in turn, has already appeared in veiled form,
in the question Orlando puts to the skeletal hand of his ancestors, of

whether it belonged to a man or a woman, "urged the war horse, or plied the needle" (71). Woolf's narrator later muses upon the needle in another figure for lesbian erotohistoriography:

> Nature, who has played so many queer tricks upon us . . . [has] added to our confusion by providing a perfect rag-bag of odds and ends within us — a piece of a policeman's trousers lying cheek by jowl with Queen Alexandra's wedding veil — but has contrived that the whole assortment shall be lightly stitched together by a single thread. Memory is the seamstress, and a capricious one at that. Memory runs her needle in and out, up and down, hither and thither. (77–78)

Taken together, these passages suggest that the hand that plies the needle, the needle that is itself a kind of finger penetrating the holes in memory and manuscript, the nerve system that controls the pen and yet is wrapped around the fibers of our whole being, are figures for a more affective and embodied form of historical inquiry. *Orlando* neither celebrates a merely cognitive or imagistic memory nor subordinates any response to material detail toward an apprehension of "the spirit of the age." Instead, the novel pursues a kind of visceral encounter between past and present figured as a tactile meeting, as a finger that in stitching, both touches and is touched, and that in reading, pokes and caresses the holes in the archival text even as it sutures them.

Orlando's aesthetic of lesbian fingerplay, as I have described it, offers up erotohistoriography as the model for a truly digital history. But insofar as it tantalizes us with the possibility of manually encountering the past, it also takes pleasure in the analog. For in analog technology, information is borne along in continuous, linear sequences of physical matter such as light waves or sound waves. Analog technology tends also to be indexical, incorporating a trace of that which is represented into the representation, as with light in a photograph, or sound waves in a recording. Digital technologies, which convert this material to binary code, create infinitesimal gaps in this continuum and enable endless shuffling. But because of its high speed and the homogeneity of its materials (numbers), digital also seems "smoother" than analog. Digital code effaces the visible seams, audible noise, palpable textures that accompany analog transitions from one material or state to another: in an analog experience of the real, the gears jam momentarily when things change, as in the small skip in spliced film or audiotape, the pops and hisses between tracks on LP records, the layers of paint overlapping or bleeding slightly as they meet in a painting, the finger interrupting a stream of text as it flips the pages of a codex. With her digits that penetrate, sew, and dangle, then, Woolf proleptically figures an analog version of the digital, even as *Orlando* retrospectively looks back toward to discredited historiographic methods and restores an eroticized materiality to the gaps and imperfect sutures between past and present.

The Sticky Fingers of Time: Analog and Digital Pleasure

Though *Orlando* precedes the digital era by quite a few decades, the independent filmmaker Hilary Brougher's feature-length film *The Sticky Fingers of Time* (1997) owes something to that novel's way of bodying as opposed to minding the gap between then and now. Significantly, Brougher made *Sticky Fingers* on a very low budget, using no special effects: if its conceit of shuffled times is digital, its technology is entirely analog.[24] Like *Orlando*, the film explores lesbian sex and time travel as figures for one another and for the erotics of apprehending history. In this small masterpiece, the slightly butch Drew (Nicole Zaray) eventually travels from her own 1990s to the 1950s and falls in love with a midcentury high femme, Tucker (Terumi Matthews). Tucker, in turn, is involved with both Isaac (James Urbaniak), an androgynous male from her own era, and Ofelia (Belinda Becker), a very feminine female from an unspecified future. The time-traveling journey begins with Drew attempting to rescue Tucker from her impending death by murder but, in the spirit of *Orlando*, becomes a romantic chase as well.

Here is a brief summary of this incredibly complicated plot. Sometime in the 1950s, as Tucker sits down to begin writing her novel *The Sticky Fingers of Time*, her live-in lover Ofelia kisses her and asks her to buy coffee. Stepping out, Tucker suddenly finds herself on her own street, but in the 1990s. Meanwhile in the 1990s, inside Tucker's former apartment, Drew has deleted the novel she had nearly finished and goes to meet her friend Gorge (Samantha Buck), so Gorge can borrow Drew's dental insurance card. After this meeting, Drew and Tucker bump into one another outside a bookstore, where Drew has just bought a vintage copy of Tucker's now-completed novel. As the two women separate, a clipping flutters out of the novel; Tucker picks it up, puts it in her purse, and follows Drew into a bar. There, they introduce themselves to one another and examine the clipping, which reveals that Tucker died of a gunshot wound in 1953. Isaac appears in the bar and surreptitiously asks Drew to help him rescue Tucker, which he cannot do himself since he has already lived through that moment in time once. He also explains that Tucker can time travel because of radiation sickness, and that Ofelia murdered her in 1953, splattering Tucker's irradiated DNA, called Code, into other, future souls — of whom Drew is now one. Drew, somewhat infatuated, follows Tucker in and out of the 1990s, with Ofelia fast behind her. Returning home, Drew finds her friend Gorge inexplicably absent. Ofelia appears and takes Drew back in time to the dentist's office, where Drew relives another murder: Ofelia's henchmen, posting as assistants, have mistakenly killed Gorge thinking she was Drew. Ofelia then takes Drew further back in time to the scene of Drew's parents' divorce, mocking Drew and then channeling her soul into a cactus. From within her cactus consciousness, Drew realizes that she has traveled to the scene of Tucker's murder once already, in a "blackout" caused by her parents' final argument, and this realization allows her soul to burst through the plant. Drew then travels to the 1950s, before Ofelia has broken up Isaac and Tucker, and steals Tucker's plane tickets to Nevada, where she had planned to see the H-bomb test that — had she arrived to see it — would have resulted in her time-traveling abilities, and hence both Drew's and Ofelia's as well. Once Drew has stopped Tucker's trip, she has effectively prevented anyone, including herself, from being able to time-travel. With Ofelia now presumably stuck in the future, Drew and Tucker settle together in the apartment, and, we can assume, live happily ever after in the 1950s.

"Fingers, why fingers?" muses Tucker at the beginning of *The Sticky Fingers of Time*. Filled with images of hands on the keys of a manual typewriter, a mouse, and a keyboard, the film seems obsessed with the act of writing, particularly the writing of lesbian pulp novels and science fiction. As with *Orlando*, its scenes of writing are obviously conventional postmodern devices to call attention to the constructedness of gender, sexuality, and time. But the film's title suggests that a certain literality, even *materiality*, gloms onto even the most rigorous deconstruction — that historical details may obstinately stick to or gum up the gears of queer theory. For *Sticky Fingers'* sticky fingers, digital clocks of a sort, are explicitly connected to time-travel. In the film's opening scene, Tucker is at the typewriter starting to write her own 1950s pulp novel, presumably the historical parallel to Drew's unfinished one. Tucker murmurs to herself, "Time has five fingers: one is for the present, two is for the past, three is for the future." Ofelia, who is her lover at this point, completes her sentence: "And four is for what could have been, and five is for what yet could be." In other words, in this film, two fingers are subjunctive. If Tucker's and Ofelia's description of the "fingers of time" were correlated with ordinary hand gestures, the index finger, one, would point to the present; the middle finger, two, would indicate the past; the heterosexual-marital ring finger would correspond to the future, as it does for Woolf's Orlando. The pinkie and the thumb, the outer limits of the hand, would signal "what could have been" and "what yet could be," respectively. But Ofelia has already scrambled the sequence, for though the audience does not know of these events yet, within the chronological order of the film she has already kidnapped Isaac from 1953, reengineered him into a time traveler by chopping off his index and middle finger and stapling prosthetic ones to the stumps, and usurped his place as Tucker's lover. Ofelia's surgery, then, has already disordered the logic of counting by hand that Tucker depends on for her novel, making Isaac's index and middle fingers into the agents of change: "what could have been" and "what yet could be" are precisely the interventions into past and future that Isaac's two primary digits allow.

One could certainly read Ofelia's act as an act of castration (and given Brougher's casting of an African American woman in the role of Ofelia, as castration of white manhood by black womanhood, a particularly pernicious cliché — about which more below). But insofar as the prosthetic fingers allow Isaac to hop the timeline, they are actually quite a bit better than the originals. Then, too, Isaac's name recalls the biblical character whose birth to an elderly and therefore presumably infertile couple already marks a certain queer fold in time, and whose status as a potential victim of infanticide reverses the Oedipal narrative. Here, though, the binding of Isaac is not a covenant between God the Father and Man his son. Instead, *time* binds Isaac to Drew: he has already returned once to the "slice of time" in which the murder has taken place and failed to rescue Tucker, and so he finds Drew and tells her that she must do so. Thus Ofelia's act seems less to castrate a masculine subject than to found a queer alternative to the sequential logic of generations, a bond between subjects who neither descend from one another nor coexist at the same moment.

The index and middle fingers may be the ones most often used for typing (if my own is any example), enhancing the film's play with the idea that writing itself is an act of intervention into time. But they are also the ones most often used in the initial stages of lesbian sex. Thus Isaac's stapled digits, the most literal reference to the film's eponymous "sticky fingers," function as a sort of temporal dildo. Or perhaps this is reductive, insofar as fingers are capable of but not limited to phallic activity, and in Isaac their sexual flexibility is matched by a certain temporal flexibility. As time-travel devices, Isaac's fingers don't seem to register the Oedipal drama of penis envy. For they "think" sexuality entirely outside the two-sex sequencing of conventional psychoanalysis, in which the mother is the past and the father is the future, and history outside the two-sex sequencing of orthodox Marxism, in which the mother is Nature on which "man" works to produce himself and his future. Exploring and reorganizing relations between now, then, and hereafter, these digits are a *tactile* unconscious, or as Walter Benjamin describes the cinema's function as optical unconscious, a surgeon's hand palpitating the organs in a patient's body.[25] In *Sticky Fingers* and the cinema alike, the patient is the present tense.

Of course, if manual sex often starts with the first two fingers, the others frequently follow, and very often the fingers eventually double back upon themselves. Likewise, Isaac's subjunctive fingers are intended to bring the past, present, and future into new conjunctions, to double time back upon itself as they insert new possibilities into the course of human events. Thus Brougher's unspoken figure for historical rupture is what may be the only sex practice invented in the twentieth century— namely, fisting. The fist is a feminized, reverse image of the Freudian toothache I described in my introduction, the pain around which an always melancholic subjectivity organizes itself: while the tooth, an instrument of penetration, turns into an orifice by way of the cavity and the dentist's drill, the hand, an instrument of receptivity in its capacity to hold things, becomes as fist an instrument of penetration. But hands, even fists, also receive touch even as they give it. Thus the film's queer "touch across time," as Carolyn Dinshaw has called it, is troped as a reciprocal tactility between disjunctive moments.[26]

Along the way, this film also pays explicit homage to *Frankenstein*. Though Drew has deleted the only copy of her novel-in-progress from her computer, Gorge remains enthusiastic about it when they meet to exchange the dental insurance card: "I love that part," Gorge says, "when Frankenstein splits his stitches and he dies, fertilizing the earth where that little girl grows tomatoes." This little snippet of dialogue, the film's slightly befuddled nod to Mary Shelley—for Gorge, like many readers, confuses the monster and his creator—seems at first glance to revise *Frankenstein* in exactly the communitarian terms that critics who see that novel as a plea for family values might have prescribed for the original monster and his creator. Rather than escaping society on an ice floe, in Gorge's account Drew's revised monster joins the human scheme of obligations and dependencies, preparing the earth for regrowth and for the next generation. The scene Gorge describes also initially seems to follow the heterosexual, masculine logic that both Shelley and Woolf would eschew. Neither Drew's novel nor this part of it ever appears directly in the film itself, so it is unclear whether the monster fertilizes the earth with his blood, his rotting corpse, or both. But given that the remainder of the film deals with disseminative modes of transmission such as radiation, it is fair to imagine that the monster sheds blood when he bursts his stitches. Here, then, in a heteronormative reading, we can see the monster figuratively inseminating the little girl. But in *choosing* to die for the next generation, the monster also accrues a particular form of Christian masculinity. He transcends the "natural" pain of childbirth, and hence the cyclical time of reproduction, and in doing so enters into a sequential temporal scheme that is the precondition for modern, Western disciplinary history. In a secular version of the Christ story that organizes the meaning of empires and nations, wounds catalyze or serve as metonyms for battle narrative, becoming the signs and guarantees of history proper. When retold across time, wounds facilitate social continuity between male generations in homosocial ways that merely biological fatherhood cannot.[27]

In this light, the monster merely serves dominant historiographical modes. His body, composed as it is of cadavers, may well contain a wounded soldier or two — but in his own death scene as Drew apparently rewrites it, historical continuity seems at first to supersede textuality, taking the more corporeal form of a delayed communion at which the little girl will presumably eat the tomatoes nourished by the monster's blood and body. Within this revised Frankenstein story, the singular and irreplaceable event of a wound on a male body does indeed install the "deep time" of at least a *generational* "before" and "after." And the possibility that this temporal schema might become *historical* appears in the scene's frame, in the form of Gorge telling this sacrifice story so that it might be handed over, handed down: this scene is all that is left of Drew's novel, and Gorge dutifully preserves it. She sublimates and displaces Frankenstein's act into a narrative fragment that might eventually count as part of official, if not precisely national, history — that is, that might be exchanged between men, across time. Indeed, this exchange is already partially underway, for the androgynously named Gorge is speaking to Drew, who bears a similarly gender-undifferentiated name. In short, the monster's masculine self-wounding has literally "engendered" a potential historicity, also structurally masculine, that the rest of the film plays out — and plays with — in terms of time travel.

Within *Sticky Fingers'* complicated intertextual moment we can certainly see a version of the dictum that "history is what hurts": Shelley's monster is stuck within a visual cultural regime that reads his soul from his deformed body and thus denies him an object for his desires, and perhaps Brougher's queer character Drew identifies with this. But we might also return to the Frankenstein scene to witness a different story — one in which bodies are the relentlessly plural sign of being *in* time rather than escaping from it, wounds a sign of being open to the possibility of change. For as the figure of the little girl suggests, these very same injuries are portals into futurity itself. And in opening himself up to a future he cannot see, the monster enacts a certain historical agency irreducible to biological reproduction between man and woman, or narrative transmission of events between men. Instead, this scene captures a tremendously polymorphous fantasy about how the queer corpus might encounter temporality and historicity. First, there is no actual event here: Gorge, a fictional character in a film, speaks of another fictional character from a nineteenth-century novel reappearing in Drew's twentieth-century novel, which Drew herself has already destroyed in despair. In fact, because Brougher (or Gorge, or Drew) has conflated the scientist and the monster, not even the "original" Frankenstein appears. Within the scene, this Frankenstein, himself assembled of cadavers with all the historical seams showing, bursts the boundaries of his own physique. A queer reader might understand this as a form of male lactation or as an ejaculation that crosses the divide between adults and children. But perhaps most importantly, we will remember that even in Shelley, the monster's body is not at all a sign of full presence outside of history, nor is it simply a sign of the wounding necessary to enter history, nor even a sign of the discontinuous body of gender nonnormativity. It is an index of temporal heterogeneity — specifically, of dead bodies persisting in the present and the future, of nonreproductive yet still insistently corporeal kinship with the departed. This revised monster's act suggests a historiographic practice wherein the past takes form of something already fragmented, "split," and decaying, to which the present and future are somehow porous in an analog way, and for which bodies are both metaphor and medium. In this sense, his body is not a "body" at all but a figure for relations between bodies past and present. It marks the return from the late eighteenth century

16. Still from *The Sticky Fingers of Time*.
Copyright Strand Releasing, 2001. Courtesy of Strand
Releasing/Crystal Pictures/Good Machine Production.

of a *corporealized* historiography, and, extending *Orlando*'s project, it suggests a future-making project of the sort that contemporary queers might embrace.

Like *Frankenstein* and *Orlando*, Brougher's film desublimates the eroticism of affective historiography, allowing us to think that history is not only what hurts but what arouses, kindles, whets, or itches. In theorizing the relations among the senses, subjectivity, and the social that make historical consciousness possible, *Sticky Fingers* argues, perhaps it is time to return to the orifice, to holes, as Woolf has put it, "big enough to put your finger through." For when Drew and Tucker time travel, they black out and wake up in another era, rubbing their eyes only to find them filled with a clear, viscous liquid, the bodily register of contact with other moments (see figure 16). It's possible that the clear substance that floods their eyes is intended to invoke tears, the bodily response most obviously correlated with the sympathetic histories practiced by the Burkean man of feeling. But the stretchy, slippery properties of this liquid make it look much more like personal lubricant of the sort with which many lesbians of the 1990s became familiar through the grassroots sex-positive lesbian presses. Taking this substance as a figure for a different kind of encounter with history, we might say that history is what pleasures. In other words, the boundaries of the properly historical, the retreating edge of a legibly historical formation, may appear in or through a directly sexual version of the gothic ecstasy that I referred to at the beginning of this chapter.

If we read Drew's Frankensteinian scene in terms of queer bodily pleasures, then, the little girl matters very much: she is, we can assume, going to eat those lovely tomatoes. In this sense, she is both a feminine subject and, shall we say, a sexual bottom. But in contrast to Freud's and Butler's formulations, Frankenstein's wound passes over from his pain to her pleasure, his openings to hers, without necessarily having to become a phallus at all. Flowing from multiple openings, his fluids fertilize tomatoes to nourish her through the mouth. In short, as with *Orlando*, holes beget holes. Here, Frankenstein's transfer of energies across time appears not as sacrifice but rather as a gender-undifferentiated discharge to be received pleasurably in the future, in a future imagined *as* pleasure. The great surprise of the scene, then, lies in the missing feast it suggests: the hint that erotic bliss may be as potentially "historical" as trauma.

Giorgio Agamben suggests that pleasure could found the new concept of time presently missing from historical materialism: "For everyone there is an immediate and available experience on which a new concept of time could be founded. This is an experience so essential to human beings that an ancient Western myth makes it humankind's original home: it is pleasure."[28] More problematically, he locates that pleasure in man's "originary home," which sounds a great deal like the Kristevian maternal body I critiqued in chapter 1. In contrast, the scene from *Sticky Fingers* offers neither mother nor father in its imagining of relations between time and history, no original, maternal body of plentitude but only a scarred and striated body on the one side, an absent prepubescent one on the other, a dumb vegetable in between, and crucially, the mouth as a tactile rather than a verbal instrument for historical transactions, for scenes of historicist binding. I have argued for the body and the hand as historiographical instruments; let us now turn to the mouth.

In work that has been crucial for queer theory, Nicholas Abraham and Maria Torok describe melancholia in corporeal terms, as the "crypting" of a lost object, an attempt to embed the object into or make it part of the body itself in a process they call "incorporation."[29] Incorporation is the pathological form of introjection, where the lost loved object serves as the means through which the subject reworks its originary erotic autonomy. In introjection, the object is a placeholder for the self whom the subject must return to loving as in primary narcissism, and this process also creates a permeable self capable of integrating the new. In the theory of introjection, time synchs up again, the uninterrupted present corresponds to an integrated self. Incorporation, on the other hand, is out of synch; it produces an unintegrated, Frankensteinian body and psyche. Interestingly, incorporation reveals itself through an oral symptom—a set of behaviors that includes binging on food, or a fetish-word, even a way of speaking, that simultaneously preserves and obscures the loss. Incorporation, then, is another kind of "fat" writing and performance, overloading both the body and the sign in ways reminiscent of Hayes's, Subrin's, and Mitchell's temporal drag.

As with melancholia compared to mourning, the "pathological" form of incorporation seems eminently queerer; it preserves the past *as* past, in a crypt imperfectly sealed off from the present, in a psyche with unpredictable leakages, in a body semiotically and sensually at productive odds with itself. But what are these odds? Despite Abraham and Torok's temporally normalizing logic, what is most crucial about the work on introjection that Torok did by herself is the fact that the past is not wholly defined in terms of trauma. Instead, it consists of latent excitations not yet traversed by the binary between pain and pleasure, preserved and suspended in this very ambivalence and capable of being released *as pleasure* rather than simply being repeated as incomplete mastery over pain. Venturing where Sigmund Freud would not, Torok has theorized a version of the possibility of a fully sensual rather than merely verbal or narrative relationship to the past. In "The Illness of Mourning and the Fantasy of the Exquisite Corpse," she works her way into the most opaque part of Freud's essay on melancholia—the section on mania where Freud notes but fails to theorize the eruptions of frenzied joy that often follow the loss of a loved one. Torok considers a series of unanswered letters in which Freud's contemporary Karl Abraham (no relation to Nicholas) pressed him to consider mania. Apparently, Abraham suggested several times that in the wake of what is supposed to be a terrible event, "mania" very often consists of a sudden influx of erotic feelings, but Freud seems not to have answered this call to examine the phenomenon. Torok suggests that the melancholic's entombed secret is not a loss at all; rather, it is "an erotic effusion" repressed and mnemonically preserved: "*The illness of mourning [i.e., melancholia] does not result, as might appear, from the affliction caused by the objectal loss itself, but rather from the feeling of an irreparable crime: of having been overcome with desire, of having been surprised by an overflow of libido at the least appropriate moment, when it would behoove us to be grieved in despair.*"[30]

In their later essay, Abraham and Torok claim that melancholic incorporation itself "perpetuate[s] a clandestine pleasure," a long-ago interrupted idyll of erotic contact with the lost object.[31] For Torok, then, the melancholic psyche is a doubled effect of pleasures past: first, pleasure is severed and remade as unpleasure or trauma; then, the object that gave pleasure itself disappears. Affect, scene, and object reemerge in the crypt, to be released in the grieving subject's sudden lust. In short, as a component of melancholia, mania revisits an inappropriate sexual response from the past.

With Torok's sense of melancholia as a lost idyll preserved, we reach the contemporary form of what I have been calling erotohistoriography: a combination of femme historiography and bottom historiography, a way of imagining the "inappropriate" response of eros in the face of sorrow as a trace of past forms of pleasure. As a mode of reparative criticism, erotohistoriography honors the way queer relations complexly exceed the present, insisting that various queer social practices, especially those involving enjoyable bodily sensations, produce forms of time consciousness — even historical consciousness — that can intervene into the material damage done in the name of development, civilization, and so on. Within these terms, we might imagine ourselves haunted by bliss and not just by trauma; residues of positive affect (idylls, utopias, memories of touch) might be available for queer counter- (or para-) historiographies. Camp performance, as I have described in the previous chapter, might be seen as a kind of historicist *jouissance*, a *frisson* of dead bodies on live ones, fading constructs on emergent ones. Or, what Annamarie Jagose has called "the figure of 'history' — its energizing of the very tropes of before and after" — might be seen in queer patterns of courtship and cruising, in sexual and more broadly tactile encounters, even in identity formations such as butch/femme or FTM, all of which suggestions *Sticky Fingers* makes.[32] Or — and — historicity itself might appear as a structure of *tactile* feeling, a mode of touch, even an erotic practice.

In *The Sticky Fingers of Time*, Drew's unfinished novel seems to have imagined this queer version of continuity, conjuring up a way for the dead to enter our bodies neither through the solely psychoanalytic means of introjection nor through the mass-popular means of psychic channeling. Instead, the lost passage on *Frankenstein* evokes Torok's notion of incorporation, of literally consuming an object that partakes of the lost body and thereby preserving it. If Frankenstein's monster enacts what seems to be a particularly melancholic futurity, the little girl's future will also emerge within the supposedly pathological delights of incorporation as she eats the ripened tomatoes. The name of the woman who narrates this scene, "Gorge," only makes explicit the incorporative logic of Drew's fantasy, for as a noun it means a narrow passage, while as a verb it means to eat to the bursting point.[33] Following the same oral logic of historical transmission, a third character hailing from the future, Ofelia, has the ability to transport others involuntarily across the timeline by kissing them. And most crucially, the film's very first intervention into linear time comes in the form of a murder that takes place in a site dedicated to the oral, if not to the erotic — a dentist's office.

In the scene where Gorge uses Drew's insurance card to have a tooth abscess examined, the Freudian "jaw tooth's aching hole" is an opening into the future for Gorge, insofar as she meets it in the form of a zombie nurse who kills her, and/or an opening into the past for the nurse, insofar as she meets it in the form of Gorge. It's also an opening into the past for Drew, insofar as Ofelia, by kissing Drew, yanks her first back to this scene and then into the cactus and her repressed past. Here teeth seem to signify two ways. In classical psychoanalytic terms, they operate as symbol for the reorganization of Drew's libido in genital terms: kissed back to the scene of a toothache, Drew emerges as all the more lesbian. In terms of temporality, Derrida has described the interval between temporal instances as a diastema, literally a break between different kinds of teeth.[34] In the dentist's office scene, then, teeth are a symbol for the collision of historical moments at the mouth, itself an intersection between the exterior and the interior of the body.

But unlike the Freudian toothache, Gorge's abscess never does get reworked into the phallus. Instead, it replicates itself in any number of references to the mouth as a temporal device. After sleeping with her ex-boyfriend one last time, for instance, Drew remarks that "relapse sucks," condensing temporal regression and the oral in a single phrase. Later, Isaac claims that "time is a pie. You can eat the slices in any order, but you can't eat the same slice twice." We might thus read the film as productively, radically melancholic in some ways, insofar as melancholia is classically regarded as a form of "relapse" to the oral phase in which teeth are absent, neither temporal spacing nor physiological boundaries are stable, and interior and exterior are thoroughly confused. Then, too, these figures make literal Torok's model of incorporating or eating the past. They invoke and dare to affirm the hunger for historical referentiality itself, that pull toward the disappearing moment, however present we know that moment never was.

In this film, orality and digitality also meet one another in a specific trope for history, one that makes good on Orlando's dreamy insertion of a tobacco flake into an ancient prayer book. *Sticky Fingers* plays several times on the film noir and pulp novel cigarette — phallic emblem, instrument of seduction, relay to *après-sex* bliss, and dykedom's most compressed display of manual and labial dexterity. But it transforms that classic cigarette scene into mutual marijuana toking. Sue-Ellen Case argued quite some time ago that we must attend to specific historical formations of erotic coupledom in order to expose poststructuralism's focus on the individual subject — or, as she puts it, we must use butch-femme to turn the Lacanian slash of self-alienation into a lesbian bar.[35] These pot-smoking scenes suggest that now it's time to turn that couple-centered lesbian bar into an even more affiliative historical joint of the sort that *Coal Miner's Granddaughter* and *The Physics of Love* also suggest. For recalling the onetime definition of a joint as "a connecting point of time," the film portrays Tucker and Drew getting wasted in bed twice, once in the 1990s and once in the final sequence.[36] These scenes redescribe the famous Shakespearean joints of time in corporeal terms not limited to the skeletal or to a single body: locations and dislocations occur through membranes and orifices; as with *The Physics of Love*'s intraveneous merging of mother and daughter, here inhalations and exhalations are the very media of temporal contact. In short, *Sticky Fingers* moves from lips and teeth to lungs, correlating Drew's entry into lesbianism with a mild hallucinogenic drug, followed up by an increasing number of shocks to her sense of chronology and temporal location. Each smoking scene hastens the attraction between these denizens of different eras, gesturing toward social possibilities exceeding but not canceling out the sexual: indeed, the toking scenes rework the visual metaphor of Walter Benjamin's "profane illumination" into something like an apostatic high.[37] Drifting the smokers across time, the joint disarticulates bodies and reorganizes subjectivities. Or as Benjamin himself might put it, as if to rework Freud's narcissistic toothache, the dream-state of being stoned "loosens individuality like a hollow tooth."[38]

In short, here historical and temporal disjunction, experienced as illicit pleasure, define and enable queer sociability. Against a developmental and specular logic of "coming out," Brougher's film suggests lesbianism as an oscillation between dreaming and waking states, and a movement among various microtemporalities that do not add up. And smoke is not the only way that history seeps in. The sticky substance that Tucker and Drew find in their eyes after time traveling literalizes the transition from an ocular logic to a tactile one; it exchanges a gay and lesbian history in which lesbians become progressively more visible, for a textural logic suggested by the film's title, in which queer history both announces itself as a suggestively lubricated touch and clings stubbornly to the (proto-?)lesbian body. Tucker also gets continual nosebleeds, a result of the radiation sickness she acquired while watching H-bomb tests in the 1950s before Drew intervened and stopped her from going. As well as needing to be lubricated, then, time travel produces a different set of bodily fluids from those considered vital to biological reproduction, itself the supposed precondition for an enduring humanity and thus for history. Yet in the face of historical rupture, these women's bodies also do not dissolve into sentimental tears. Instead, they discharge something else, some new form of subjectivity neither imprisoned within nor fully free from past forms. The oozy eyeballs and bloody noses turn the certainty of chronology and continuity into unpredictable temporal flows, and they move the biological location of futurity away from the uterus, vaginal canal, or tear ducts, and onto new bodily sites.

These effluvia and their sites of emergence, in turn, evoke a loss of control reducible neither to genitalized orgasm nor to sentimentalism's hydraulic release of desexualized emotions. In *Sticky Fingers* time, and eventually history, are gathered and redispersed through the edges and breaks of the body itself. The film's various seepages suggest corporeal connections across bodies but beyond sex, across historical moments but beyond generationality, across social movements but beyond concepts of activism that relegate sex practice and erotic style to the margins of what can count as political. They are examples of what, following the film critic Laura Marks, might be called *haptic* historiography, ways of negotiating with the past and producing historical knowledge through visceral sensations.[39]

The Dialectics of Feeling

If Woolf emphasizes hands to invoke the pleasures of both reading and writing history, Brougher's use of them also calls forth a historical-material development in which the index finger is key: the invention of the camera. As Walter Benjamin puts it in his essay on Baudelaire, "A touch of the finger now sufficed to fix an event for an unlimited period of time."[40] While previously I discussed the role of the camera in turning reproductive sequence into historical consequence, here I would like to discuss its uses for alternative modes of affiliation across time. For the camera also unfixed the event of representation itself, reducing a series of laborious steps into one push of a button that would then trigger a hidden sequence of automated motions. Indeed, Benjamin traces the temporal work of the camera back to the invention of the match, suggesting that the profane illumination or historiographic flash he describes in his *Theses on the Philosophy of History* does indeed have its literal referent in the act of lighting up: "The invention of the match around the middle of the nineteenth century brought forth a number of innovations which have one thing in common: one abrupt movement of the hand triggers a process of many steps."[41] By the time of the movie camera, the role of the index finger was paradoxical: pushing a button both stopped time, staying the process of change and decay as it captured images one by one, and initiated the inexorably forward movement of frames as the film stock scrolled through. Benjamin also argued, famously, that in stopping time film and photography possessed the power to reveal previously invisible structural elements of a given moment in history, even as their very apparatus effaced material process, labor, and duration. But in his analysis these haptic experiences of "switching, inserting, pressing, and the like" were eventually supplanted by the optic experiences engendered by a city filled with images.[42] By the time Benjamin wrote "The Work of Art in the Era of Mechanical Reproduction," he had relegated the hand to a mere metaphor, speaking of the audience's ability to "grasp" formerly inaccessible artworks and bring them closer.

In contrast, *The Sticky Fingers of Time*, like *Orlando*, both literalizes and lesbianizes the hand that can freeze and reorder time, yet it refuses to develop the results of this act into a properly image-bound dialectic. To put it more simply, Brougher's film retains its medium's commitment to the indexical—not only to the history of the index finger, but to the indexical as the very quality linking film to historiography. For film contains a trace of the light hitting an object. The film's moments of bodily encounters with temporal alterity recall Benjamin's concept of the mimetic faculty, perhaps the most directly corporeal of the several revolutionary cognitive practices he advocates. For Benjamin, mimesis combines similarity on the visual plane and sensuality on the tactile plane. In his essay "On the Mimetic Faculty," he traces the human gift of analogy— another aspect of the aforementioned analog—which relies on the meanings produced by physical contiguity. Analogy, far from being a merely linguistic trope, consists of making and understanding likenesses, from the one-to-one correspondences of children's gestural imitations, through the more abstract signs of dance, through representation via runes and hieroglyphs, to the "nonsensuous similarity" of language itself, a binding element between perceiver and perceived that retains a trace of indexicality.[43] Countering the Saussurian model in which sound-patterns have an arbitrary relation to what they call forth in the mind, Benjamin suggests the possibility of a motivated or material (yet also nonrepresentational) bond between signifier and signified: the semiotic, a lost or decayed imitative element. In short, he grants even speech and writing an indexical trace, a time-binding of past and present.

While Benjamin's theory of mimesis in language has not inspired a school of thought, several media critics in his tradition—most notably Andre Bazin and Roland Barthes—have recognized that cinematography itself is mimetic in the sense Benjamin describes. The camera cannot represent or mime its object without direct contact with the light rays that have touched that object, yet it immediately ceases to be dependent on that object and preserves the trace of a past moment only as light. Crucial to the semiotic, then, is a repressed link to the body (here, the eyes), a buried moment of physical contiguity not unlike Torok's aforementioned erotic idyll. Psychoanalysis tends to locate this moment out of history, in a universalized primal relation to the mother. But Benjamin's essay on Surrealism, which can be read as a companion to the one on mimesis, suggests that the semiotic can be both historicized and brought into view, developed like invisible ink (or like Braille) through a tactile version of thinking.

For as extensions of the mimetic faculty, Benjamin's more fully elaborated concepts of the optical unconscious and the dialectical image paradoxically demand a heightened sense of attention to the body. In his view, the Surrealist project was to think as if intoxicated or dreaming, to master the world of commodities by seizing the revolutionary energies of outmoded objects, juxtaposing them with natural, mythic, or futuristic signs, making them touch one another, sensing the ways in which objects from different times or domains inadvertently repeat one another or exist in a metonymic relationship.[44] Mimesis, that is, is the Surrealistic "grab," the prehensile "seize" of appropriation. It seems more like incorporation, which Torok describes as "instantaneous and magical," than like introjection, with the latter's steady accretion of new capacities and meanings.[45] In these terms, mimesis might be thought of both as the invisible adhesive that binds of otherwise incongruous elements (and thus as the mortar of the dialectical image) and as the physical means of dissolving frozen images back into mobile practices, dead identities into live social acts (and thus as an acid bath for congealed meanings). Broadly thought, Benjaminian mimesis denotes a kinesthetic apprehension of the object-world, albeit one subject to changes in technology that variously demand, repress, or transform the kinetic element of perception, and in doing so historicize this object-world. This tactile register lends itself to the kind of antinarrative leaps across time, the achronic "correspondences" that Benjamin so valued: these are felt as well as seen. Whatever "appears" as a formless brush of one thing against another, a sensual meeting irreducible to resemblance, is a sign of something that the discursive regimes and narrative genres of official history cannot contain — even as they depend on it.

Following Benjamin (as well as Sir James Fraser), Michael Taussig reminds us that mimesis itself has two elements — copying, which depends on the visual apprehension of sameness, and contagious magic, which is more like infiltration and depends on contact. *Sticky Fingers* plays with this double sense of mimesis, with the way that lesbian bodies only seem to copy one another visually, while actually oozing into one another and in doing so mutually reconstellating one another and themselves. As if to follow the logic of the copy, Brougher gave the parts of Drew and Tucker to two actresses who look quite a bit alike. These characters also live in the same apartment at two different moments, and one name actually suggests artistic replication ("Drew" as the past tense of "draw"). But Drew is actually *made of* Tucker, rather than just resembling her, as is Ofelia. Recall that in the film's 1953 plot, the H-bomb test scrambles Tucker's "Code," the DNA-like semiotic substance that makes up the human soul, and this reorganization allows her to travel across the timeline. Knowing this, Ofelia has murdered Tucker, splattering her Code so that it recombines with the Code of people in the future, including herself and Drew. In contrast to the replicative function signaled by Drew's name, then, Tucker's suggests a more active relation between bodies ("Tuck her," "Fuck her," or even "Touch her"), and indeed her body, in the form of its Code, has "touched" Drew's long before they meet. Tucker has likewise touched Ofelia, whose name itself lingers on the sound "feel" (and also brings us back to *Hamlet*'s temporal juggernauts). Finally, it is by tactile appropriation, that is, by the lure of lesbian sex, that Tucker eventually draws Drew into the 1950s to fuck her forever. The film thus moves from copy to contact, turning this latter form of contagious magic into an encounter across time rather than just space.

In this case of tactile appropriation, history — the political unconscious consisting not only of repressed social conflict but also and crucially in this film of effaced or foreclosed social bonds of which lesbianism is only one — opens up to a lesbian hand. Or, following Taussig again, "the history of mimesis flows into the mimesis of history."[46] In other words, we might think of mimetic historiography as a nonrepresentational encounter with traces of the past or future. The very inaccessibility of other times to touch guarantees a binding that cannot be reduced to the literal, the physical — yet cannot be thought elsewise than with the erotic at the center. Mimetic historiography does not privilege the steady cumulation of meaning over time but works in fits and starts, torques and seizures. And mimesis itself is historically contingent: as Benjamin recognized in his description of the role of cinema as a mimetic technology and as Taussig echoes in his phrase "the history of mimesis," the sensorium itself is temporally heterogeneous. Indeed, we might think of Raymond Williams's "structures of feeling" not only as traces of residual, dominant, and emerging modes of production but also as more literal assemblages of older and newer sensations dependent on modes of *re*production — that is, enabled or disabled by mediating technologies and social forms as they come and go, in what I'd like to call a *dialectics* of feeling. To put it simply, we feel through and with representational, technological, and social forms whose histories are uneven and overlapping. This, too, involves the power of the analog, where edges show and make themselves felt.

Sticky Fingers hints at the historical specificity of mimesis and at the erotic power of scrambling mimetic modes when Tucker, hiding in Drew's apartment, attempts to put a compact disc onto a turntable and then to listen to the entertainment center as if it were a radio — here, there are no means of digital conversion that could seamlessly blend one medium and another. Immediately thereafter, Tucker surprises any understanding of her as a diehard lesbian by having sex with her now ex-boyfriend Isaac (doubling Drew's "relapse" with her own ex-boyfriend). Tucker's screwball mixup in Drew's bedroom, prefigured by electronic components and their sensory regimes, moves eroticism beyond the play between male and female, or even the presence and absence of components like the penis, and toward the play between sensations available then and not now, or vice versa.

More broadly, the film's very cinematography mimics the dialectic between seepage and rupture, older and newer modes of sensory engagement, that I have described. Rather than splicing together black-and-white and color film stock to move between the 1950s and the 1990s, for instance, Brougher's cinematographer shot the 1950s sequences in the same color film as the 1990s ones, after which her editor took the color out from the 1950s scenes. As the film's opening scene shifts into the 1990s, the colors and the era literally bleed into Tucker's face, and just as she has found herself with a nosebleed in the black-and-white 1950s, her gummy eyes greet the colorful 1990s. The 1990s scenes and those set in Ofelia's historically indeterminate milieu are not differentiated by color or stock at all, so they too simply fold "naturally" into one another. But the 1970s scenes that Ofelia forces Drew to witness look different, for they were shot on a different color film stock, Fuji color-negative, which Brougher saw as a useful way to duplicate the red-yellow tones and flatness of filmic images from that era. Here, the analog technique of splicing suggests in formal terms that the 1970s are the only era truly out of time or sequence, the one least accessible to the travelers.

And this turns out to be the case: just as Sharon Hayes offers up a dead slogan from the feminist movement, just as Subrin's *Shulie* seems to stall out before "women's lib," *Sticky Fingers* theorizes the limits of erotohistoriography by way of that era. In a scene near the end of the film, Ofelia kisses Drew, thrusting her backward in time to a hotel room in the Poconos, where Drew's family once spent a summer vacation that ended in her parents' divorce. At the time, Drew had passed out during her parents' final argument. But in this revisit, Ofelia and her assistants bind Drew's arms and legs tightly, forcing her to stand in the hotel doorway and watch what she missed when she blacked out as a child: her mother, dressed in a crochet vest and turtleneck, storms out of the hotel shouting, jumps in the family station wagon, and drives off by herself. Drew's mother's actions suggest that like many heterosexual white women of her time, she has come to realize that her marriage is a trap — as she leaves, she shouts that it's not the kids, it's that her husband simply doesn't listen to her. In other words, in this return to the past, what had been a *personal* loss for Drew is here subtly reframed as a political moment, a moment in social time.

Yet unlike other slices of the historical pie in this film, this one is indigestible; unlike other historical portals, this one is impenetrable. For after Drew turns away from the scene, Ofelia transmits Drew's Code into a cactus — an unusable instrument of penetration if ever there was one, whose spiny "fingers" may stick but cannot hold anything. From inside the cactus, Drew relives the blackout that had allowed her to escape from her parents' final argument as a child and learns that during that blackout

17. Still from *The Sticky Fingers of Time*.
Copyright Strand Releasing, 2001. Courtesy of Strand
Releasing/Crystal Pictures/Good Machine Production.

she had time traveled to discover Tucker's murdered body on the street in
1953. Thus the 1970s were inaccessible to Drew even in their own present
tense: having blacked out and gone elsewhere in time, Drew neither
remembers nor even initially experiences her mother's primal feminist
scene yet remains, like Elisabeth Subrin, Sharon Hayes, and other artists I
have discussed, haunted by it.

As Drew watches her mother's departure from the doorway of the
hotel room, Ofelia stands behind her (see figure 17). On the face of it,
this staging seems to put past (the mother), present (Drew), and future
(Ofelia) in their proper relation. But we can also read this sequence as a
rupture of the pattern in which a butch-femme or straight feminist past, a
queer 1990s present, and a multiracial cybernetic future mutually illuminate one another. For insofar as Ofelia is played by an African American
actress, she — like *Shulie*'s "Negroes" — links the problem of the timeline with the problem of the color line. As Frances Negrón-Muntaner
has explored in detail, Brougher's decision to cast an African American
woman in the role of Ofelia has implications of which the film is not fully
in control.[47] I cannot do justice to Negrón-Muntaner's intricate, psycho-
analytically informed argument, which pivots on an understanding of
Ofelia as the black phallus who guarantees the time-hopping that engenders a white lesbian relationship. Nor do I wish to perform a racial/
racist "rescue" of the film. Rather, I'd like to use Negrón-Muntaner's
critique to question the terms of this chapter thus far. Is claiming pleasure
for historiography a queer act that nevertheless recapitulates the film's
erasure of a specifically black social time, or repeats its disavowal of the

founding violence so often enacted upon people of color in the name of white pleasures?

It's fair to say that the color-blindness that Brougher claims animated her choice of actors is also a form of historical blindness: intentionally or not, she cast Ofelia as the "time freak" (the film's words) from a de-historicized future, while casting the two white women and the white man as representatives of particular decades. Ofelia seems to have control over the timeline, but she has no access to the markers of historicity; her red satin kimono and straightened updo could come from almost any twentieth-century moment. This may be an attempt to avoid the cheesiness of futuristic costuming, but it does contrast with the loving attention to period detail lavished on the other characters, the props, and the setting. Just as Subrin's "Negroes" are trapped in the post office, Ofelia's own era, whenever it is, is limited to interior domestic scenes in a suburb. For instance, a long scene takes place in Ofelia's home on Staten Island, with no evidence of the public street life that marks the film's 1950s and 1990s alike, or of the protofeminist antidomesticity that marks Drew's mother's 1970s in this film. Neither does Ofelia have an interior life: despite her suggestively Shakespearean moniker, she is the least melancholic character. While the others brood their way across the timeline, she continually and enigmatically smiles. Nor does she black out like Drew, or bleed like Tucker, or leak around the eyes like both white women. Ofelia, then, can exist in the past and the future and perhaps in the subjunctive tense, but she neither fully resides in her own historical moment nor has a body that opens out into historical time. In fact, the whole thrust of the film is to get Drew back to the moment before Tucker sees the H-bomb, thereby preventing Ofelia from ever breaking the timeframe of her nonhistory to murder Tucker in 1953. And Drew is successful; she steals Isaac's and Tucker's plane tickets to Nevada, leaving Isaac out of the love triangle, herself and Tucker happily stuck in the 1950s in sanitary white coupledom, and Ofelia out of both time and love. African American female interventions — especially if we read Ofelia as, allegorically, the force of black feminism and/or lesbianism in and before the 1970s — are effaced in both the film's present and its past and relegated to an unspecified future that may not even happen. Ofelia has "no future" in a way that belies the power of queerness alone, as Lee Edelman has described it, to signal destruction of linear political imaginings.[48] Or, as the film puts it, Ofelia now has "nothing to kill but time itself."

Ofelia's character asks us to consider: is queer "time binding" — even, specifically, the elliptical time-hopping that seems to animate the white butch-femme styles that Drew and Tucker play with — a way to willfully forget interventions into lesbian history by people of color? Is it a way of claiming correspondences across time that represses what to a white body might not even be tangible? Perhaps we might even pause to ask whether some white butch-femme practices of the 1990s and beyond, grounded as they have been in a certain kind of time-play with the 1950s rather than in any genuine engagement with the coeval gender systems of other con-temporary ethnic groups, may also engage Jim Crow as well as Joan Crawford or Johnny Cash. Or perhaps we might ask, *whose* 1950s are available for this kind of play? In other words, if the film is read as an excursus on lesbian history that transforms the latter into a genuine eroto-historiography, Ofelia's sudden blockage in the 1970s of the very time-binding she has seemed to catalyze throughout the film may tell a dif-ferent story. For even when the butch-femme renaissance of the 1980s and 1990s questioned gender separatism, its theorists and practitioners did not always engage with racial segregation, with the history or pres-ent tense of lesbians of color.[49] Furthermore, though I would like to be able to imagine a broadly applicable historiographic practice grounded in bodily pleasures reclaimed, the specifics of particular racialized histories include bodily experiences that do not necessarily center on the sexual in the way I have described and may thus demand more careful working out.

Erotohistoriography *Noir*

Here is one such example of what such working out might look like (the other will follow in the next chapter). In the 1970s scene I have de-scribed, Drew stands at the doorway of the hotel room, unable to enter the past, with Ofelia standing behind her as an augur of things to come. Ofelia's own body thereby registers the very future to which Drew's back is turned like the Benjaminian angel of history. Looking backward in time, Drew witnesses the personal catastrophes of a divorce and the social irruption of the women's movement. But she cannot see the H-bomb, the global catastrophe that has made all the film's characters possible. As a woman of color Ofelia has the only body that even remotely registers what the film elides — the decimation of and damage to Asian populations in Japanese and Hawaiian nuclear test sites, of Native American popula-tions in Nevada sites, of poor and brown bodies compromised by nuclear and other toxic waste dumped into regions whose populations are politically marginalized. Though Tucker's typewriter, Drew's computer, and even Isaac's time-traveling fingers could represent technological developments that have led to greater expressive freedom for women and queers, the nuclear holocaust that haunts the film is, as Benjamin puts it, "proof that society has not been mature enough to incorporate technology as its organ."[50] The only significant piece of vintage stock footage in the entire film is a short filmstrip of an atomic bomb test, which is spliced into a montage at the beginning and therefore never appears diegetically within the film. The H-bomb, then, is even less accessible in the formal terms of editing than the scenes shot on the Fuji stock make the 1970s. As Ofelia looks out the doorway into the past, perhaps only she can see beyond the deracinated 1970s that Drew witnesses, and even beyond Tucker's sanitized 1950s, into the technological development that has caused one of the United States' most potent historical blackouts and, arguably, a continuation of its genocidal policies toward people of color.

How does Ofelia feel historical or historically, if she is blocked from both triumphalist linear narrative and from erotohistoriography, white-lesbian-style? In cinema, Gilles Deleuze suggests, tactility can figure a release from the visual and its enchainment with cause-effect relations, only if the hand can "relinquish its prehensile and motor functions to content itself with a pure touching."[51] Shelley, and to a greater extent Woolf, offer up literary versions of this relinquishment: the monster's body figures a "pure touching" of past and present, and Orlando's hand pokes, prods, caresses, penetrates as opposed to grasping. But Ofelia rejects this pastoral vision of what an appendage might do. For her body alone incorporates an organ that registers the greatest number of temporalities at once and can both penetrate and encircle. In addition to engineering Isaac's interestingly les-bionic fingers, Ofelia has designed a prehensile tail for her own body. Perhaps this detail unwittingly invokes racist equations of African Americans and animals. But juxtaposed with Ofelia's status as symbol of the future, the self-manufactured tail hints at what Mark Dery and others, following Sun-Ra, have called "Afro-futurism"—a critical dialogue between technoculture and racial justice crucial for populations consistently troped as primitives.[52] Ofelia teasingly remarks that her tail "even has extra chakras," which at least locates the tail in *some* culture or other. Given the number of inside jokes in the film, this culture is very likely that of the 1990s yoga craze, with all its appropriations of non-Western practices and icons. But Ofelia's teasing suggestion also tells of other possibilities. Iconographically serving as a

18. Still from *The Sticky Fingers of Time.*
Copyright Strand Releasing, 2001. Courtesy of Strand
Releasing/Crystal Pictures/Good Machine Production.

weapon, an emblem of godlike or human powers, an element of the
Indian flag, the chakra encompasses the differential times of body, religion, and nation; that is, it condenses linear time without losing history.

While Ofelia's tail is not a time-travel machine per se, it does constitute
the film's stickiest "finger of time"; it is the digit that most effectively stalls
the machinery of escape from the past and future into the present. Midway through the film, when Isaac takes Drew to Ofelia's Staten Island
home of the future, Drew tries to sneak back into her own timeframe. As
she touches a doorknob, Ofelia's tail suddenly strikes out like a whip and
encircles Drew's leg and then folds back to drag her away from the door
(see figure 18). Following Taussig, we can see Ofelia's tail as a historiographic whip, quite literally "dislocating the chains of [historical] concor-
dance with one hand, reconstellating them in accord with a mimetic snap,
with the other," as she consistently refuses to grant Drew access to and
ownership over a continuous past and forces her to understand relations
between events Drew cannot remember.[53] Ofelia has already remarked to
Drew in the 1970s scene, "You can't travel. You're not strong enough."
Only Ofelia herself, she seems to suggest, has the capacity to sustain
competing marks of historicity on her own body, to have a physiology,
sartorial style, and gestural repertoire that do not unfold inevitably out of
one another — even by way of the discontinuous resemblances of Surrealism, the dialectical image, or camp. Ofelia's tail is at once the sign of an
invented past and a self-generated future, of atavism and prolepsis, of the
natural and the constructed, of phallicism and invagination, of remain-
ders and ruptures. Far from *being* an anachronism, like Tucker and Drew

in their temporal switchings, Ofelia fits into neither and both of their historical moments and *wears* an anachronism on her body, as if to materialize the meeting of history with bodies, desire, and even—insofar as the tail is prosthetic—commodities. Yet the vestigial/futuristic tail is also the paradoxical sign of society's longed-for maturity, what Benjamin calls its ability to incorporate technology into its organ, except that here society, technology, and the social organ include the sexual body.

Like the body of Frankenstein's monster, like *Orlando*'s many fingers, Ofelia's tail is a crucial binding device that leashes bodies to one another even across time. With her ability to literally take hold, to seize, to grasp the past and bring it into conjunction with the present, to rub the two violently together, Ofelia is the sign of an embodied, frictive historical method that cannot be contained even by the film's oral and manual logics. Hers is a truly *epidermal* temporality, one that substitutes black skin's tangibility for its visibility and the historical burden the latter has borne. Furthermore, unlike Drew or the United States, Ofelia does not "black out." Though this may suggest that she does not have an unconscious, as Negrón-Muntaner argues, I think it also indicates her status as the film's best historiographer, the one who doesn't black out blackness. Ofelia neither forgets nor repudiates the past, but she also refuses to dissolve it into something with which she unproblematically identifies. Through the looking-glass of Frankenstein's tale is Ofelia's tail, which refuses the (often racialized) sacrificial logic of even queer becoming. As an erotohistoriographic tool, Ofelia's tail counts more than any other digit and points to the way that the movement of history on and between particular bodies can encode and incite collective desires.

As it turns out, Ofelia has the most promisingly Frankensteinian body of all the ones I have described in this chapter. First, she resembles Victor Frankenstein in her capacity to engineer the human and her occasional appearance in a white lab coat. Second, born like the monster of a scientific experiment (here, in the form of the H-bomb), Ofelia turns against her progenitor Tucker, whose Code has created her. Possessed of a physique that amalgamates flesh and technology, past and future, and seemingly chained to the past as she vengefully chases Tucker and Drew across the timeline, Ofelia, like the monster and his creator, turns her white masters into slaves. Her zombie nurses, her technological subordination of Isaac, her lashing tail suggest that if the encounter with history has erotic dimensions, these must be also squared with the use of particular bodies—black bodies, slave bodies—to motor modernity's "progress."

Reading backward through Ofelia, it is possible to see Shelley's *Franken-stein* not only as a novel about relations between men across space and time but as a novel about relations between black people and white peo-ple. Indeed, as the literary critic Elizabeth Young has persuasively demon-strated, *Frankenstein*'s monster was a powerful metaphor in both aboli-tionist and anti-abolitionist discourse, where it figured the construction of a black underclass with the potential to turn against its "masters."[54] *Frankenstein*'s questions about absolute power and enslavement, though, interlace not only with its subtle intimations of racial difference (figured most powerfully, perhaps, by the image of a monster with "yellow skin and black hair" bounding across a relentlessly white Arctic snowscape) but also with its famous homoeroticism. If Victor and the monster are master and slave, they are also mutually desirous, albeit in terms of the paranoia, projection, and identification that often accompany disavowed lust.[55] Ofelia's tail, then, also shadows forth the specter of interracial sadomasochism that at least retrospectively haunts *Frankenstein*. Sado-masochism, or leathersex, is all about wearing the skins of the dead: as "skin drag," leathersex invokes the "stitching" of skin onto body, and its traffic in skins can be read as a discourse on blackness even when it does not involve people of African descent. Conversely, Ofelia's tail reminds us that *Frankenstein* haunts sadomasochism, for if s/m's skins are not pre-cisely those of the human dead, they do come to life, warming up and moving with the body they clothe.

What happens, then, when sex mimics the postures and costuming of chattel slavery? Would that be temporal drag's most embarrassing perfor-mance, erotohistoriography's inverse nightmare? Or with s/m, might we risk claiming the most monstrous — some would say — mode of bodying forth a past we can barely look in the face?

four. Turn the Beat Around

Sadomasochism, Temporality, History

As the black Frankensteinian historiographer holding the whip, Ofelia hints at what might be erotohistoriography's limit-case — sadomasochistic role-play, especially between black people and white people. By "role-play," I mean not only the conscious assumption of "top" and "bottom" personae who respectively give and receive pain but also the use of props and costuming that suggest specific social forms of power such as police officer or prison guard, and/or historically specific time periods such as Nazi Germany or the Spanish Inquisition. The latter activities comment on "history" in simultaneously corporeal and symbolic ways. Sadomasochism has certainly been read as the cumulative effect of traumatic relations between parents and children, as a rehearsal of horrifying misuses of power at particular historical moments, and/or as a commentary on the asymmetrical organization of power in everyday life. But however one views S/M, it is inescapably true that the body in sadomasochistic ritual becomes a means of invoking history — personal pasts, collective sufferings, and quotidian forms of injustice — in an idiom of pleasure.[1] This is its scandal and its promise. And, I will risk saying, this mixture of scandal and promise may be especially potent in scenes of interracial S/M. As Saidiya Hartman argues of black physicality, the very ravished, wounded, discontinuous, fragmented, subjected body that anchors the scene of white subjectification also, potentially, "holds out [more] possibility of restitution [than] the invocation of an illusory wholeness or the desired return to an originality plentitude."[2]

In this chapter, I want to focus on this extremely marginalized sexual practice, which I understand in predominantly temporal terms. First, returning to chapter 1's suggestions about habitus as an incarnation of class, I will treat S/M as a deployment of bodily sensations through which the individual subject's normative *timing* is disaggregated and denaturalized. Through an analysis of Isaac Julien's short film *The Attendant* (1992), I will argue that this disorganization is also collective: sadomasochistic sex performs dialectic of a rapid-tempo "modernity" and a slower "premodernity," the latter indexed by any number of historical periods and, crucially, by forms of labor and affiliation that do not accede to capitalist imperatives. Second, returning to erotohistoriography, I will consider sadomasochism as a kind of erotic time machine that offers a fleshly metacommentary on the dual emergence of modernity and its others, on the entangled histories of race, labor, nationhood, and imperialism as well as sexuality. I will argue for sadomasochism as — at least in Isaac Julien's hands — a finely honed erotohistoriographic instrument for encountering the horrors of the translatlantic slave trade.

The Beat Goes On: Timing Sadomasochism

Sadomasochism is a sexually "minor" practice, an erotic dialectic between two or more people that ostensibly focuses on the ritualized exchange of power.[3] But as originally figured by the Marquis de Sade in his fictional writings, s/m also shuttles (or plays at shuttling) between the power relations proper to the French Revolution and those proper to the *ancien regime*: Simone de Beauvoir writes that members of the disempowered French aristocracy of which Sade had been a member revived their status as "lone and sovereign feudal despot[s]" symbolically, in the bedroom.[4] Indeed, not only did Sade resurrect an obsolete social system in his orgiastic scenes but he also wrote his major works in an era that saw a revolutionary and secular experiment with the Western sociotemporal order — the installation of the French Republican calendar from 1793 to 1805. Though this new calendar was made law in 1793, it began retroactively on September 22, 1792, replacing the Christian dating framework that began with the birth of Christ. It interrupted the rhythm of the Christian Sabbath by instituting ten-day weeks, while also standardizing the length of months to thirty days and recalibrating days, hours, minutes, and seconds on the decimal system.[5]

Sade, then, lived through, wrote within, and reinvented sex at a moment when time itself was starkly revealed as not eternal or "timeless" but contingent and rationalized.[6] Even as his sexual reinventions depend on the trappings of the deposed aristocracy, in many ways they also depend on the Republican conception of time as arbitrary and heterogeneous, and thus malleable, even retroactively so. In fact, Sade used sexual practice itself to measure, mediate, and mimic the possibility that temporal schemae might, in a given historical moment, compete with one another.

Beauvoir, for instance, remarks that the sadomasochistic scene depends on a certain depersonalization, which the mirror both figures and effects: the Sadean sadist, she writes, fails to "coincide" exactly with her own movements when she sees them in the mirror, while the masochist uses the mirror to avoid merging with his own emotions; otherwise, "freedom and consciousness would be lost in the rapture of the flesh."[7] In other words, various techniques of visual distantiation, which in contemporary s/m culture might also include the blindfold, the strobe light, or hallucinogenic drugs, produce a temporal noncoincidence between action and result that, in turn, makes possible the awareness of the body as object. Here, the s/m mirror scene introduces an interval, a liberating gap between an effect and the "self" as its cause. The time of proprioception and the time of visual apprehension compete with one another, and their syncopation enables the estranged consciousness crucial to "freedom."

Thus in sadomasochism the historical asynchrony achieved by sexually allegorizing a lost form of imperial power (such that the feudal era appears to interrupt modernity) meets the temporal asynchrony achieved through prying apart impulse and action. In this juncture lies a potential for sex *itself* to become a kind of historiography, perhaps even an "ahistoriography."[8] I recognize that this position seems diametrically opposite from the one taken by Sade's most rigorous admirers, who tend to see Sade as relentlessly opposed to all things purportedly durational: familial generations, inherited property, even literature.[9] But in my view Sadean sex, in its very insistence on reanimating historically specific social roles, in the historically specific elements of its theatrical language, and in using the body as an instrument to rearrange time, becomes a kind of *écriture historique*. s/m becomes a form of writing history with the body in which the linearity of history itself may be called into question, but, crucially, the past does not thereby cease to exist. In this respect, Sade was tacitly ahead of current queer theory, which has shied away from exploring any convergence between this stigmatized form of sexual practice and the seemingly weightier matters of time and history—perhaps precisely because the accoutrements and intersubjective dynamics of s/m so often call up the ghosts of chattel slavery.

Backbeat: Theorizing Sadomasochism

Sadomasochism's absence from the historical turn in queer theory—though s/m was once a staple of queer theorizing "beyond identity"—deserves some attention. One reason for this absence may be that s/m was so central to a relatively ahistorical, deconstructive, and psychoanalytic queer theory that was itself responding critically to historically determinist or monolithic analyses of sexual behavior. For example, some defenders of sadomasochism refuted Andrea Dworkin's and Catharine Mackinnon's description of male sexuality as primally and inevitably rapacious, a description that cast male sexuality as historically unchanging.[10] Furthermore, while many radical lesbian feminists and critical race theorists had condemned the sadomasochistic use of icons from the Spanish Inquisition, slavery, and the Holocaust as a perpetuation of genocidal culture, white gay male theorists (following, if not always giving credit to, Beauvoir) suggested that the real force of s/m lay in its capacity to undermine psychic structures rather than to shore up historically asymmetrical power relations.[11] Leo Bersani, for instance, has famously argued for the refusal of sex to figure or guarantee any particular sociality. Instead, Bersani deduces from Lacan, Freud, Blanchot, Bataille, and to a certain degree from Dworkin and Mackinnon themselves, that all sexuality is fundamentally masochistic, insofar as desire and erotic contact threaten the very structure of the ego.[12] Like Edelman, whose work on futurity draws from him, Bersani severs the links between erotics and psychic wholeness, sex and revolution, fucking and utopia or even dystopia.[13]

Even when Bersani's early work does invoke the relationship between sexual practice and history, it is only to point out that in Freud the libido's violent disruptions are not the product of a timeless human nature but rather echo earlier sexual events in the subject's life, so that the unconscious actually contains a "history of the self's structure."[14] Yet because Freud explains the formation of selfhood temporally, but not quite historically, the undigested past that threatens the coherent self is not a moment experienced collectively; it is merely one point on an individual, if universalized, timeline of developmental events. Preserving this impetus to think of sex as a refusal of sociality and presumably thereby of shared pasts, in his later work Bersani remarks that sadomasochism detaches the master-slave relation from historically specific "economic and racial superstructures," thereby revealing the sheer eroticism of that relation.[15] He hints only in the negative that s/m could potentially reconstitute historical analysis, calling it a bad-faith "theatricalized imitation of history," as if the very representation of historical events through means other than solemn realism inevitably betrays their meaning.[16] He does not seem to consider s/m a catalyst for any genuinely historicist inquiry or a mode of connecting otherwise separate historical moments, any more than he considers sex itself a blueprint for community: for Bersani, sex is fundamentally antirelational not only spatially but also temporally. Given queer theory's own resistance to take s/m seriously in terms of history, it has been easy for critics who would condemn queer theory in the name of a more properly historicist analysis to fasten on sadomasochism as a sociosexual and critical fad, whose fading from academic interest ought to be viewed with relief.[17] In this light, the queer theoretical turn toward metacommentary on history and historiography, and away from what seems to be the solipsistic, merely psychoanalytic power of a particular sex act, looks on the face of it like critical and, perhaps more importantly, political progress.

In fact, there is something of a schism in s/m theory itself, and even within individual theorists, between a will to condemn sadomasochism's historical trappings, as second-wave feminists and critical race theorists have tended to do, and a will to ignore or trivialize them, as white gay male theorists who use it as a paradigm for the antirelational thesis have done. But are we truly locked into a choice between viewing sadomasochism as either an equivalent to the historical forces that oppress or the agent of their complete dematerialization and privatization into psychic drives? I would suggest that we need to continue to theorize s/m, to historicize its theorizations, and, most urgently, to *theorize its historicisms*. Even Bersani eventually points out that s/m refuses the very detachment from economic and racial superstructures that he claims for it earlier, insofar as it "profoundly — and in spite of itself — argues for the continuity between [historically specific] political structures of oppression and the body's erotic economy."[18] In this remark, which posits continuity between history and eroticism rather than a simply causal relationship, bodily response is somehow linked to history. Following this logic, I'd like to posit that s/m may bring out the historicity of bodily response itself. By "historicity" I mean not only the conditioning of sexual response over time, as second-wave feminists and critical race theorists would have it, but the uses of physical sensation to break apart the present into a fragments of times that may not be one's "own," or to feel one's present world as both conditioned and contingent. How might we link up sadomasochism's temporary destruction of the subject, then, to the uses of *time* — irreducible to history yet indispensable for any formalization or apprehension of it?

Queer theory written by white lesbians offers one way into the question: for these critics, sadomasochism is an analeptic mode of (re)constituting a posthumanist self that, in contrast to the ego central to Bersani's analysis, may never have been coherent enough to shatter in the first place. Thus scholars and artists such as Kathy Acker, Lynda Hart, and Ann Cvetkovich have described sadomasochism as a phantasmatic return to a sexual trauma for the purpose of organizing it into an experience.[19] Revisiting s/m's "backwardness" in terms of Freudian *Nachträglichkeit*, Hart has provided the most sophisticated articulation of sadomasochism as a form of psychic healing from sexual trauma. To describe the effect of a sadomasochistic reworking of rape or incest, she invokes Lacan's "future anterior," the grammatical tense expressing something that is not yet present but "will have been so" in the future: "what takes place [now . . .] is not the past definite of what was, because it is no more, nor is it the present perfect of what has been in what I am, but rather the future anterior of what I will have been for what I am in the process of becoming."[20] In other words, in a sadomasochistic "scene" at least one player gets to articulate a future in terms of the changes that take place as she (re)encounters a sexually violent past. The scene remakes her identity neither as the unchangeable victim of trauma nor as a heroine who transcends her past but as a *process* that can be recognized only retrospectively from the stance of an imagined future in which she is freed from torment but still capable of change. For Hart, who follows Cathy Caruth's theories of trauma, the sadist is *witness to* as well as *executor of* violence, which is also key to this temporal Möbius strip, because this witness secures a different "will have been" for the survivor by embodying that retrospective stance: as if to echo Beauvoir's description of Sade, Hart's witness turns a certain visual distantiation into the kind of temporal dislocation that can secure an open future. In this sense, Hart's analysis seizes on Sade's depersonalizing techniques as means not only of producing temporal dissonance in the present but of recasting the future in terms other than those dictated by the past. Here and in other lesbian-queer formulations, sadomasochistic release may have a function somewhat akin to Luciano's vision of nineteenth-century sentimental culture: just as the mourner slows time down and experiences this slowing as a return to an eternal human condition, the masochist's sensations seem to alter the flow of time so that there is an "after" to violence appearing as its "before," a consensual might-have-been triumphing over a personal history of being victimized.

However problematically redemptive the white lesbian-feminist theoretical move might be in Bersani's or Edelman's view, it is important for my purposes because it restores a temporal axis to what, in the white gay male argument, tends to be s/m's largely structural role as a force of negation. This strand of lesbian queer theory acknowledges, albeit often implicitly, that sadomasochism is a, perhaps *the*, set of sexual practices that most self-consciously manipulates time. But these theorists have predominantly focused on s/m's relationship to the family romance, specifically to incest—and thus not to the signifiers freighted with a more legibly national and global history that frequently mark sadomasochistic sex. It was earlier, so-called second-wave and Third World feminists who in their very condemnations actually confronted the way that sadomasochistic fantasies and/or practices index national and imperial pasts.

Of course, the argument that sadomasochism's "historical" costumes, props, and reenactments aggrandize personal pain by connecting it to collective suffering is not obsolete, nor is an understanding that s/m may perform a distorted version of the statement "the personal is political" by visually suturing individual trauma to a historically specific structure of systematic oppression. But whatever the uses of Holocaust, slave, or Inquisitor paraphernalia do—whether one approves or disapproves of them—they certainly enact a kind of time traveling. s/m roles move their players back and forth between some kind of horrific *then* in the past and some kind of redemptive *now* in the present, allegedly in service of pleasure and a freer future. Sadomasochistic eroticism, whatever its moral valences, depends on two linked temporal phenomena. One is a feeling of return to an archaic and more chaotic psychic place, often allegorized as a historical moment that is definitively over: for instance, the powerlessness of a masochist's infancy can be depersonalized and displaced somewhat if it is costumed as an antebellum enslavement he did not go through literally. But conversely, sadomasochism can also aim for a certain visceral fusion, a point of somatic contact between a single erotic body in the present tense and an experience coded as both public and past: for instance, a modern-day Jewish woman might participate in a reenactment of some horror from the Holocaust, experiencing anti-Semitism in more scripted and overt ways than she does in her everyday life, testing her limits, feeling a corporeal, painful, and/or even pleasurable link to her ancestors. Here, the aim is not displacement but a certain condensation of public and private, collective and individual subjectivities.

In this latter respect, s/m might be a way of feeling historical that exposes the limits of bourgeois-sentimental, emotional reactions to historical events.[21] Sadiya Hartman has linked empathy to possession, arguing that the liberal white subject's ability to identify with the suffering or overjoyed black body is "both founded upon and enabled by the material relations of chattel slavery."[22] s/m would seem an even more inappropriate response, a hyperbolic possession of feelings not one's "own." Yet even as it flouts the pieties of correct emotionality, substituting moans of pleasure for tears, s/m also refuses to eschew feelings altogether as a mode of knowledge. s/m, as affect corporealized, rings some changes on what it might mean to theorize historical consciousness—a slippery concept, but one that I take to mean both a latitudinal understanding of individual experience as part of a contingent set of institutional structures (as in Fredric Jameson's "cognitive mapping"), and a longitudinal way of connecting that experience to a collective past or future, albeit in a relationship other than simple cause and effect.[23] Sadomasochist players may implicitly insist on the body's role, and even the role of sexual pleasure, in such consciousness, for sadomasochism reanimates the erotic dimension of affect that is both solicited and repressed in sentiments like nostalgia, patriotism, or pride in one's heritage. Despite the centrality of sadomasochism to a paranoid criticism that often seems to insist on a separation between pleasure and analytic rigor, eroticism and historical memory, s/m relentlessly physicalizes the encounter with history and thereby contributes to a reparative criticism that takes up the materials of a traumatic past and remixes them in the interests of new possibilities for being and knowing. Or at least Isaac Julien seems to think so.

A Text Is Being Beaten: *The Attendant*
and the Marquis de Sade

Julien's film *The Attendant* was originally made for the BBC series *Time-Code* in 1992, which invited filmmakers to produce short, dialogue-free works using the then-new digital technology of Digital D1.[24] In keeping with the New Queer Cinema's anti-identitarian (anti)formalism, *The Attendant* features a situational sexual encounter occurring in the off-hours of a museum, a soundtrack shorn of dialogue or voice-over, a fragmented storyline, and characters who travel outside diegetic time. This film also posits, extremely controversially during the last throes of the "sex wars" of the 1980s and early 1990s, that a black British man might willingly incorporate the iconography of the transatlantic slave trade into his sexual fantasies and activities. When *The Attendant* was first shown, many reviewers saw colonialist history as some kind of catalyst for contemporary sadomasochism, or the latter as a reiteration of the former, and read the film as a rebuke to the New Queer Cinema itself: as one reviewer declared, "Insofar as a passion for historical revisionism can be judged a true test of New Queer Cinema, Julien lets us know that he's only queer by half. Some histories are simply a lot harder to revise than others."[25]

Yet the film's most remarkable quality for a millennial queer audience, almost two decades later, may be that it explores sadomasochism as a means not of revising the past but of meeting up with it in the first place. That is, *The Attendant* exploits rather than apologizes for the historical excesses of some sadomasochistic practices, the subject about which sadomasochism's most radical theoreticians and defenders have remained so silent. Julien seems to recognize that sadomasochism is an unusual sexual technique not only because its rise and elaboration can be traced to a particular historical figure (the Marquis de Sade) and moment in time (the French Revolution) but also because it is a hyperbolically historical, even metahistorical way of having sex. For *The Attendant* bravely solicits the historiographical possibilities I have described. The film suggests that affect and eroticism themselves may be queer insofar as they refuse to acquiesce always and in ordinary ways to industrial, commodity, or "modern" time. It intimates that sadomasochism overtly engages with the dialectic between an era's dominant temporal modality and other historical moments and their temporal fields. And it gestures toward the possibility of encountering specific historical moments viscerally, thereby refusing these moments the closure of pastness.

In *The Attendant*, a museum guard, a middle-aged man of African descent played by Thomas Baptiste and referred to in the credits only as the Attendant, has a sexual encounter with a white man played by John Wilson, called the Visitor. Their attraction to one another is fueled by, even as it seems also to reanimate, a painting displayed at the museum, F. A. Biard's abolitionist painting of 1840, variously titled *The Slave Trade*, *Scene on the Coast of Africa*, or *Slaves on the West Coast of Africa*, depending on the source one consults.[26] This painting, the film's very first image, shows a slave market. There a white, presumably European man straddles

19. Still from *The Attendant*.
Copyright Isaac Julien, 1992. Courtesy of Isaac Julien and
Victoria Miro Gallery, London / Metro Pictures, New York.

a prone, black, presumably African man, as other black and white men look on. In the periphery of this scene, more white men whip, bind, inspect, and brand black men — though in the background there also appears to be a black man whipping another black man, indexing the presence of West African slave traders. In the museum, this painting suddenly and literally comes alive when, during an ordinary day on the job, the Attendant meets the seductive gaze of the Visitor. As the two men's eyes connect, the painting metamorphoses into a *tableau vivant* of an interracial sexual orgy, with participants posed exactly as they were on the canvas, only now wearing modern s/m gear (see figure 19). After the museum finally closes, the Attendant and the Visitor consummate their lust by whipping one another in a room off the main gallery — or the Attendant may simply imagine this happening; the film leaves this ambiguous.

On the face of it, *The Attendant* is clearly a filmic response to specific critics and intends to trouble several different early 1990s audiences. In the moment of its release, it questioned contemporary antiracist accusations that interracial sadomasochism simply repeated and extended violence against people of color, and instead asked black and white men to examine the traumatic histories encoded in their interracial desires without demanding that they simply cease desiring. In this respect, it also interrogated Kobena Mercer's critique of Robert Mapplethorpe's photographs of black and white men, some in sadomasochistic poses, which Mercer described as fetishistic and racist.[27] And the film critiqued Marlon Riggs's *Tongues Untied* (1989), which vilified sadomasochism as a white thing and proclaimed that black men loving black men was *the* revolutionary act: *The Attendant* answers Riggs, ironically, with a piece containing no dialogue, in which tongues (and bodies) may be tied, but speak volumes anyway. Yet Julien's film has much to say about sadomasochism beyond reclaiming the right of black men to fantasize about it and to practice it across the color line, important as that project was and continues to be. Fittingly enough for a film without dialogue, it does not make its claims for sadomasochism on the level of content; it eschews both Riggs's verbal polemic and his straightforward presentation of sexually proper activities. As José Esteban Muñoz has shown in his discussion of *Looking for Langston* (1988), Julien's consummate formalism is part of his counterhistoriographic work: "the concept of time and space that is generated [in *Looking for Langston*] occupies overlapping temporal and geographic coordinates that we can understand as a queer black cultural imaginary . . . Its filaments are historically specific and the overall project is more nearly *trans*historical."[28] Here, the "trans" is not short for "transcendental" but means simply across or in between histories.

Seen in this light, *The Attendant* brings out a certain formal dialectic within sadomasochism, one that hyperbolically clarifies the *temporal* aspects of power and domination and yet also offers new modes of temporal apprehension and historical consciousness. Hart has written that s/m's "(form)ality depends on a stillness, a waiting that is acted out through both the suspense of deferred gratifications [and] the reenactment of suspense within the sexual scene itself."[29] In other words, sadomasochistic sex pivots on the oxymoron of acting out a passive position: inaction becomes a form of action as the receiver, often forced to lie still, anticipates physical contact or receives it in an unguarded moment. Carla Freccero has elegantly parsed the difference between this kind of awaiting and simple inaction: "Passivity — which is also a form of patience and passion — is not quite the same thing as quietism. Rather it is a suspension, a waiting, an *attending* to the world's arrivals (through, in part, its returns)."[30] This is *The Attendant*'s attendance.

From the beginning, Julien's film plays with the dialectic between spectatorship and participation, perception and action, fixity and motion, servitude and revolution, timelessness and timing. Its very title figures this contradiction: to be "attendant" is to wait for, to expect, but also to go, follow, accompany, wait on, to be in constant motion on behalf of another. The opening shot of *The Attendant* extends this dynamic. In color, it reveals the Biard painting from afar, glowing in an otherwise black frame. As the picture appears to draw closer, a faint shaft of light to the left reveals that this is actually a zoom shot of a slide projected onto a wall. Julien seems to have shot the projected slide of a painting not only to self-reflexively indicate the layers of mediation that attend any act of perception but also to bridge the gap between painting and film, thereby prefiguring the scenes where the people in the Biard piece begin to move. The next frame shows a title card reading *The Attendant*, with a shadow flickering across the letters, again juxtaposing stillness and motion. This is followed by still black-and-white shots of a museum from the outside, taken from below and emphasizing the motionlessness of marble steps, white columns, and Greek statuary. Inside, motion is restored as people mill about a room containing paintings and marble busts, each patron walking in a straight line for a while, turning at a right angle, and continuing on. These walkers seem to be imitating both the frames around the pictures and the curatorial practice of producing a linear historical sequence punctuated by moments of spectatorial contemplation. As these scenes clarify, *The Attendant* is certainly about film itself, about the rupture of the still image, about arresting a temporal flow and then recatalyzing it — and eventually, it reveals the inherent eroticism of this very dynamic.

For instance, the encounter between the Attendant and the Visitor takes place as a set of three tableaux, identifiable as scenes rather than stills only by the slight movements therein: first, we see the Visitor with his whip poised over the prone Attendant, whose mouth and eyes move, then the two lovers in reversed positions with the Attendant on top, and finally the Attendant and the Visitor frozen, standing side by side. This scene of scenes, in turn, takes place in a room with two Tom of Finland drawings on the wall, flanking the tableau with still art as if to emphasize the two-dimensionality of the lovers' encounter. We also see another *tableau vivant* of sorts in a more opaque aspect of the film: as the Attendant checks museum visitors' bags, he imagines or recalls himself singing an operatic aria from a theater box to an audience consisting of black and white men dressed in disco and s/m gear who are frozen in static poses on a stage below him. I will make more of this last scene a little later, but for now, let me register it as simply one of many moments of the film's play with flow and freeze.

As much as *The Attendant* is concerned with sexual politics, then, it also explores the relationship between film and the static "high arts" of painting, line drawing, and sculpture, which appeared historically prior to the moving, popular art of film yet continue to inform it. Julien's film is a striking meditation on the passive and active modes not only of sex but also of perception: it explores the dialectic between contemplation and intervention as they inflect sadomasochistic scenes and then open these scenes into history. For the art forms Julien explores require different and often competing modes of apprehension. In the Kantian tradition, still art solicits a single temporal mode, the slow time of contemplation that lifts the viewer out of her historical moment and into some eternal, disinterested realm of understanding. While film can engage this perceptual practice to a certain extent, it also mobilizes other ways of receiving its sensory input. Crucially, it both solicits a certain bodily mimicry in its audiences and formally reiterates historically specific gestures and bodily experiences. For instance, the material of the projected film negative, segments strung into duration, mirrors the factory assembly line and even, it has been argued, the stopwatch time of Taylorist projects aimed at improving human efficiency.[31] To give another example of how cinematic genres register and recapitulate the bodily impact of macrosocial change, the melodrama — a genre *The Attendant* directly invokes in later scenes — engages a slow time of absorption in detail, but not precisely that of disinterested contemplation, for melodramatic absorption is tied to the repetitive routines of domestic labor.[32] Julien's innovation is to link the dynamics among film as a temporal medium, the temporalities of the cinema's various narrative genres, and the time of still art to sadomasochistic practice itself.

In that *The Attendant*'s formal properties shuttle between stasis and motion, stopping and going, the film is not so much sadomasochistic (that is, it does not traffic in the real time of historically specific s/m cultures) as eminently Sadean. In fact, without ever referencing Sade, *The Attendant* joins a history of critical treatments of this allegedly foundational figure, to whom sexual theorists keep going back to read and develop philosophy in the bedroom, perhaps precisely because this writer's own disruptions of time make him a site and a cite of eternal return.[33] The most pertinent to the film are those of Beauvoir and Marcel Hénaff.

Following up on her own insights about the importance of mirrors in the Sadean scene, Beauvoir argues that Sadean sadomasochism depends on "tableaux rather than adventures."[34] In her view, Sade's novels and the vignettes within them aim to imitate the image, to create a place outside of narrative wherein the object awakens to the senses without any surrounding explanatory or causal apparatus, which inaugurates an "enchanted domain" outside of time.[35] Yet this does not account for Sade's insistence that eroticism consists precisely in *mobilizing* the tableau, as Beauvoir herself seems to recognize when she discusses Sade's use of mirrors to multiply his scenes and achieve a certain temporal asynchronicity. Indeed, Marcel Hénaff suggests that the tableau was useful to Sade precisely because of its "double emphasis on motion and motionlessness."[36]

In *The Attendant* the cross-genre dialectic between still and moving art that I am describing gains erotic force and becomes a form of historiography by citing the Sadean *tableau vivant* rather than by citing Sade himself. As a genre of performance art, the *tableau vivant* is key to the joinder of Julien and Sade, of sex and a historicized sense of time. In its early-nineteenth-century inception as a parlor game, it involved players frozen into what were called "attitudes," poses that imitated actual paintings or illustrations of either fiction or history and, presumably, conjured forth the original characters' mental states. It thereby brought the high art of painting into scandalous contact with the low art of acting, the cognitive work of apprehending historical events or interpreting fiction into proximity with more physical, even sexual reactions to the often female bodies on stage. In other words, as the film critic James Tweedie writes in his discussion of another New Queer Cinematic film, the *tableau vivant* is "a medium of historical return that never sloughs off the mediating presence of actual bodies," and therein lies its shock value.[37] Because Julien's re-animation of the Biard painting links sadomasochism to the history of race slavery, it suggests the *tableau vivant*'s potency as a medium of return not just to history but to genocide: Julien hints that the aesthetic form itself is perversely tied to the intertwined histories of race and sexuality, that perhaps slave auctions were the first *tableaux vivants* staged for nonreligious purposes.[38] Yet however much the *tableau vivant* inevitably calls forth the myriad of situations in which black bodies have been forced into spectacularized stillness, Julien seems to be arrested in part by the genre's physicality. His *tableau vivant* of the slave trade insists that the sufferings of black people are in the first instance fleshly—and thereby not fully reducible to the heterosexist, sentimentalist account that the violation of their family ties constitutes the worst offense against them. Conversely, the *tableau vivant* also offers a queer image of aliveness, of sheer animacy unfettered by the narrative drives of biography or history, and in so doing conjures up the possibility of a future beyond both reproduction and writing.[39]

The Attendant makes a historical return to a medium of both historical return and extrafamilial futural conjugation. This is also a way of commenting on the history of commodification that subtends the slave trade. Julien's recapitulations of the Biard painting as a set of sadomasochistic orgies most obviously evokes Hénaff's description of the Sadean tableau: playing on the dual meaning of "table," Hénaff claims that Sade's ekphrastic sex scenes initially lay out bodies and body as if on a slab, enabling the viewer to classify part-objects and thereby create a spatialized, cognitive chart of erotic elements.[40] As in Hénaff's description of the tableau as both butcher block and taxonomic chart, the black man at the center of Julien's reconstituted tableau is laid out for the simultaneous gazes of the cinematic spectator, the Attendant, and the multiracial group of men inside the picture who gather around the body. Behind a black man wearing a harness that quarters his chest and emphasizes his pectoral muscles, a white man in shining black leather or rubber squats to the right of his head and cradles his chin. Another white man kneels, touching the black man's belly with one hand and gesturing with the other. This dynamic recalls and reworks the typical auction scene portrayed in the original painting, where sellers routinely called spectatorial attention to various parts of slave bodies as signs of their capacity for hard work. But if this tableau plays on "table" in some of the ways Hénaff suggests, it also reminds us that the table is, in Marx, the commodity fetish par excellence: once commodified, the Marxian table "stands on its head, and evolves out of its wooden brain grotesque ideas, far more wonderful than 'table-turning' ever was."[41] And Marx's table, in turn, recalls the slave forced to show off his physical prowess by dancing minstrelsy on the auction block.

Without directly invoking Marx's scene of animated objects, Hénaff suggests that the tableau paradoxically establishes and eliminates distance, presumably because it seems to invite the spectator into the scene (just as, we might note, commodities seem to invite the buyer to touch them). Hénaff writes that for Sade, this spatial collapse "is identified with an aggression that forces the engraving to move, features to come to life . . . Engraving becomes scene; the pictorial evolves toward the theatrical, and motionless tableau toward *tableau vivant*."[42] Again, though

Hénaff is speaking in terms more psychoanalytic than Marxist, the aggression he describes suggest Walter Benjamin's description of commodity culture as a scene of grabbing, touching, bringing the once auratic object close.[43] This becoming-tableau is exactly what happens to *The Attendant*'s reworked slave auction. As the Attendant enters the gallery and passes by the framed tableau, the characters inside blink and follow him with their eyes, but it is not clear that he sees this. He walks by a second picture, a close-up tableau mimicking a smaller section of the Biard painting. Here a white man wields a whip over a black man facing away from him, with other black and white men in the background. This group, too, watches him go by. When the men in these two S/M scenes begin to move, it is only their eyes that do so; they leave ambiguous the question of whose desire, aggression, and perhaps even valuation mobilize them. Is it the Attendant's? The film viewer's? Or someone else's?

At this point in the film, though, the live characters remain framed, literally trapped in the still scene of the tableau as though stuck in the historical past, hemmed in by its representation, immobilized by the fixity of a relatively static art. Even the movement of their eyes threatens to have only the effect of animating the commodity, of setting tables to dancing as Marx describes. Yet Hénaff, following Hegel's famous discussion of the master/slave dialectic, contends that the tableau's duality as static and moving picture figures a certain Hegelian threat to the sadomasochistic master: that in fulfilling his desire to animate the scene, he will thereby cause its end and thereby his own death as a master. How, then, to escape this end? Lynda Hart argues that S/M involves "the unexpected element, the *switching* . . . which takes the participants by surprise."[44] *The Attendant* moves beyond simply bringing the dead to life and thereby forcing them either to inhabit the commodity form or to perform its obverse by killing the master, insofar as the film makes this switching literal: shortly after the Biard painting awakens, the crack of a whip announces that the Attendant and the Visitor have begun to play. The two men then appear frozen in the sequence of *tableaux vivants* I have described, with each playing "top" once before they stand side by side. These men not only wield switches, they *are* switches. Yet what we miss seeing is, precisely, the "action," the reanimation of sex that would kill off the master entirely. Perversely, the master too must play dead to keep the possibility of mastery alive.

In fact, *The Attendant* suggests that a large part of sadomasochism's power lies less in pain itself than in the pause, which the film figures most insistently as the frozen moment of suspense between the crack of a moving whip and its contact with a body that will flinch. And indeed, as Hénaff has perhaps most thoroughly explored and as Julien's piece clearly recognizes, genuinely Sadean sadomasochism plays with and literalizes power *as* time. A dynamic between restraint and release shapes sadomasochistic sexual actions, which are syncopated by reward and sometimes punishments; bottoms are rewarded for physical endurance and for waiting; tops for anticipating the bottom's needs and for maintaining suspense. In fact, one of the most powerful aspects of sadomasochism is the way it makes the pause itself corporeal. Here we might recall Gilles Deleuze's description of the masochistic aesthetic, turning away from Sade and toward Sacher-Masoch. While Deleuze, like Hénaff, describes Sadean sexuality as dependent on an acceleration and multiplication that aims to annihilate the object, Deleuze also claims that the erotic writings of Sacher-Masoch celebrate a suspension of time that preserves the object of desire indefinitely: "The masochist is morose . . . by which we mean that he experiences waiting in its pure form."[45] Perhaps this is simple melancholia, a solipsistic fixation on the lost object — except that unlike the melancholic, the masochist anticipates a future. As if to claim masochism over melancholia, Julian uses s/m to "take back" time, specifically the suspension of black people *from* the time of history. He uses s/m to produce a *suspended temporality*, that is, a temporality of anticipation, poise, readiness . . . in short, of attendance.

And so we can now see s/m as a dialectic between the will to speed up and annihilate and the will to slow down and dilate. Here is where history, as opposed to a more abstract or metaphysical temporality, enters the scene. I suggested at this chapter's outset that sadomasochism lays bare the dynamic between a historically specific modernity (the French Revolution) and its precursor, precondition, or repressed double (figured as the *ancien regime*): that its temporal dialectic engages with historicity. In fact, Hénaff too locates Sadean acceleration in history, noting that it conforms to an industrial capitalism in which exchange value is increased by shortening the time necessary for production.[46] In *The Attendant*, the Biard painting registers the precondition for this shortening of the time of production — the exploitation of labor, which under slavery did not occur in a directly capitalist mode of production itself but in a feudal mode that fed the mechanized textile industry and was instrumental in its profits.[47] This exploitation, however "precapitalist" its exterior forms seemed, involved what the historian Walter Johnson calls "violent acts of resynchronization" irreducible to Taylorism: the wresting of languages, affiliations, local histories, and skills into an undifferentiated black labor force.[48] Slaveholders stole and reshaped, among other things, African people's quotidian rhythms of sleeping, waking, eating, and mating; their biographical timelines for entering the workforce, coupling, reproducing, nursing, childrearing, and dying; their seasonal times of agriculture and holidays; their market times of buying, selling, and trading.[49] Slaveholders also suspended the geographical movements of an entire segment of the U.S. population in order to feed the machine of rapid-paced industrial production: the slow time of so-called premodernity, here, is not prior to or even resistant to so-called modernity but is the latter's condition of existence. Thus we might also read Julien's stoppages as a critical response to the repressed history of industrialization, or a formalistic way of reclaiming bodies, temporalities, and histories that in another era would have been appropriated, even *stopped*, for the making of so-called modern time. He encodes this reclamation on the soundtrack, as an insistent heartbeat, a sonic figure for a body not yet or no longer alienated from its ancestral habitus, or even from a biorhythmic pace: or perhaps simply as a beat going on despite social death. This element of the soundtrack is also a kind of defibrillator that forces the stilled heart of sentimentalism back into action, allowing us to take the pulse of an alternative history.

Finally, the film has another register, this time visual, for an alternative historiography beyond the "official" histories promulgated within the classical space of a British museum that preserves the work of a heroic abolitionist painter but nothing of the slaves whose freedom he supposedly cherished. Enter, not the conquering hero of abolition, but the angel of history.

The English Beat: Attending to History

In *The Attendant*, moments before the Biard painting comes alive and just as the Attendant and the Visitor begin to cruise each other, miniature Cupid-like angels with large wings appear above the two men's heads, frozen in the act of brandishing bows and arrows. These angels, dressed in silver lamé boots and loincloths and black leather pectoral harnesses, turn in small circles like statuettes on a music box.[50] With these pixilated figures that invoke Walter Benjamin's famous Angel of History, who flies with her back to the future as the human-made catastrophes of the past pile up at her feet, Julien's film marks several transitions.[51] Eventually, the angels move us from spaces that secure racial purity (the museum) to those fostering interracial sexual contact (the side galleries), from still art to theater, from present to past, and from the quotidian to the supernatural. One of Julian's rather campy angels carries a pitchfork, perhaps to shovel up Benjamin's pile of historical debris, perhaps to remind us that history is also the devil's doing.

Yet though these angels turn, they seem to be frozen on an invisible, moving base. This emphasis on stillness might be an example of mere fetishism, or reification, or any number of other modes of obfuscating the social. But in fact it was Benjamin himself who historicized the pause, recognizing that it provides an antidote both to the traditional historicist models of progress and to the "revolutionary" ideology of a complete break from the past—and, we might add, to the restorative pause that feeds modernity's model of progress. Benjamin wrote that "a historical materialist cannot do without the notion of a present which is not a transition, but in which time stands still and has come to a stop."[52] In this formulation, the pause does not signal an interval between one thing and another; it is itself a thing, analytically and experientially available, that reveals the ligaments binding the past and the present. In Benjamin, making time stand still takes the form of recognizing and diagnosing a dialectical image: in the words of Benjamin's translator, the pause creates a "configuration . . . pregnant with tensions" between a heretofore misrecognized or lost element of the past and something occurring right now and, crucially, in a temporal relationship other than causality.[53]

The little angels are not, all by themselves, the film's dialectical images. But their arrows literally point us toward one, and toward another way of accessing and understanding the convergence of sex and historicist thinking in sadomasochism. Edmund Jephcott, the translator of "Theses on the Philosophy of History" for *Illuminations*, where the essay first appeared in English, substituted the term "pregnant" for the German *gesättigten* ("saturated"). This translation is particularly revealing for *The Attendant*: the film presents us with a configuration not so much pregnant as "erect" with tensions. Just before the museum closes, before the Attendant and the Visitor consummate their lust, the Attendant looks at his pocket watch. The watch casing appears as a gold circlet in an otherwise black-and-white filmic frame. Later, the film cuts to a male body, shot in color from mid-torso down, wearing crystal beads draped across his belly and gold lamé shorts with a distinct bulge in them (see figure 20). The little frozen angels spin on each thigh of the body whose bulge is on such

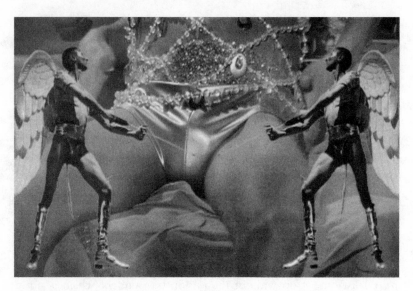

20. Still from *The Attendant.*

Copyright Isaac Julien, 1992. Courtesy of Isaac Julien and
Victoria Miro Gallery, London / Metro Pictures, New York.

dramatic display (and who is neither Attendant, nor Visitor, nor museum
guest, nor obviously lifted from any painting). The angels point their
arrows down toward this "target." Here, color correspondence between
the Attendant's gold watch and the gold-clad bulge has taken the place of
narrative continuity: time and sex form what Deleuze has called a crystal-
image: something that glints up from we don't know what historical
moment, even within the film's terms, to meet the Attendant's present
and, possibly, the future of the film's showing.[54]

The bulge corresponds to nothing we have seen so far — not to the
slave ship in the painting, not to the reanimated slave / s/m scene, and not
to the flogging scenes between the Visitor and the Attendant. It is, in
some ways, a tongue-in-cheek response to Robert Mapplethorpe's famous photograph "Man in the Polyester Suit" (1980), which shows a
black man shot from the torso down, his flaccid penis emerging from the
fly of his trousers. But the bulge also recalls and makes sense of an earlier
set of images that had, up to this point in the film, remained entirely
incongruous. At the beginning, just before the Attendant checks the Visitor's black leather bag and they exchange their first glance, we hear an
extradiegetic chorus singing "Remember me, remember me." A close-up
of the Attendant's impassive face and steady gaze fades to a shot of him in

21. Still from *The Attendant*.
Copyright Isaac Julien, 1992. Courtesy of Isaac Julien and
Victoria Miro Gallery, London/Metro Pictures, New York.

a black tuxedo and corsage, standing in an opera box, singing and gesturing outward. He seems to be addressing his performance toward the stage below him, where another, younger black man stands with his arms out, surrounded by black and white men frozen in various poses against a shiny curtain (see figure 21): these are all the same men who will later appear in the sadomasochistic reenactment of the Biard painting. Bare at the chest, they are dressed in metallic loincloths. The chorus the Attendant sings to them is the aria "When I am laid in earth," popularly known as "Dido's Lament," from Henry Purcell's opera *Dido and Aeneas*.

For several minutes as the seduction scene progresses, this operatic moment hovers entirely outside the film's plot. As it turns out, the gold shorts and the bejeweled torso must belong to someone in the assembled group on the opera stage: the figure wears pale nylons over his skin so it is difficult to tell which one. The opera scene is one possible referent for the aria's chorus, "Remember me but ah! forget my fate." Perhaps the Attendant is asking the audience to remember his performance but to forget that he ends up curating the art of other people rather than making his own. Perhaps the younger man in the loincloth represents a queer past that the Attendant has temporarily given up. Perhaps the chorus solicits the Anglo segment of Julien's audience to remember the role of their ancestors in the transatlantic slave trade. Or perhaps it is a warning to s/m players about the political implications of mimicking slave relations. Yet later, the "Remember me" chorus reappears when the Biard painting comes alive: the chorus seems to be waking up the Attendant, the s/m players in the frame, and Biard's original painted figures, and the afore-mentioned heartbeat contributes to this effect. Perhaps, then, what we have is a more complicated injunction. The intertwined sounds seem to implore these men of the past and the present, asking them to move across time and take up their obligations to one another. In keeping with Sade's antagonism toward inheritance, they ask the dead slaves to release any hold on their descendants that would deny later generations the capacity to recalibrate pain into pleasure. But then, too, in keeping with Benjamin's pursuit of new collective memory-forms, the sounds ask the living players never to confuse pleasure with historical amnesia.

As a figure for and a catalyst of this kind of reciprocal movement across time, the gilt-veiled phallus functions as the film's critical caesura, dou-bling the long caesura of the aria's opening, "When I am laid . . . am laid . . ." *The Attendant*'s visual pause links sex not only to the abstract, generic, Western "time" signaled by the gold watch but also to a specifi-cally national history. For it directs our attention toward the Attendant's performance of "Dido's Lament," and thereby toward Purcell's opera *Dido and Aeneas* or, as Julien puts it, "another scene on the coast of Africa."[55] Both the libretto and the performance history of this opera tell a story of sex and empire, but not the straightforward story of African slave capture that we might expect from the Biard painting. As Joseph Roach argues in detail, the seventeenth-century librettist Nahum Tate intended *Dido and Aeneas* to be a gloriously British opera, and he reworked Virgil's *Aeneid* according to Geoffrey of Monmouth's massive *History of the Kings of Britain*.[56] In the original epic, Aeneas takes advantage of the African queen Dido's generosity in sharing all the resources of her great city of Carthage. But he eventually abandons her, plunders Carthage with his men, and sails away, intending to use her riches to found Rome. Mon-mouth wrote that Aeneas was the grandfather of Brutus, whom he named as the founder of Britain — and this "fact" inspired Tate to imbue Virgil's epic with details from English national history.[57]

The opera, then, tells a tale of interracial love, the exploitation of Africa, and European nation making: Roach has called it an "allegory of Atlantic destiny."[58] He reads "Dido's Lament" as Purcell's paean to Euro-pean political memory, to conquerors who conveniently remember only their "deep love for the people whose cultures they have left in flames."[59] Moreover, the opera's performance history sits at the disavowed intersection of European and African history: it premiered in 1689, a watershed year in the development of liberal democracy, when a parliamentary act confirmed England's first Bill of Rights. And this, in turn, was just after James II, fleeing England in December 1688, ceded to the original investors the largest share of the Royal African Company that captured slaves on the Guinea Coast to trade with the West Indies. James's flight precipitated the defeat of the Royal African Company's monopoly over the slave trade, which opened it up to other English companies, allowing the Dutch and French to aggressively pursue trade in the region in a competition that ultimately drove up the price of slaves.[60] In sum, the opera *Dido and Aeneas* is an Anglicized tale of European empire building whose initial performance coincided with signal events in both English liberal democracy and its disavowed crutch, the transatlantic slave trade. Thus even in its original context, the lament — though it appears in the form of an aria that, like all arias, suspends narrative and historical time — can be read as both a rebuke to free-market capitalism and its need for slavery, and as an elegy for African culture. "When I am laid in earth / May my wrongs create / no trouble in thy breast / Remember me, but ah! forget my fate": these lyrics at once suggest the destruction of Carthage in the person of Dido, the death of bodies in the slave trade, and the transformation of objects and labor into abstract commodities marketed to kindle memories other than those of the social relations that produced them. The Attendant's appropriation of the lament, though, changes the emphasis of the opera somewhat. In beseeching us to "remember me, but ah! forget my fate," Dido/the Attendant actually seems to be asking her audience not to regard her or her city as simply dead, simply left in flames. In fact, in Virgil's original *Aeneid*, Dido promises to return from the dead and makes good on this promise when Aeneas enters the underworld. Julien, unlike Tate, seems to honor her request and her triumph. The reanimations of slave scenes bring the static, supposedly "dead" historical object of slavery, the dead bodies of the enslaved, and the dead commodity-object back to life.

And in turn, *The Attendant*'s revivifications take place beyond the merely visual, or even sonic, register. They rely on a technique that Alison Landsberg has referred to as "prosthetic memory," or portable, often mass-produced experiences disseminated by films and museums to consumers who never lived through the events represented.[61] Prosthetic memories are neither the scars of originary trauma nor the proprietary result of long, slow cultural inculcation like that of family heritage or ethnic birthright: they belong to nobody and everybody at once and are detachable from the context that produced them.[62] They come from the body's engagement in mimetic activities, participatory affective and sensory relationships that ring changes on, variously, emotions, identity, and affiliation. (Think, for instance, of the United States Holocaust Museum's technique of issuing an identity card to each museumgoer, who is encouraged to go through the exhibit without looking at the back of the card for the fate of his/her historical counterpart, so that his/her sensations lose their anchor to any preconceived outcome.) These changes, however momentary, bind and unbind historical subjectivity: collective experiences are implanted and disseminated, such that they overflow their containment both as individual traumas and as events over and done with. Prosthetic memories counter the work of the historical monument, for they travel with and in protean sensations. It's notable, then, that Julien chooses to stage his meditation on colonial oppression and sadomasochistic fantasy in what Landsberg calls the "experiential site" of a museum flanked by statuary (and even on an operatic stage populated by frozen actors).[63] For situating S/M fantasy in the museum suggests complex relays between sadomasochism and the pain/pleasure dynamic of cultural memory, between the ostensibly separate publics constituted around sex and those hailed by the heritage industries.

However, Landsberg assumes that experiential sites try to duplicate the exact sensory and emotional experiences of the original sufferer, with as little modification as possible, and certainly without either humor or eroticism as part of the equation: in her analysis prosthetic memory is essentially curative. But whatever is going on in a sadomasochistic scene where players appropriate the signs of, say, the Spanish Inquisition, it isn't exactly the incorporation of these events into the participants' set of experiential data. It's doubtful that S/M players routinely emerge from their scenes with a sense of having been through a historical process or feeling empathy for the sufferers they have imitated. Instead, and complicating Landsberg's analysis, even a sadomasochism that eschews historical role-playing or the solicitation of personal memories openly deals *in* prosthetics — stand-ins in group sex, imitation body parts in the use of penetrative instruments of various kinds, extensions and reduplications of the so-called natural body in leather.

To return to Freud for a minute: one of his definitions of perversion is temporal: various pleasures are a kind of loitering at the way-stations toward male orgasm. But another definition is spatial and invokes the prosthesis: "[the perversions] extend, in an anatomical sense, beyond the regions of the body that are designed for sexual union."[64] In other words, perverts transport genital sensations outside their proper zones and use other parts of the body (fingers, anuses, fists, nipples) as substitutes for genital satisfaction. Many sadomasochistic players elongate the erotic zones in this way by using parts such as arms, fingers, hands, and even the entire body itself in ritualized practices of stretching and suspending. These actions, again, corporealize the experiences of delay or duration. Other sadomasochists extend sex beyond the physiological body itself with props such as dildos, piercing needles, and whips.

These spatial extensions of the body, in turn, have a temporal logic of their own. For a transgender lesbian top, for example, the dildo can serve as a prop for the prosthetic memory of a masculinity she feels as a birth-right but has not lived biologically. The dildo or even the hand itself can restore an "amputated" masculinity, which is often felt as a discontinuous past that has been temporarily interrupted by the butch top's female body but now resumes in the moment of sexual contact.[65] In other words, the dildo extends the butch or daddy top into her "own" masculine past, the imagined time of another life. Just as s/m exceeds the spatial boundaries of a player's "own" body, too, it can exceed the temporal boundaries of her "own" lifetime. Thus, rather than *being* a site for the inculcation of prosthetic memory, s/m may *literalize* the prosthetic aspect of all memory. In other words, while s/m cannot return its players back to a prior histor-ical moment any more than a museum can, it can remind us of what the museum itself represses: memory is not organic or natural at all but depends on various prompts and even props. Nor is "history" inevitable; dominant historiography simply demands that the props for modernity be hidden so as to make it seem so. In turn, s/m shows us, memory can prop up projects unrelated to the history it supposedly references.

The most visible prosthetics in Julien's film are whips, predominantly in the hands of white men. This image of the whip travels: appearing first in the original Biard painting, it reappears in the *tableau vivant* of the sadomasochistic orgy in the hand of the Visitor and is finally wielded by the Attendant. But through a flashback, we learn that when the Attendant originally searched the arriving Visitor's personal items, presumably for cameras or dangerous items, he either saw or fantasized about the shaft of the whip protruding slightly from the black leather case that the Visitor carried, and stroked its length (here, perhaps, is the film's only dildo). This brief scene seems to pun on the historical "baggage" borne by the whip, which, in the hands of the Visitor and the white men in the tableaux, catalyzes a historical flashback, a racial "memory" of the power of actual or de facto ownership that white men once wielded over black men. In the hands of the Attendant, however, the whip also invokes and invites the sexual pleasure that white men, however much they disavowed it, may have taken in disciplining black men: the Attendant's whip recalls and reverses the pointing finger of the white man in the earlier tableau of the sadomasochistic orgy. Held by the Attendant, the whip also indexes the erotic energy that enslaved black men managed to preserve and transmit to their successors despite their sufferings.

The whip, like the dildo I have described, works in *The Attendant* as a power line connecting historical as well as personal pasts to the present. As a trope it not only links sadomasochism's power/sex dynamic to slavery but also suggests that historical memories, whether those forged from connecting personal experiences to larger patterns or those disseminated through mass imagery, can be burned into the body through pleasure as well as pain. This is why Julien reanimates the dead in *sex* scenes rather than in the scenes of revenge or fear mongering in which a classically Derridean "hauntology" usually traffics.[66] Julien's commitment to an eroticized hauntology is, I think, his major contribution to a queer-of-color critique that would hold sensuality and historical accountability in productive tension.[67] Saidiya Hartman formulates the problem, and by implication Julien's project, succinctly: "This re-membering takes the form of *attending* to the body as a site of pleasure, eros, and sociality, and articulating its violated condition."[68] This "attending" is both rigorously responsible and utopian, a practice of somatic critique and of carnal hope.

Julien, like Hilary Brougher in *The Sticky Fingers of Time*, seems to figure this mode of corporeal historical cognition—let us call it a new, phenomenological historical materialism—in phallic terms: whips give, penetrate, pierce. But it is Walter Benjamin and not Julien who equates historicizing with masculine sexual dominance. "The historical materialist," Benjamin writes, "leaves it to others to be drained by the whore called 'Once upon a time' in historicism's bordello. He remains in control of his powers, man enough to blast open the continuum of history."[69] Here, in a metaphor reminiscent of Thomas Paine's withering claim that history defiles the male body, Benjamin aligns fiction, fairy tale, and myth with a threatening female sexuality also troped in the commercial terms of a whorehouse: it is as if a (presumably nonmaterialist) "historicism" pimps out a feminized mysticism strong enough to emasculate the scholar, while the genuine materialist holds to a spermatic economy that will maximize his own sexualized cognitive power. Julien, on the other hand, suggests that history may enter through the bottom after all — and on the wings of fairies. Indeed, the way his angels do not turn their backs consistently to anything, but turn around and around, suggests a certain opening up of the body to other times, past and future, that Benjamin's work seems sometimes to refuse. In the crotch shot, the historiographic navel of the film's dream, the miniature angels moving in circles on the man's thighs have their bows taut, arrows pointed directly at his bulge, suggesting that he too is as likely to be penetrated as to penetrate. Eventually, this dialectical image, juxtaposing real and heavenly bodies, begins to undulate; the man whose torso is in the frame brings his hands around to carefully pull away the crystal beads that cover his stomach, and he moves his hips up and down, up and down, as if to receive penetration from above, or to give it from below.

With these images of bodily porosity, Julien also brings forth the possibility of the tactile historicism I have called "erotohistoriography." In fact, Julien comments, "Although the current images of 'whips' and 'chains' in the representational practices of s/m have been borrowed from [the] colonial iconography [of slavery], the refashioning of these accoutrements (i.e., rubberisation, polished surfaces, latex, polished metal) has transformed them into sexualised, stylised fetish clothing for the queer body."[70] In other words, he notes that s/m's restylings occur on the level of the visual *and* the tactile. Here, then, the whip is important not just as an elongation of the body, nor merely as a prosthetic, nor even as a sadist's mnemonic device, but as itself the switchily "passive" recipient of a black queer touch that makes it shine with new meanings. In *The Attendant*, the shine of the gold lamé bulge resonates with the shine of the rubber and leather worn by the participants in the framed sadomasochistic orgies, the silver boots worn by the angels, the curtain of the opera stage, the gold casing of the watch, the picture frames around the paintings and *tableaux vivants*. This proliferation of visual and tactile rhymes cannot be coordinated into anything like a linear historical narrative (backward into slavery, forward into utopia). Instead, they represent a kind of short-circuiting, a jolt seen or felt, a profane illumination or kinetic leap into history otherwise. If s/m in its sensory elements encodes and transmits the bodily knowledge of personal and collective trauma, Julien seems to argue, it can also release this knowledge for new bodily experiences in the present tense. In his analysis the register of touch can literally open up slavery's historical baggage and distribute its contents differently.

As with *Orlando* and *Sticky Fingers*, *The Attendant* also signals the vital role of tactility in a queer-of-color historiography with the motif of the hand. In one scene, we see a manicured, dark-skinned hand caressing a marble bust on its stony lips, cheek, and chin (we are later to learn that this hand belongs to the Attendant's co-worker and live-in lover or wife, an African American woman known as the Conservator and played by Cleo Sylvestre). The next shot shows a hand in a black leather glove, presumably the Attendant's, caressing the hilt of a black whip that is held in a bare white hand; no faces appear in the frame to locate these hands. These images of bare and gloved, black and white hands appear elsewhere in the film: at one point we see a torso (the Attendant's?) wearing a suit, hands smoothing those same black leather gloves; another shot shows the Conservator in long black opera gloves slowly applauding from a balcony; yet another shows the black leather gloves now on the white Visitor, who raises his gloved hands up to dab his eyes; even the crotch shot includes the actor's hands encased in nylon. This proliferation of veiled hands suggests the kind of blind groping, the movement by instinct and "feel," that queer-of-color historians have had to use as methods for finding and making meaningful the mostly uncataloged materials of their collective pasts.

Julien's images of hands, their robing and disrobing, their insistence on touch, invoke just this kind of memorial practice: they figure a memory that is insistently corporeal but not organic or hereditary. These images also remind us that s/m is at base a practice of skinplay. Its colloquial designation "leathersex" suggests a certain doubling and distantiation of the skin, for even as leather hides the skin, it also is skin. It makes the idea of skin visible, engenders a certain fascination with the epidermal "once removed": thus s/m is always, as Kobena Mercer reminds us, a racialized practice.[71] For Mercer, both leathersex and pornographic photography problematically figure the sheen of black skin as an eroticized and incommensurate difference. For Julien, I would argue, this racial*ized*, reduplicative aspect of both visual media's history and the iconography of s/m is not always rac*ist*. First, Julien transfers the "epidermal schema" from people to props: gloved hands, the hilt of a whip wrapped in black leather, the crotch covered by gold lamé. More importantly, he exploits the skin-liness of s/m, its ability to capture the way queers polish and rub and elasticize the signs of dominant histories and cultures, to figure interracial eroticism as a tactile practice and not just a visual one. Black skin, here, is rescued from its entrapment in the visual, put back into motion and lambency, given porous qualities that overtake racist fetishizations of color and even shine.[72] As with *Frankenstein*, the dead come back to life as and through layers of skin; here, leather serves as a doubling of black skin and binds contemporary Afro-British and African American subjects to their enslaved (or even slave-trading) ancestors. This view of s/m as skinplay, in turn, suggests some things about film as a medium and, eventually, about the temporal in both Julien's film and s/m in general.

In her work on the haptic, discussed in the previous chapter, Laura Marks has persuasively argued for a tactile notion of the medium of film as "impressionable and conductive, like skin."[73] As a material trace of an object — a record of the impression of light on something — film, she argues, is also capable of leaving traces on its viewers. In this view, which literalizes the notion of spectatorial absorption, film takes an impression of the objects it represents and then disseminates this impression into the bodies of viewers in a process that involves both contagious and imitative mimesis. The idea of film as a conduit for the trace is also a distinctly erotic one, as it foregrounds a tangible exchange irreducible to the "purely" visual yet, paradoxically, never fully present as touch. The film stock and the screen are like membranes between the object and the viewer, at once suggesting and withholding contact.[74] The screen, to put it simply and to stretch Marks's claims a bit, is like the skin of the s/m top. Julien's work resonates with this analysis momentarily, when he shows the Conservator eavesdropping on the encounter between the Visitor and the Attendant, her ear pressed against a wall and her hand touching it. The wall, too, is a porous membrane, for the Conservator seems enchanted, at once part of the scene and apart from it (remember that she, too, may have fantasies about interracial contact as she caresses the marble bust in an earlier scene). Julien calls this "aural voyeurism," but I think its aural sense is ultimately troped as tactile: it is as if, with her white-gloved hand touching the wall that separates her from the sex scene, the Conservator "overfeels" as much as overhears the scene.[75] Likewise, the crotch shot at the center of the film breaks up the merely temporal pause, the still shot, into motion, light, the invitation to touch, and yet withholds full contact with the penis underneath its gold sheath. This tease is what Benjamin's one-way "blasting" into history would disallow. The crotch shot is not only a dialectical image but a dialectical membrane between the viewer and the body that shamelessly beckons us toward the bordellos of myth and history, "Once upon a time," and specific historical moments like the disco costumes' 1970s, the painting's 1840, and the opera's 1689.

The Attendant ends with a black man apparently suffused with homoerotic and sadomasochistic desire inhabiting the role of a diasporic queen as written by a celebrant of British imperialism. Here is where the temporal aspect of sadomasochism contributes to a different kind of historiography, one that may not be fully containable within the rubric of hauntology. Roach offers one more element in what he calls his "genealogy of performance" for *Dido and Aeneas*, an element of the very lament sung by the Attendant that obliquely illuminates the role of sexuality in the cultural memory of a conquered people.[76] He notes that the bass line of the lament is a chaconne, which the *Oxford English Dictionary* defines as a now obsolete, stately dance in triple time that in European usage served as the finale to a ballet or opera.[77] But Roach argues that the European theater's grand finale apparently had its origins as a dance with sexual meanings in Spain and, prior to that, in Peru, the West Indies, or Africa, depending on the historian one consults.[78] Even as Dido prepares for suicide, then, her body carries and transmits the historical memory of pleasures that exceed the parameters of her own lifetime, her individual love affair, her geopolitical location, and her death. This memory, both a "might have been" and a "what could be again," is preserved in the form of a transatlantic beat, however domesticated it has become. In other words, her song performs an even more animate "Remember me" than its lyrics, an incitement to memory that appears at the level of meter and bass line. The lament thereby raises its own dead, even as its words frame the story of England's rise on the backs of dead and dying African slaves. And in fact, *The Attendant*'s score isolates, reformulates, and elevates that bass line from the very beginning: the opening "Remember me" and all its echoes throughout the film are accompanied by a haunting ground bass, as violins thrum "long-short-long, long-short-long" on the same note over and over again while the aria rises above them.

In putting whips into the hands of the characters who eventually sing and hear this lament, Julien has transposed that bodily memory back into a beat we can see as well as feel, or perhaps that we are enjoined to feel while we see it. The other sonic "beat" that punctuates the film's work on time and history is the aforementioned pounding heartbeat; both the chaconne and the heartbeat are slow, steady, thudding. Perhaps the heartbeat and the dance are, respectively, overly organic or sentimental figures for the feeling body whose recalcitrant rhythms might disrupt the march of national allegory. But the heartbeat, especially, suggests the visceral effect of past history on present bodies and perhaps even vice versa. And the Attendant's lament, floating down to the disco-themed stage, also answers its own call: it beams the stately chaconne back toward the bodies capable of re-enlivening it, not in its original form but in living transformation. These bodies also fulfill — in a contemporary idiom — Dido's promise to return from the dead, insofar as they register an era before AIDS and the power that disco had to connect moving bodies back then, and they bring that era momentarily back to life. The actors on stage suggest a literal "disco-theque," a library of records unavailable as written text or even visual document, but accessible in and as rhythm. The operatic lament that eddies around them calls to mind Wai Chee Dimock's description of how meaning literally re-sounds over time: "An effect of historical change, noise is a necessary feature of a reader's meaning-making process. And even as it impinges on texts, even as it reverberates through them, it thickens their tonality, multiplies their hearable echoes, makes them significant in unexpected ways."[79] Except that with sadomasochism, "noise" is more than sonic; within the practice of sadomasochism, it becomes kinetic. Whippings, for instance, thicken the body's sensations, multiply its felt responses, and make bodily experience significant in unexpected ways.

It may seem here that I teeter toward a racist conception of black bodies as the receptors or repositories of some essential beat. Honestly, I think Julien himself may encourage that tilt, challenging his audience's desire not to be racist, its wish to abstract race politics from those of desire, or desire from racialization. By playing with the sonic and visceral qualities of "beats" in a film without dialogue, he also refuses us the easy comforts of an authentic "voice." But most important, Julien's association of diasporic African experience and sadomasochistic practices — the latter of which I have argued here are grounded in rhythm — expose rhythm as a form of cultural inculcation and of historical transmission rather than a racial birthright. In fact, here rhythm, perhaps itself the essence of what Bourdieu means by habitus, becomes an immanent but not natural, material but not essential, replicative but not procreative means of intergenerational continuity despite the transience of the body and the nonsuccessive emergence of these generations. *The Attendant* thereby figures time as a modality of power rather than a neutral substance, and the body as a perhaps inadvertent conduit for effaced histories of pleasure, rather than a figure for some ahistorical being or a mere mannequin on which icons of oppression are scandalously hung for fun.

Sadomasochism is, in Julien's final analysis, a complicated form of what Toni Morrison calls "skin memory."[80] Julien offers a particularly synesthetic mode of historiography, in that he uses the genre of a "silent" film (or more precisely a film without dialogue) to exploit the phenomenological aspects of the temporal politics he explores, to turn what would otherwise be visual representation or sonic resonance into a form of re-vivification. Invoking the chaconne, the disco beat, the crack of the whip, and the heartbeat, *The Attendant* insists that sound *feels*. The film takes black and queer tactile restylings of the visual into yet another sensory realm, demonstrating that s/m's sonic touches and tactile sounds can aggregate temporalities *within* the body, rather than simply on its surfaces. In other words, s/m is not merely another form of temporal drag performance: it reorganizes the senses, and, when it uses icons and equipment from traumatic pasts, reorganizes the relationships among emotion, sensation, and historical understanding. Its clash of temporalities ignites historical possibilities other than the ones frozen into the "fate" of official histories.

Ultimately, Julien suggests that s/m may bring the body to a kind of somatized historical knowledge, one that does not demand or produce correct information about or an original experience of past events, nor even engender legibly cognitive understandings of one's place in a historically specific structure. Instead, and crucially, it enacts the oscillation between historically specific forms of time (or between a historically specific form of time and its constructed or fantasized opposite) and illuminates some past consequences and futural possibilities of this movement. Sadomasochism, that is, stages a certain shuttling between the times of imperial will and bodily responses that conform to and defy it, the times of retroactive healing and of suspense, the times of sentimentality and of libidinalized revolution, the times of the "primitive" and the futuristic, the times of forced synchronization and of resistance to that, the times of industrial capitalism and of the feudal relations it ultimately depends on. s/m has the potential to produce — or at least to figure — lived history as that which emerges out of a competition between temporalities.[81] And it refuses to synthesize these temporalities into a single imperative, even as Julien suggests that the imperative tense of "Remember me" is at play in interracial s/m, at least for the black participant.

What I hope to have shown through this analysis of *The Attendant* is how Julien brings out and seizes on the temporal aspect of sadomasochism, both to undermine the British empire's monumentalizing history of itself *and* to suggest a queer-of-color historiography grounded in bodily memories of a nonoriginary pleasure — one perhaps never given the legitimacy of becoming an experience — as well as pain. His methodology and insights might be crucial for a revitalized queer studies in which we recognize the power of temporal as well as spatial demarcations, see temporal difference in relation to subjugated or simply illegible attachments, and view time as itself material for critical and cultural practices that counter the insistent rhythm of (re)production. These critical and cultural practices include sex itself. The *ars erotica*, as Michel Foucault has called them, are ways of intimating, of understanding and constructing knowledge with the body as instrument. At least in sadomasochism, their object is not only the embodied self but also the structures in which that self is embedded and the contingencies that make a given self possible. As s/m makes particularly clear, these structures and contingencies, the shorthand for which is "history," include time — prescribed and possible chronometrics of bodily sensation, syntaxes of encounter, and tenses of sociability. As a critical technique or mode of analysis enacted with the body erotic, then, sadomasochism offers up temporal means for reconfiguring the possible: the "slow time" that is at once modernity's double and its undoing, the sensation that discombobulates normative temporal conditionings that serve the status quo, the deviant pause that adds a codicil of pleasure to a legacy of suffering. These are not, to be sure, reparations for past damages (as if perfect redress were possible), or the means of transcending all limitations. They are, however, ways of knowing history to which queers might make fierce claim.

Coda

In the works I have brought together in this book, sexually dissident bodies and stigmatized erotic encounters — themselves powerful reorientations of supposedly natural, physiological impulses — perform the contest between modernity's standard beat and the "sudden rise" of possibilities lost to the past or yearning toward the future. W. E. B. Du Bois, in a recently rediscovered essay, "Sociology Hesitant" (1905), recognized this dialectic as the proper object of the then-new discipline of sociology, the study of "modern" man.

Implicitly distancing himself from the linear logic of anthropology, Du Bois articulates human existence as effectively rhythmic. For him, life consists of the dynamic between the structures of "law, rule, and rhythm" in a given culture and the "something Incalculable," the "traces of indeterminate force" that render agency possible.[1] Du Bois described these two elements not in terms of fate or free will but as a primary and secondary rhythm. Primary rhythm is inexorable; Du Bois correlates it with the death rate. But the AIDS epidemic has surely shown us that there is nothing natural about that particular rhythm; indeed, Du Bois fails to recognize that there are very few natural tempos on a macrosocial level, though the individual body may offer them in the form of things like pulse and heartbeat. More importantly, Du Bois correlates the secondary rhythm, the incalculable one that contains the seeds of change, with chance. He writes that it presents a "nearly the same uniformity as the first . . . [and] differs from [the first] in its more or less sudden rise at a given tune."[2] The musical metaphor recalls the haunting bass line in *The Attendant*, or perhaps the rise of Dido's lament above that bass line. But Du Bois's concrete example of the secondary rhythm is actually "a woman's club."[3] He doesn't flesh out the example, but he very likely means one of many progressive-era gatherings of black women who aimed to educate themselves, advocate for reform, and help their poor.[4]

A women's club offers unofficial, improvised forms of affiliation that can interrupt the seemingly inexorable meter of a given culture — here, the United States' explicit programs for the gradual, some might say only partial, assimilation of black people — without offering a simple respite before a renewal of the same terms. But the explicitly queer texts this book has examined short-circuit this current time with erotic activities out of reach of the unconscious soldier-speaker with whom I began this book, and likely unthinkable in Du Bois's women's clubs: drug-taking and drag, fisting and s/m. These bodies and encounters are, themselves, kinetic and rhythmic improvisations of the social: not drives, not identities, and not even collectives. They are scenes of uptake, in which capitalist modernity itself looks like a failed revolution because it generates the very unpredictabilities on which new social forms feed.

I can imagine a counterargument to all of this: aren't all of these practices and concepts simply fantasies of temporal and material immediacy, themselves retrospectively constructed from a place of melancholia about the inevitability of linguistic or semiotic mediation? To which I might reply, no, but yes. No, because it's important to me not to see any of these speculative modes of using time or doing history as, even in fantasy, primal; I don't think any of the texts I examine posit discredited, visceral ways of knowing as only *prior* to dominant ones, but rather as their repressed alternative. The artists I discuss acknowledge the affective dimension of cognitive work in part by literalizing it as sex. But they also understand that erotic sensation is only a disavowed form of affect, and scholars have learned to understand affect as a cultural artifact. Erotic practices, these artists seem to be arguing, are no more immediate than language, yet we know a lot less about how to do things with sex than we know about how to do things with words. But also: yes, risking the fantasy of immediacy actually allows us to rethink mediation. The works I have examined here also understand the carnal aspect of ideology; that is, they recognize that if ideology is common sense, "sense" must be understood to include both emotions and physical sensations, each of which come to "feel right" in large part through temporal regulation. Bodies, then, are not only mediated by signs; they come to "matter" through kinetic and sensory forms of normativity, modes of belonging that make themselves felt as a barely acknowledged relief to those who fit in, while the experience not fitting in often feels both like having the wrong body and like living in a different time zone.

Thus unbinding time does not mean simply unleashing a biological instinct or psychic drive, be it sex or death. Nor does unbinding history mean simply showing how whatever looks like sex is actually a superstructural result of unequal economic relations. Rather, unbinding time and/from history means recognizing how erotic relations and the bodily acts that sustain them gum up the works of the normative structures we call family and nation, gender, race, class, and sexual identity, by changing tempos, by remixing memory and desire, by recapturing excess. Finally, erotic inquiries of this sort also challenge our most cherished modes of scholarly procedure. We end up having to admit the possibility that performance, affect, and even sex itself, through the work they do with time and history, might be knowledge practices. And ultimately, I think that this is just what queer critique must do: use our historically and presently quite creative work with pleasure, sex, and bodies to jam *whatever* looks like the inevitable.

appendix. Distributors for Films and Videos

The Attendant (1992, dir. Isaac Julien). 35 mm, b/w and color, 8 mins.
Distributed on video by Frameline Distribution.
145 9th St., #300, San Francisco, CA 94103 USA.
Telephone: +1 (415) 703-8650. E-mail: info@frameline.org.

Coal Miner's Granddaughter (1991, dir. Cecilia Dougherty). Video, b/w,
   120 mins.
Distributed by Video Data Bank.
112 S. Michigan Ave., Chicago, IL 60603 USA.
Telephone: +1 (312) 345-3550. E-mail: info@vdb.org.

K.I.P. (2002, dir. Nguyen Tan Hoang). Video, color, 4 mins.
Distributed by Video Out Distribution.
1965 Main St., Vancouver, BC V5T 3C1 Canada.
Telephone: +1 (604) 872-8449. E-mail: info@videoout.ca.

The Physics of Love (1998, dir. Diane Bonder). Video, color, 25 mins.
Distributed by friends of the late Diane Bonder.
Contact: Kathy High, Associate Professor of Video and New Media, Arts Depart-
   ment, Rensselaer Polytechnic Institute. West Hall 104, 110 8th St., Troy, NY,
   12180 USA.
Telephone: +1 (518) 209-6209. E-mail: kathy@kathyhigh.com.

Shulie (1997, dir. Elisabeth Subrin). Video, color, 36 mins.
Distributed by Video Data Bank.
112 S. Michigan Ave., Chicago, IL 60603 USA.
Telephone: +1 (312) 345-3550. E-mail: info@vdb.org.

The Sticky Fingers of Time (1997, dir. Hilary Brougher). 35 mm blow-up from
   16 mm film, color, 90 mins. Distributed on DVD by Strand Releasing.

Information about and contact with Allyson Mitchell: www.allysonmitchell.com.

notes

preface

1. Graves, "It's a Queer Time," hereafter cited in text by line number.

2. See Chauncey, *Gay New York*.

3. Nora, "Between Memory and History," 9.

4. On alternative temporal schemae, see Boellstorf, *A Coincidence of Desires*.

5. Foucault, "The Life of Infamous Men," 77.

6. The best description of this aspect of Sedgwick's work can be found in Stockton, "Eve's Queer Child."

7. Crimp, "Mourning and Militancy," 18, his emphasis.

8. I refer to the trajectory from part 2, chapter 3 of Butler's *Gender Trouble* titled "Freud and the Melancholia of Gender" to her book *The Psychic Life of Power*.

9. Moraga, *Giving Up the Ghost*.

10. While it would be easy enough to cite Edelman's *No Future* as the synecdoche for this kind of work, I'm also referring to my own piece with Berlant, "Queer Nationality," whose ending section on zines celebrates negation.

11. Sedgwick, "Paranoid Reading and Reparative Reading."

12. This sentence channels three very important theories of, respectively, pastness, futurity, and lateral movements in and with time: Love, *Feeling Backward*; Muñoz, *Cruising Utopia*; and Stockton, "Growing Sideways, or Versions of the Queer Child."

13. Sedgwick, "Paranoid Reading," 8, her emphasis.

14. Derrida, *Specters of Marx*, 38.

15. The phrase "epidemic of signification" is Treichler's; see *How to Have Theory in an Epidemic*, 11 and passim. ACT UP's signs, fliers, stickers, and T-shirts often relied on resignifying dominant phrases or images. See Crimp and Rolston, *AIDS DemoGraphics*.

16. La Planche and Pontalis, "Binding," 50–51. For an elegant discussion of Freudian "binding" in relation to narrative and sexuality, see Tuhkanen, "Binding the Self."

17. I thank one of my anonymous readers from Duke University Press for this formulation.

18. Lentricchia and DuBois's *Close Reading* contains a good bibliography for close reading of the New Critical sort and beyond it. For a sampling of the New Critics, whose aim was to close off the text from historical context, see Ransom, ed., *The New Criticism*.

19. On the corporeal excess indexed by popular genres, see Williams, *Hard Core*.

20. Rosen, *Change Mummified*, 20 and 178.

21. Ibid., xi.

22. Ibid., 99.

23. Ibid., 173.

24. Deleuze and Guattari, "What Is a Minor Literature?"

25. I take this account of style's political function from Coviello's introduction to his *Intimacy in America*.

26. Chakrabarty, *Provincializing Europe*, 18.

27. Ibid., 41.

28. D'Emilio, "Capitalism and Gay Identity."

29. Chakrabarty, *Provincializing Europe*, 66, my emphasis.

30. On habitus, see Bourdieu, *Outline of a Theory of Practice*, and Mauss, "Body Techniques."

31. Chakrabarty, *Provincializing Europe*, 71.

32. On the repressed erotics of close reading, see Armstrong, "Textual Harassment."

33. Edelman, *No Future*.

34. Freeman, *The Wedding Complex*.

35. Benjamin, "Theses on the Philosophy of History," 261.

36. Halberstam offers a list of several social forces and institutions structured by the homogeneous time she calls "straight time" in her book *In a Queer Time and Place*.

37. Povinelli, "Notes on Gridlock."

38. Among these works are not only the ones already cited but also Boellstorff, *A Coincidence of Desires;* essays in Bruhm and Hurley, eds., *Curiouser;* Castiglia and Reed, "'Ah, Yes, I Remember It Well'"; Chambers, *Loiterature;* Cvetkovich, *An Archive of Feelings;* Dinshaw, *Getting Medieval;* Elliott, *Popular Feminist Fiction as American Allegory;* essays in Eng and Kazanjian, *Loss;* Felski, *Doing Time;* Ferguson, ed., *Feminism in Time* special issue of *Modern Language Quarterly;* Ferguson, *Aberrations in Black;* Fradenburg, *Sacrifice Your Love;* essays in Freeman, *Queer Temporalities;* Gordon, "Turning Back"; Grosz, *The Nick of Time;* Grosz, *Space, Time, and Perversion;* Grosz, *Time Travels;* Holland, *Raising the Dead;* Jagose, *Inconsequence;* Love, "'Spoiled Identity'"; McGarry, *Ghosts of Futures Past;* Nealon, *Foundlings;* Patel, "Ghostly Appearances"; Ricco, *The Logic of the Lure;* Spivak, "The Staging of Time in *Heremakhonon*"; Wiegman, "Feminism's Apocalyptic Futures"; Wiegman, "On Being in Time with Feminism"; and Weston, *Gender in Real Time*.

introduction

1. Reese, "Siting the Avant-Garde."

2. Experimental filmmakers' techniques include "single framing . . . painted or scratched film . . . extended dissolves . . . long-takes . . . flicker editing . . . cut-ups . . . fake synch . . . outdated filmstock . . . found footage . . . out-of-focus lens . . . [and] intermittent projections." Ibid., 6.

3. Nguyen's liner notes to *Nguyen Tan Hoang: Complete Works* cite the tape as *Kip Noll, Superstar: Part I* (1981), dir. William Higgins, Catalina Video.

4. Deleuze contrasts the "movement-image," in which movement is a result of time, with the "time-image," in which movement reveals time and its heterogeneity. See *Cinema 2*.

5. One of the first activist movements to inform, shape, and intervene on queer theory figured itself explicitly as a spatial intervention: Queer Nation ironically inhabited the nation-form while laying bare the queerness at the heart of supposedly straight spaces. Indeed, as Berlant and I have argued, "We're here, we're queer, get used to it," and "We are everywhere," two of Queer Nation's chants, captures its spatial program of expanding queer territory beyond the gay ghetto toward schools, shopping malls, and straight bars and exposing the structural reliance of all kinds of public places, up to and including the nation itself, on the effaced presence of gay bodies. See Berlant and Freeman, "Queer Nationality." Important accounts of lesbian, gay, and/or queer identity emerging within new geopolitical formations of space include Berubé, *Coming Out Under Fire*; Boyd, *Wide Open Town;* Chauncey, *Gay New York*; D'Emilio, *Sexual Politics, Sexual Communities*; Faderman, *Odd Girls and Twilight Lovers*; Howard, *Men Like That*; Kennedy and Davis, *Boots of Leather, Slippers of Gold*, and numerous other community histories. The major schools of early 1990s queer theory were also initially attuned to space. The trope of the "border" organized such classic texts as Moraga's and Anzaldúa's coedited volume *This Bridge Called My Back* and Anzaldúa's *Borderlands = La Frontera*. Critical and theoretical work taking the closet as paradigmatic includes not only Sedgwick's *Epistemology of the Closet* but also Creech, *Closet Writing/Gay Reading*; Rambuss, *Closet Devotions*; and Russo, *The Celluloid Closet*. The stage metaphor can be seen at work in the merger of queer theory and performance studies, inflecting such 1990s publications as Butler, "Imitation and Gender Insubordination"; Robinson, "It Takes One to Know One"; Muñoz, *Disidentifications*; and Harris, *Staging Femininities*.

6. La Planche and Pontalis, "Binding," 52.

7. Luciano, *Arranging Grief*, 9.

8. Zerubavel, *Hidden Rhythms*.

9. Thompson, "Time, Work-Discipline, and Industrial Capitalism"; see also Hareven, *Family Time and Industrial Time*.

10. Bourdieu, *Outline of a Theory of Practice*, 78.

11. Butler, "Imitation and Gender Insubordination."

12. Nietzsche, *On the Advantage and Disadvantage of History for Life*. On the monument, see also Luciano, *Arranging Grief*, 169–214.

13. Borneman, *Belonging in the Two Berlins*.

14. Berlant, "Slow Death."

15. Kristeva, "Women's Time."

16. Luciano, *Arranging Grief*, 25–68.

17. Bhabha, "DissemiNation."

18. Zaretsky, *Capitalism, the Family, and Personal Life*, 33.

19. Luciano, *Arranging Grief*, 177.

20. See Floyd, "Making History."

21. An early and important consideration of how discourses of racial atavism and decline inflected early sexology is Somerville, *Queering the Color Line*. On lesbians as figures of cybernetic and other futurities, see the essays in Doan, ed., *The Lesbian Postmodern*.

22. For Vivien, see, for instance, Vivien, *The Muse of the Violets*; Robin Vote is a character in Barnes's *Nightwood*; the quoted text is from Eliot, "The Love Song of J. Alfred Prufrock," in *The Waste Land and Other Poems*, ed. Frank Kermode (New York: Penguin 2003), 2–8, at 6.

23. Laplanche and Pontalis, "Deferred Action." The classic essay on *Nachträglichkeit* is Freud, "Remembering, Repeating, and Working-Through."

24. Abelove, "Some Speculations." On the narrativization of sex, see Morrison, "End Pleasure."

25. Love, *Feeling Backward*.

26. Queer Marxist critics such as Morton have borrowed this term from Ebert, *Ludic Feminism and After*.

27. See Morton, "Pataphysics of the Closet," as well as other essays in the same volume and other Morton essays published elsewhere; Case, "Towards a Butch-Femme Retro-Future"; Champagne, "A Comment on the Class Politics of Queer Theory"; and Hennessy, "Queer Theory, Left Politics."

28. See, for instance, Floyd, "Making History."

29. Derrida, *Specters of Marx*. For formulations indebted to Derridean spectrality, see Freccero, *Queer/Early/Modern*; early and important interventions into presentist/presence-ist historiography are collected in Fradenburg and Freccero, eds., *Premodern Sexualities*. For a reading of *différence* as dialectical history see Terdiman, *Present Past*.

30. Benjamin, "On Some Motifs in Baudelaire."

31. Williams, "Structures of Feeling."

32. Jameson, *The Political Unconscious*, 102.

33. Lyotard, *The Differend*.

34. Jameson, "The End of Temporality."

35. Ibid., 712.

36. Ibid., 713.

37. Here the work of Bersani is exemplary. See, especially, "Is the Rectum a Grave?"

38. Freud, "On Narcissism," 64.

39. Freud, *The Ego and the Id*, 17.

40. Butler, "The Lesbian Phallus," 60.

41. Some of the stars of the original films from which Higgins's compilation was made died of HIV-related infections or AIDS. *K.I.P.* can also be read as homage to Crimp's famous essay "Mourning and Militancy," which argues that the AIDS-era gay community ought to acknowledge its grief as well as its rage, particularly its grief over the loss of a sexual culture.

42. Freeman, "Queer Belongings," 297.

43. Shakespeare, *Hamlet*, 1.5.188. All lines hereafter cited in the body of the chapter.

44. Stone, *The Family, Sex, and Marriage in England*. For a broader discussion of kinship as a means of forming and maintaining the state, see Stevens, *Reproducing the State*.

45. Hunt, "A Thing of Nothing," 30–31.

46. Shakespeare, *A Midsummer Night's Dream*, 1.2.65. All lines hereafter cited in the body of the text.

47. Mauss, "Body Techniques," 102.

48. Stone, *The Family, Sex, and Marriage*, 318.

49. Mauss, "Body Techniques," 104, his emphasis.

50. Benjamin, "Theses on the Philosophy of History," 260.

one. Junk Inheritances, Bad Timing

1. See Doane, *The Emergence of Cinematic Time*.

2. See Hirsch, *Family Frames*.

3. Smith, *American Archives*, 11.

4. Hirsch, *Family Frames*, 6–7.

5. Smith, *American Archives*, 120.

6. *Coal Miner's Granddaughter* (dir. Dougherty).

7. Kotz, "Inside and Out," 3.

8. Another work engaged with the project of theorizing a queer degenerative cinema is *Video Remains* (2004, dir. Alexandra Juhasz). On the New Queer Cinema, see the essays in Aaron, ed., *New Queer Cinema*.

9. Rich, "New Queer Cinema" (1992), rep. in Aaron, *New Queer Cinema*, 15–22. For a useful description of the formal attributes and temporal politics of the New Queer Cinema, see Pendleton, "Out of the Ghetto."

10. It also occasionally, though certainly not always, revealed and troubled the role of whiteness and Western nationalisms in dominant constructions of homosexuality. On the racial politics of the New Queer Cinema, see Muñoz, "Dead White."

11. Rich, "The New Queer Cinema," 16, 19. This lacuna is currently being filled in cinema studies, particularly in essays on the work of Todd Haynes: see De-Angelis, "The Characteristics of New Queer Filmmaking"; Gorfinkel, "The Future of Anachronism"; Landy, "'The Dream of the Gesture'"; Luciano, "Coming Around Again"; and O'Neill, "Traumatic Postmodern Histories."

12. Felski, "Nothing to Declare."

13. Annamarie Jagose has argued, for example, that the nineteenth-century field of sexology defined sexuality itself as "a sequential effect" (*Inconsequence*, 24). That is, sexologists understood object-choice as the outcome of a series of biological, psychological, and moral aberrations; they posited gender identity as the cause of sexual object-choice; and they consistently figured female and lesbian sexualities as masculine derivatives.

14. Wings, "A Maverick among Mavericks," 82–83.

15. For a discussion of how intimacy is a matter of timing, see Zerubavel, "The Language of Time."

16. Bhabha, "DissemiNation."

17. Wings, "A Maverick among Mavericks," 83.

18. Renan, "What Is a Nation?" 53.

19. Voloshinov, *Marxism and the Philosophy of Language*, 23.

20. *Oxford English Dictionary* online, 2nd ed., 1989, "accent," *n*. 1.

21. *The Physics of Love* (dir. Diane Bonder).

22. Harris, *Lover*. For page citations from the 1993 preface, I have used the reprinted edition published by New York University Press. For page citations from the novel, I have used the original, unprefaced first edition by Daughters, Inc.

23. On queer dykes' rebellion from the feminist mother, see Creet, "Daughter of the Movement."

24. Harris, "Introduction to Lover," xix. Hereafter cited in text, parenthetically.

25. Harris, *Lover*, 5. Hereafter cited in text, parenthetically.

26. I owe this insight about Christianity to Molly McGarry.

27. Kara Thompson's prospectus for a dissertation titled "A Romance with Many Reservations: American Indian Figurations and the Globalization of Indigeneity" alerted me to the complex structure of the convolute, Benjaminian and otherwise.

28. Bouquet, "Figures of Relations."

29. Stockton, "Growing Sideways, or Versions of the Queer Child," 300.

30. See Kristeva, "Women's Time."

31. Zaretsky, *Capitalism, the Family, and Personal Life*, 32. See also Brown, "Women's Work and Bodies in *The House of the Seven Gables*."

32. Gillis, "Making Time for Family," 8. See also Gillis, "Ritualization of Middle Class Life in Nineteenth Century Britain"; and Hareven, *Family Time and Industrial Time*.

33. Gillis, "Making Time for Family," 8–9; on the Sunday drive, ibid., 12. On Christmas, see Nissenbaum, *The Battle for Christmas*, esp. 90–175.

34. Gillis, "Making Time for Family," 13.

35. Hirsch, *Family Frames*, 7.

36. Elsaesser, "Tales of Sound and Fury," 62. Note that Elsaesser is referring to the mise-en-scène, but it's also clear that mid-twentieth-century women were encouraged to replicate this effect in their own homes. Dana Luciano's "Coming Around Again" alerted me to the importance of this article.

37. I am indebted to Kendra Patterson Smith's seminar paper of 2005, "Queer Relics: Martyrological Time and the Eroto-Aesthetics of Suffering in Bertha Harris' *Lover*" (unpublished), for an illuminating discussion of the role of the female hagiographic genre in *Lover*.

38. Kristeva, "Women's Time," 206.

39. Ibid., 207.

40. Ibid., 209.

41. Ibid., 210.

42. Felski, "Nothing to Declare."

43. Lochrie, "Mystical Acts, Queer Tendencies," 190.

44. Irigaray, "Sexual Difference," 5, emphasis hers.

45. Irigaray, "Questions to Emmanuel Levinas," 181.

46. James, "I Forgot to Remember to Forget," 18. See also Halberstam, "Forgetting Family."

47. Lorde, "The Uses of the Erotic."

48. See Deleuze and Guattari, *Anti-Oedipus*.

49. Casarino, "Time Matters." The essay takes up Giorgio Agamben, Louis Althusser, Walter Benjamin, Gilles Deleuze, Karl Marx, and Antonio Negri.

50. Bloom, "Clinamen, or Poetic Misprision."

51. Casarino, "Time Matters," 190.

52. Bloom, "Clinamen, or Poetic Misprision, 42.

53. Negri, *Marx beyond Marx*, 71, cited in Casarino, "Time Matters," 200.

54. On touches across time, see Dinshaw, *Getting Medieval*.

55. Casarino, "Time Matters," 202–3, my emphasis.

56. Jameson, "Pleasure," 71.

57. Ibid., 72.

58. Ibid., 73.

two. Deep Lez

1. Hayes has since taken *In the Near Future* to Vienna, Warsaw, and London.

2. I take this phrase of J. L. Austin from the art historian Julia Bryan-Wilson, who uses the term "infelicity" to describe Hayes's textual utterances. See Austin, *How to Do Things with Words*, and Bryan-Wilson, "Julia Bryan-Wilson on Sharon Hayes," 279.

3. The bill sat in committee and never reached the floor from 1923 to 1946 (when it failed) and 1950 (when the Senate passed a version so watered down that supporters rejected it); it was finally introduced to the states for ratification in 1972 and failed to meet the required number of state ratifications by its deadline of 1979 and extended deadline of 1982; it has been languishing in committee ever since. See Mansbridge, *Why We Lost the E.R.A.*, 1–19.

4. On criticisms of the ERA, see ibid.

5. See Martin, "Extraordinary Homosexuals and the Fear of Being Ordinary."

6. The filmmaker Elisabeth Subrin (about whom much more follows) articulates this question beautifully in "Trashing *Shulie*," 61.

7. Wiegman, "On Being in Time with Feminism," 164.

8. Case, "Toward a Butch-Femme Retro-Future."

9. Butler, *The Psychic Life of Power*, 3.

10. Wiegman, "On Being in Time with Feminism," 172.

11. Crimp, "Mourning and Militancy."

12. See Roof, "Generational Difficulties," 71–72, and Heller, "The Anxieties of Affluence," 322.

13. *Shulie* (dir. Elisabeth Subrin).

14. On Shulamith Firestone's activities from 1967 to 1970, see Echols, *Daring to Be Bad*. For the purposes of clarity, in this chapter I use "Shulie" to designate the fictive subject of both the 1967 documentary and the 1997 reshoot, and "Firestone" to designate the historical agent that the 1967 documentary could not imagine. Similarly, "video" refers to Subrin's reshoot, and "film" to the 1967 original. Wherever possible, I have also distinguished between the earlier and later works with dates in the parentheses.

15. Elisabeth Subrin, personal conversation, fall 1999.

16. See Ross, "The Uses of Camp," and Dyer, *Heavenly Bodies*.

17. Subrin, "Trashing *Shulie*," 66.

18. Butler, *The Psychic Life of Power*, 133.

19. Ibid., 146, her emphasis.

20. See the essays in Eng and Kasanjian, *Loss*.

21. The classic statement privileging symbol over allegory is Samuel Taylor Coleridge, *The Statesman's Manual* (1816), 437. Of the many deconstructions of that distinction, the most famous is de Man, "The Rhetoric of Temporality." For theories of allegory from which we might extrapolate the queer practices of camp and world making, respectively, see Fletcher, *Allegory*, and Benjamin, "Allegory and Trauerspiel."

22. Taylor, in *The Archive and the Repertoire*, describes performance in terms of "a nonarchival system of transfer that I came to call the *repertoire*" (xvii). Though I developed my argument before encountering her book, I think that temporal drag is, indeed, a repertoire for the passing down or handing over of fading gendered and sexualized lifeways and scenarios.

23. Some plodding remarks on terminology: neither "lesbian" nor "dyke" covers, precisely, the commitment to playing with age that — as I discuss further on — marks *Shulie* and many 1990s cultural productions made by queer females. Yet "queer" still remains frustratingly neutral and does not do justice to the specifically femme sensibilities also at work in some of these texts. Hence some neologisms.

24. Rosenbaum, "Remaking History."

25. See Krauss, "The Originality of the Avant-Garde"; also, more generally, the early 1980s feminist debates on postmodernism published in the journal *October*.

26. Firestone, *The Dialectic of Sex*, 31.

27. Rich, *Chick Flicks*, 384.

28. Wiegman, "On Being in Time with Feminism," 170.

29. Echols, *Daring to Be Bad*, 65–69.

30. Žižek writes that "a true historical break does not simply designate the 'regressive' loss (or 'progressive' gain) of something, but *the shift in the very grid which enables us to measure losses and gains* (his emphasis): *The Plague of Fantasies*, 13, cited in Scott, "Fantasy Echo," 289; see also Bhabha, *The Location of Culture*, 253–54.

31. Engels, "Socialism," 694, quoted in Firestone, *The Dialectic of Sex*, ix (unpaginated).

32. Firestone, *The Dialectic of Sex*, 3.

33. Ibid.

34. Ibid., 44.

35. Ibid., 35.

36. Ibid., 42.

37. Ibid., 21.

38. Creet, "Daughter of the Movement."

39. Garrison suggestively describes the historical transformation of feminisms as "radio waves" rather than oceanic ones. See "U.S. Feminism — Grrrl Style!"

40. Subrin, "Trashing *Shulie*," 62.

41. Important articulations of this include, of course, Bhabha, *The Location of Culture*; McClintock, *Imperial Leather*; and Chakrabarty, *Provincializing Europe*.

42. The phrase "waiting room of history" is from Chakrabarty, *Provincializing Europe*, 8.

43. Zines I am thinking of here include *I Heart Amy Carter* (Tammy Rae Carland), *Snarla* (Johanna Fateman and Miranda July), and *William Wants a Doll* (Arielle Greenberg). Other 1990s zines whose titles suggest the aesthetic I am describing can be found at the Sallie Bingham Center for Women's History and Culture Zine Collection at Duke University: *I Kicked A Boy* (Mandy, Rae, and Reba), *Winky Pinky* ("Tera Winkypinky"), and *Power Candy* ("Ericka"). A representative though not exhaustive sampling of 1990s zines can be found in Taormino and Green, eds., *Girl's Guide to Taking Over the World*.

44. Elisabeth Subrin, personal conversation, fall 1999.

45. Riot Grrrl did not initially understand its work as a politics of style, but needless to say, the media pounced on Riot Grrrl fashions, ignoring the feminist messages that the movement espoused. Here I hope at least to retranslate that aesthetic back into a political language of sorts, along the lines of Hebdidge's *Subculture*. As well, it's important to note that Riot Grrrl chapters still exist and thrive, despite my periodizing past tense.

46. See Sedgwick, *The Coherence of Gothic Conventions*, *Between Men*, and "Queer Performativity." See also Barber and Clark, "Queer Moments," 5.

47. Probyn, "Suspended Beginnings," 99.

48. *Swallow* (dir. Elisabeth Subrin); *Judy Spots* (dir. Sadie Benning). For a seminal meditation on the politics of mourning for lost cultures that nevertheless insists on maintaining clear distinctions between generations, see Crimp, "Mourning and Militancy."

49. On shared parenting as a solution to what we would now call gender trouble, see Gilligan, *In a Different Voice*; and Chodorow, *The Reproduction of Mothering*.

50. Firestone, *The Dialectic of Sex*, 109.

51. Ivy, "Have You Seen Me?"

52. Firestone, *The Dialectic of Sex*, 1.

53. Bikini Kill, *Revolution Girl-Style Now* (1991). Released in cassette tape form and independently distributed from hand to hand.

54. See Edelman, *No Future*.

55. www.girlpower.gov (visited January 7, 2008). Changed to www.girlshealth .gov (visited March 26, 2009).

56. "Girl power," draft entry, *Oxford English Dictionary* online, September 2008.

57. Hanna, "Gen x Survivor," 131.

58. Ibid., 134.

59. Lichtman, "Deeply Lez," 22–23.

60. "The owl of Minerva begins its flight only with the onset of dusk." Hegel, *Elements of the Philosophy of Right*, 23.

61. Hilderbrand, "Retroactivism."

62. Halberstam's examples are the lyrics to Le Tigre's "Hot Topic" (*In a Queer Time and Place*, 163), the Butchies' cover of Chris Williamson's "Shooting Star" (*In a Queer Time and Place*, 171), and a 2002 Queer Arts Festival project that paired luminaries of the 1970s and 1980s lesbian folk scene with dyke bands in mutually appreciative performances and interviews (*In a Queer Time and Place*, 181).

63. A bibliography of performance historiography would include, at least, Girard, *Violence and the Sacred*; Jackson, *Lines of Activity*; Roach, *Cities of the Dead*; Taussig, *Mimesis and Alterity*; and Taylor, *The Archive and the Repertoire*.

64. Reckitt, "My Fuzzy Valentine," n.p.

65. Ibid.

66. McKay, "Allyson Mitchell," 48.

67. "Somehow a microchip in my brain got coded with the information that this can be hot." Mitchell, quoted in McKay, "Allyson Mitchell," 47.

68. Moon and Sedgwick, "Divinity," 216.

69. Ibid., 218.

70. Ibid.

71. Ibid.

72. Berlant, "Slow Death."

73. McKay, "Allyson Mitchell," 47.

three. Time Binds, or, Erotohistoriography

1. On the gendering of "sensory" history, see Smith, *The Gender of History*.

2. Halberstam, *Skin Shows*, 30.

3. Habermas, *The Structural Transformation of the Public Sphere*, 43–50.

4. The phrase "publishing the family" is from Howard, *Publishing the Family*.

5. Goode, *Sentimental Masculinity and the Rise of History, 1790–1890*, 161.

6. Gordon, *Ghostly Matters*.

7. Goode, "Dryasdust Antiquarianism," 63 and *Sentimental Masculinity*, 71.

8. In fact, Goode notes that Mary Wollstonecraft's *Vindication of the Rights of Men* condemned sentimental history. *Sentimental Masculinity*, 13 and 30.

9. Ibid., 79–86.

10. Ibid., 45–46. In *The Gender of History* Smith attributes some of these modes of doing history to amateur female historiographers.

11. Goode, *Sentimental Masculinity*, 105.

12. Bentley, "Family, Humanity, Polity," 327–28.

13. Goode, *Sentimental Masculinity*, 39.

14. Ibid., 34.

15. Shelley, *Frankenstein*, 155. Hereafter cited in text by page number.

16. Goode, *Sentimental Masculinity*, 84–85.

17. My thanks to Timothy Morton for pointing out the relevance of this passage to my larger discussion.

18. For a history of "the spirit of the age," see Chandler, *England in 1819*, 105–8 and 125.

19. Ibid., 274.

20. Woolf, *Orlando*, ix, vii. Hereafter cited in text by page number.

21. Vita Sackville-West's son Nigel Nicolson called *Orlando* "the longest and most charming love letter in literature" in his *Portrait of a Marriage*, 202.

22. Both quotes are from Carla Freccero, *Queer/Early/Modern*, 102.

23. I follow Ann Cvetkovich's call for thinking an expansive receptivity in terms of actual lesbian sex acts in "Recasting Receptivity."

24. Material about the production of *The Sticky Fingers of Time* is taken from the commentary of the director, Hilary Brougher, and the cinematographer, Ethan Mass, on the DVD of the film distributed by Strand Releasing.

25. Benjamin, "The Work of Art in the Age of Mechanical Reproduction," 233.

26. Dinshaw, *Getting Medieval*, 21. See also Pellegrini, "Touching the Past."

27. Fradenburg and Freccero, "The Pleasures of History," 373.

28. Agamben, "Time and History," 104. Thanks to Gregory Dobbins for bringing this essay to my attention.

29. Abraham and Torok, "Mourning *or* Melancholia." Following Torok via Butler, we might think of drag, tattooing, piercing, hormones, and other body modifications up to and including phalloplasties as ways of incorporating lost attachments.

30. "Erotic effusion," Torok, "The Illness of Mourning," 103; long quote, 110, her emphasis.

31. Abraham and Torok, "Mourning *or* Melancholia," 131.

32. Jagose, *Inconsequence*, xi.

33. Thanks to Brad Epps for pushing me to think about these names.

34. Derrida, *Specters of Marx*, 64.

35. Case, "Toward a Butch-Femme Aesthetic," 295.

36. *Oxford English Dictionary* online, 2nd ed. (1989), "joint," n. 6 (*Obs. rare*).

37. Chisholm, "The City of Collective Memory," 124. I take my analysis of smoke in part from the Harlem Renaissance writer Bruce Nugent's short story "Smoke, Lillies [*sic*] and Jade," first published in 1926 in the journal *Fire!*, and Faulkner's use of breath and dust in *Absalom, Absalom!* (1937).

38. Benjamin, "Surrealism" (1929). The translation "hollow tooth" is Richter's, in his *Walter Benjamin and the Corpus of Autobiography*, 35.

39. Marks writes that "haptic *perception* is usually defined by psychologists as the combination of tactile, kinesthetic, and proprioceptive functions, the way we experience touch both on the surface of and inside our bodies . . . In haptic *visuality*, the eyes themselves function like organs of touch." Marks, *The Skin of the Film*, 162.

40. Benjamin, "On Some Motifs in Baudelaire," 175.

41. Ibid., 174.

42. Ibid.

43. Benjamin, "On the Mimetic Faculty," 334.

44. Benjamin, "Surrealism."

45. Torok, "The Illness of Mourning," 113.

46. Taussig, *Mimesis and Alterity*, xviii.

47. Negrón-Muntaner, "Ofelia's Kiss."

48. Edelman, *No Future*.

49. Some foundational thinking about butch-femme in the 1980s came from women of color: see Moraga and Hollibaugh, "What We're Rollin' Around in Bed With"; Moraga's *Loving in the War Years;* and the oral histories in Kennedy and

Davis, *Boots of Leather, Slippers of Gold*. Yet the racial axis of butch-femme gender practices disappeared from view in slightly later classic works such as Case, "Toward a Butch-Femme Aesthetic"; Faderman, *Odd Girls and Twilight Lovers*; and Rubin, "Of Catamites and Kings."

50. Benjamin, "The Work of Art in the Age of Mechanical Reproduction," 242.

51. Deleuze, *Cinema 2*, 12.

52. See Dery, "Black to the Future," 180.

53. Taussig, *Mimesis and Alterity*, 19.

54. Young, *Black Frankenstein*.

55. See Sedgwick, *Between Men*.

four. Turn the Beat Around

1. I am indebted to Anne Cheng for providing a succinct account of this chapter's aims in her reader's report for the version of this chapter published in *differences*; several of her observations have inflected this paragraph.

2. Hartman, *Scenes of Subjection*, 74.

3. For descriptions of "power exchange" as the basis of sadomasochism, see Califia, *Public Sex*; Samois, *Coming to Power*; and Thompson, *Leatherfolk*.

4. Beauvoir, "Must We Burn Sade?," 16.

5. Zerubavel, "The French Republican Calendar," 870.

6. Thus the French Revolution belies O'Malley's claim that this new understanding of time occurred with the inception of railroads and standard times — though he may be right that "modern," secular time was not *popularly* understood this way in the eighteenth century or in the United States. See O'Malley, *Keeping Watch*.

7. Beauvoir, "Must We Burn Sade?," 43.

8. See Rohy, "Ahistorical."

9. The positions of Bataille, Blanchot, and Bersani, who see Sade as an antagonist to the idea of durability itself, especially in the form of the social contract, are elegantly summed up by Ferguson in "Sade and the Pornographic Legacy."

10. Dworkin, *Intercourse*; Mackinnon, *Feminism Unmodified*. For criticism, see Califia, *Public Sex*.

11. For arguments that sadomasochism repeats the historical violence it cites, see Miriam, "From Rage to All the Rage"; Reti, "Remember the Fire"; and Star, "Swastikas."

12. Bersani, *The Freudian Body*, 38. Bersani later revises this to describe anal sex as the consummate practice of self-shattering. See "Is the Rectum a Grave?"

13. See Edelman, *No Future*.

14. "The peculiarity of Freudian analysis is to propose a history of the self's structure which includes, as one of its stages, a solidifying of character structures . . . [it]

partially demystifies the notion of such structures by explaining them historically rather than just deducing them from the concept of an ahistorical human nature" (Bersani, *A Future for Astyanax*, 58).

15. Bersani, *Homos*, 89.

16. Ibid., 90.

17. Critiques of queer theory along these lines include Morton, "Changing the Terms"; Nussbaum, "The Professor of Parody"; and Siegel, "The Gay Science."

18. Bersani, *Homos*, 90.

19. See, for instance, Acker's *Blood and Guts in High School*; Cvetkovich, *An Archive of Feelings*; and Hart, *Between the Body and the Flesh*.

20. Clément, *The Lives and Legends of Jacques Lacan*, 122, cited in Hart, *Between the Body and the Flesh*, 161.

21. The concept of "feeling historical" is elaborated in Nealon, *Foundlings*.

22. Hartman, *Scenes of Subjection*, 21.

23. Jameson, "Cognitive Mapping."

24. Julien, "Confessions of a Snow Queen," 120.

25. Burston, "*The Attendant*," 65.

26. Julien misidentifies the title of the painting as *Scene on the Coast of Africa* in his article "Confessions of a Snow Queen." That title refers to an engraving after Biard's painting, made by Charles E. Wagstaff in 1844. Biard's painting is also referred to in several exhibit catalogs as *Slaves on the West Coast of Africa*.

27. See Mercer, "Skin Head Sex Thing," and the essay that Mercer reconsiders in the latter, "Imaging the Black Man's Sex."

28. Muñoz, *Disidentifications*, 60.

29. Hart, *Between the Body and the Flesh*, 103.

30. Freccero, *Queer/Early/Modern*, 104, my emphasis.

31. See O'Malley, *Keeping Watch*.

32. On melodrama and spectatorial absorption, see Doane, *The Desire to Desire*.

33. I thank H. N. Lukes for this point, in conversation.

34. Beauvoir, "Must We Burn Sade?," 51.

35. Ibid.

36. Hénaff, *Sade*, 106.

37. Tweedie, "The Suspended Spectacle of History," 380. Rebecca Schneider speculates that "the 'still' in theatrical reenactment—especially the heritage of *tableaux vivants*—offers an invitation . . . to constitute the historical tale differently," "Still Living," 65.

38. Writing about "the obscene theatricality of the slave trade," Saidiya Hartman suggests as much. See Hartman, *Scenes of Subjection*, 17.

39. See Fleissner, *Women, Compulsion, Modernity*, 198.

40. Hénaff, *Sade*, 105.

41. Marx, *Capital, Volume One*, 320.

42. Hénaff, *Sade*, 105.

43. Benjamin, "The Work of Art in the Age of Mechanical Reproduction."

44. Hart, *Between the Body and the Flesh*, 141, her emphasis.

45. Deleuze, *Masochism*, 63.

46. See Hénaff, *Sade*, 134.

47. An important discussion of how the politics of time affected people of African descent living under slavery can be found in Smith, *Mastered by the Clock*.

48. Johnson, "Time and Revolution in African America," 152.

49. Ibid., 153.

50. See Orgeron, "Re-Membering History in Isaac Julien's *The Attendant*."

51. Benjamin, "Theses on the Philosophy of History," 257.

52. Ibid., 262.

53. Ibid.

54. Deleuze, *Cinema 2*, 69.

55. Julien, "Confessions of a Snow Queen," 120.

56. See also Price, "*Dido and Aeneas* in Context."

57. Specifically, the ascension of William and Mary to the throne. See Roach, *Cities of the Dead*, 42.

58. Ibid., 44.

59. Ibid., 46.

60. Calder, *Revolutionary Empire*, 347–48, cited in Roach, *Cities of the Dead*, 42. It should be noted that scholars of early music have disputed the 1689 premiere date for the opera; see a series of debates in the journal *Early Music*, beginning with Pinnock, "'Unscarr'd by turning times'?"

61. See Landsberg, *Prosthetic Memory*.

62. In this sense, the concept of prosthetic memory confronts the most conservative implications not only of the antisadomasochistic notion that reenactments of trauma cannot transform the victim but also of habitus, or even "performativity," neither of which fully accounts for how a liberatory rather than random or reactionary difference might appear in the nonidentical repetitions that constitute identity. Like performativity, prosthetic memories are less than voluntary, and more than merely compelled, but as vicarious modes of being they float more freely than either habitus or performativity would allow.

63. Landsberg, *Prosthetic Memory*, 2.

64. Freud, *Three Essays*, 16.

65. Hart cites Stephen Best's description of how prostheses lengthen not only space but time; see Best's "The Race for Invention," 202, cited in Hart, *Between the Body and the Flesh*, 96. An extraordinary fictional example of experiencing female masculinity as a return to a prior state of being male can be found in Radclyffe Hall's short story "Miss Ogilvy Finds Herself" (1926, published 1934).

66. See Derrida, *Specters of Marx*.

67. Roderick A. Ferguson offers a useful definition of queer-of-color critique as a mode of analysis that (1) exposes liberal capitalism's reliance on a tacitly white heterosexual matrix; (2) interrogates the way Marxist analysis naturalizes heterosexuality in order to produce its utopian formulations of property relations untainted by capitalism; and (3) remembers the primacy of racist evolutionary thinking to both liberal and Marxist discourses of progress. In other words, queer-of-color critique is a mode of historical materialism *otherwise*, one that I think Julien anticipates in this and other films. See Ferguson, *Aberrations in Black*, esp. 1–10.

68. Hartman, *Scenes of Subjection*, 77, my emphasis.

69. Benjamin, "Theses," 262.

70. Julien, "Confessions of a Snow Queen," 122–23.

71. Mercer, "Skin Head Sex Thing," 174–75.

72. I take some of my thinking here from the essays in Ahmed and Stacey, *Thinking through the Skin*.

73. Marks, *The Skin of the Film*, xii.

74. This is, of course, an indexical view of film, insofar as the concept of index suggests the material presence of the original in the thing itself. Marks, *The Skin of the Film*, 242.

75. "Aural voyeurism," Julien, "Confessions of a Snow Queen," 120.

76. "Genealogy of performance," Roach, *Cities of the Dead*, 25.

77. "Chaconne," *Oxford English Dictionary* online, 2nd ed. (1989). Some would call the bass line a passacaglia, but the two are so closely related and composers often used the terms interchangeably. Thanks to Catherine Fung for drawing my attention to the passacaglia.

78. Roach, *Cities of the Dead*, 47.

79. Dimock, "A Theory of Resonance," 1063.

80. Morrison, *Love*, 67.

81. The formulation is Johnson's, in "Time and Revolution in African America," 152.

coda

1. Du Bois, "Sociology Hesitant," 40, 40, 44.

2. Ibid., 44.

3. Ibid.

4. For a local history of black women's clubs, see Hendricks, *Gender, Race, and Class*.

bibliography

Aaron, Michele A., ed. *New Queer Cinema: A Critical Reader*. New Brunswick, N.J.: Rutgers University Press, 2004.

Abelove, Henry. "Some Speculations on the History of Sexual Intercourse during the Long Eighteenth Century in England." *Deep Gossip*, 21–28. Minneapolis: University of Minnesota Press, 2003.

Abraham, Nicholas, and Maria Torok. "Mourning *or* Melancholia: Introjection *versus* Incorporation." *The Shell and the Kernel: Renewals of Psychoanalysis*, vol. 1, ed. Nicholas T. Rand, 125–38. Chicago: University of Chicago Press, 1994.

Acker, Kathy. *Blood and Guts in High School*. New York: Grove Press, 1984.

Agamben, Giorgio. "Time and History: Critique of the Instant and the Continuum." *Infancy and History: The Destruction of Experience*, 91–105. New York: Verso, 1993.

Ahmed, Sara, and Jackie Stacey, eds. *Thinking through the Skin*. London: Routledge, 2001.

Anzaldúa, Gloria. *Borderlands = La Frontera: The New Mestiza*. San Francisco: Spinsters/Aunt Lute, 1987.

Armstrong, Isobel. "Textual Harassment: The Ideology of Close Reading, or How Close Is Close?" *Textual Practice* 9, no. 3 (1995): 401–20.

Austin, J. L. *How to Do Things with Words*. 2nd ed. Cambridge, Mass.: Harvard University Press, 1975.

Barber, Stephen M., and David L. Clark. "Queer Moments: The Performative Temporalities of Eve Kosofsky Sedgwick." *Regarding Sedgwick: Essays on Culture and Critical Theory*, ed. Stephen M. Barber and David L. Clark, 1–56. New Brunswick, N.J.: Rutgers University Press, 2002.

Barnes, Djuna. *Nightwood*. (1936). New York: New Directions Publishing, 1961.

Beauvoir, Simone de. "Must We Burn Sade?" *The Marquis De Sade*, ed. Paul Dinnage, 9–82. New York: Grove Press, 1953.

Benjamin, Walter. "Allegory and Trauerspiel." *The Origin of German Tragic Drama*, 159–235. London: Verso, 1985.

———. "On Some Motifs in Baudelaire." (1939). *Illuminations*, ed. Hannah Arendt, 155–200. New York: Schocken Books, 1968.

———. "On the Mimetic Faculty." (1933). *Reflections: Essays, Aphorisms, Autobiographical Writings*, ed. Peter Demetz, 333–36. New York: Schocken Books, 1978.

——. "Surrealism: The Last Snapshot of the European Intelligentsia." (1929). *Reflections: Essays, Aphorisms, Autobiographical Writings*, ed. Peter Demetz, 177–92. New York: Schocken Books, 1978.

——. "Theses on the Philosophy of History." (1940). *Illuminations*, ed. Hannah Arendt, 253–64. New York: Schocken Books, 1968.

——. "The Work of Art in the Age of Mechanical Reproduction." (1935). *Illuminations*, ed. Hannah Arendt, 217–51. New York: Schocken Books, 1968.

Bentley, Colene. "Family, Humanity, Polity: Theorizing the Basis and Boundaries of Political Community in Frankenstein." *Criticism* 47, no. 3 (summer 2005): 325–51.

Berlant, Lauren. "Slow Death (Sovereignty, Obesity, Lateral Agency)." *Critical Inquiry* 33, no. 4 (summer 2007): 754–80.

Berlant, Lauren, and Elizabeth Freeman. "Queer Nationality." *boundary 2* 19, no. 1 (1992): 148–80.

Bersani, Leo. *The Freudian Body: Psychoanalysis and Art*. New York: Columbia University Press, 1986.

——. *A Future for Astyanax*. Boston: Little, Brown, 1969.

——. *Homos*. Cambridge, Mass.: Harvard University Press, 1995.

——. "Is the Rectum a Grave?" *October* 43 (winter 1987): 197–222.

Berubé, Allan. *Coming Out Under Fire: The History of Gay Men and Women in World War Two*. New York: Free Press, 1990.

Best, Stephen. "The Race for Invention: Blackness, Technology, and Turn-of-the-Century Modernity." Ph.D. dissertation, University of Pennsylvania, 1997.

Bhabha, Homi. "DissemiNation: Time, Narrative, and the Margins of the Modern Nation." *Nation and Narration*, ed. Homi K. Bhabha, 291–322. New York: Routledge, 1991.

——. *The Location of Culture*. New York: Routledge, 1994.

Bloom, Harold. "Clinamen, or Poetic Misprision." *The Anxiety of Influence: A Theory of Poetry*, 19–45. New York: Oxford University Press, 1973.

Boellstorff, Tom. *A Coincidence of Desires: Anthropology, Queer Studies, Indonesia*. Durham, N.C.: Duke University Press, 2007.

Borneman, John. *Belonging in the Two Berlins: Kin, State, Nation*. New York: Cambridge University Press, 1992.

Bouquet, Mary. "Figures of Relations: Reconnecting Kinship Studies and Museum Collections." *Cultures of Relatedness: New Approaches to the Study of Kinship*, ed. Janet Carsten, 167–90. Cambridge: Cambridge University Press, 2000.

Bourdieu, Pierre. *Outline of a Theory of Practice*. Cambridge: Cambridge University Press, 1977.

Boyd, Nan Alamilla. *Wide Open Town: A History of San Francisco to 1965*. Berkeley: University of California Press, 2005.

Brown, Gillian. "Women's Work and Bodies in the House of the Seven Gables."

Domestic Individualism: Imagining Self in Nineteenth-Century America, 63–95. Berkeley: University of California Press, 1992.

Bruhm, Stephen, and Natasha Hurley, eds. *Curiouser: On the Queerness of Children*. Minneapolis: University of Minnesota Press, 2004.

Bryan-Wilson, Julia. "Julia Bryan-Wilson on Sharon Hayes." *Artforum International* (May 2006): 278–79.

Burston, Paul. "*The Attendant*." Review. *Sight and Sound* 3, no. 4 (1993): 64–65.

Butler, Judith. "Critically Queer." *GLQ* 1, no. 1 (1993): 17–32.

——. "Freud and the Melancholia of Gender." *Gender Trouble: Feminism and the Subversion of Identity*, 57–65. New York: Routledge, 1990.

——. "Imitation and Gender Insubordination." *Inside/Out: Lesbian Theories, Gay Theories*, ed. Diana Fuss, 13–31. New York: Routledge, 1991.

——. "The Lesbian Phallus." *Bodies That Matter: On the Discursive Limits of Sex*, 57–91. New York: Routledge, 1993.

——. *The Psychic Life of Power: Theories in Subjection*. Stanford, Calif.: Stanford University Press, 1997.

Calder, Angus. *Revolutionary Empire: The Rise of the English-Speaking Empires from the Fifteenth Century to the 1780s*. New York: Dutton, 1987.

Califia, Pat. *Public Sex: The Culture of Radical Sex*. 2nd ed. Pittsburgh: Cleis, 1994.

Casarino, Cesare. "Time Matters: Marx, Negri, Agamben, and the Corporeal." *Strategies* 16, no. 2 (2003): 185–206.

Case, Sue-Ellen. "Toward a Butch-Femme Aesthetic." *The Lesbian and Gay Studies Reader*, ed. Henry Abelove, Michèle Aina Barale, and David Halperin, 294–306. New York: Routledge, 1994.

——. "Towards a Butch-Femme Retro-Future." *Cross Purposes: Lesbians, Feminists, and the Limits of Alliance*, ed. Dana Heller, 205–20. Bloomington: Indiana University Press, 1997.

Castiglia, Christopher, and Christopher Reed. "'Ah, Yes, I Remember It Well': Memory and Queer Culture in *Will and Grace*." *Cultural Critique* 56 (2003): 158–88.

Chakrabarty, Dipesh. *Provincializing Europe: Postcolonial Thought and Historical Difference*. Princeton, N.J.: Princeton University Press, 2000.

Chambers, Ross. *Loiterature*. Lincoln: University of Nebraska Press, 1999.

Champagne, John. "A Comment on the Class Politics of Queer Theory." *College English* 59 (1997): 350–51.

Chandler, James. *England in 1819: The Politics of Literary Culture and the Case of Romantic Historicism*. Chicago: University of Chicago Press, 1999.

Chauncey, George. *Gay New York: Gender, Urban Culture, and the Making of the Gay Male World, 1890–1940*. New York: Basic Books, 1994.

Chisholm, Dianne. "The City of Collective Memory." *GLQ* 7, no. 2 (2001): 195–203.

Chodorow, Nancy. *The Reproduction of Mothering: Psychoanalysis and the Sociology of Gender*. Berkeley: University of California Press, 1978.

Clément, Catherine. *The Lives and Legends of Jacques Lacan*. Trans. Arthur Gold-
hammer. New York: Columbia University Press, 1983.

Coleridge, Samuel Taylor. "The Statesman's Manual: A Lay Sermon." (1816). *The
Complete Works of Samuel Taylor Coleridge*, vol. 1, *Aids to Reflection and The
Statesman's Manual*, ed. W. G. T. Shedd, 421–51. New York: Harper and Broth-
ers, 1884.

Coviello, Peter. *Intimacy in America: Dreams of Affiliation in Antebellum Literature*.
Minneapolis: University of Minnesota Press, 2005.

Creech, James. *Closet Writing/Gay Reading: The Case of Melville's Pierre*. Chicago:
University of Chicago Press, 1993.

Creet, Julia. "Daughter of the Movement: The Psychodynamics of Lesbian s/m
Fantasy." *differences* 3, no. 2 (1990): 135–59.

Crimp, Douglas. "Mourning and Militancy." *October* 51 (1989): 3–18.

Crimp, Douglas, and Adam Rolston. *AIDS DemoGraphics*. Seattle: Bay Press, 1990.

Cvetkovich, Ann. *An Archive of Feelings: Trauma, Sexuality, and Lesbian Public
Cultures*. Durham, N.C.: Duke University Press, 2003.

———. "Recasting Receptivity: Femme Sexualities." *Lesbian Erotics*, ed. Karla Jay,
125–46. New York: New York University Press, 1995.

D'Emilio, John. "Capitalism and Gay Identity." *Powers of Desire: The Politics of
Sexuality*, ed. Christine Stansell, Ann Snitow, and Sharon Thompson, 100–113.
New York: Monthly Review Press, 1983.

———. *Sexual Politics, Sexual Communities: The Making of a Homosexual Minority in
the United States, 1940–1970*. Chicago: University of Chicago Press, 1998.

DeAngelis, Michael. "The Characteristics of New Queer Filmmaking: Case Study
—Todd Haynes." *New Queer Cinema: A Critical Reader*, ed. Michele Aaron, 41–
52. New Brunswick, N.J.: Rutgers University Press.

Deleuze, Gilles. *Cinema 2: The Time-Image*. Trans. Hugh Tomlinson and Robert
Galeta. Minneapolis: University of Minnesota Press, 1989.

———. "Masochism: An Interpretation of Coldness and Cruelty." *Masochism: An
Interpretation of Coldness and Cruelty, Together with the Entire Text of Venus in
Furs, by Leopold Von Sacher-Masoch*, trans. Jean McNeil and Aude Willm, 15–
116. New York: George Braziller, 1971.

Deleuze, Gilles, and Félix Guattari. *Anti-Oedipus: Capitalism and Schizophrenia*.
Minneapolis: University of Minnesota Press, 1993.

———. "What Is a Minor Literature?" *Out There: Marginalization and Contemporary Cultures*, ed. Russell Ferguson, Martha Gever, Trinh T. Minh-Ha, and
Cornel West, 59–69. Cambridge, Mass.: MIT Press, 1990.

De Man, Paul. "The Rhetoric of Temporality." *Blindness and Insight: Essays in the
Rhetoric of Contemporary Criticism*, 187–228. Minneapolis: University of Minnesota Press, 1983.

Derrida, Jacques. *Specters of Marx: The State of the Debt, the Work of Mourning, and* the *New International*. Trans. Peggy Kamuf. New York: Routledge Classic Editions, 2006.

Dery, Mark. "Black to the Future: Interviews with Samuel R. Delany, Greg Tate, and Tricia Rose." *Flame Wars: The Discourse of Cyberculture*, ed. Mark Dery, 179–222. Durham, N.C.: Duke University Press, 1995.

Dimock, Wai Chee. "A Theory of Resonance." PMLA 112, no. 5 (October 1997): 1060–71.

Dinshaw, Carolyn. *Getting Medieval: Sexualities and Communities, Pre- and Post-Modern*. Durham, N.C.: Duke University Press, 1999.

Doan, Laura, ed. *The Lesbian Postmodern*. New York: Columbia University Press, 1994.

Doane, Mary Ann. *The Desire to Desire: The Woman's Film of the 1940s*. Bloomington: Indiana University Press, 1987.

——. *The Emergence of Cinematic Time: Modernity, Contingency, the Archive*. Cambridge, Mass.: Harvard University Press, 2002.

Du Bois, W. E. B. "Sociology Hesitant." (1905). *boundary 2* 27, no. 3 (2000): 37–44.

Dworkin, Andrea. *Intercourse*. New York: Free Press, 1997.

Dyer, Richard. *Heavenly Bodies: Film Stars and Society*. New York: St. Martin's, 1986.

Ebert, Teresa. *Ludic Feminism and After: Postmodernism, Labor, and Desire in Late Capitalism*. Ann Arbor: University of Michigan Press, 1996.

Echols, Alice. *Daring to Be Bad: Radical Feminism in America, 1967–1975*. Minneapolis: University of Minnesota Press, 1989.

Edelman, Lee. *No Future: Queer Theory and the Death Drive*. Durham, N.C.: Duke University Press, 2004.

Elliott, Jane. *Popular Feminist Fiction as American Allegory: Representing National Time*. Basingstoke, UK: Palgrave, 2008.

Elsaesser, Thomas. "Tales of Sound and Fury: Observations on the Family Melodrama." *Home Is Where the Heart Is: Studies in Melodrama and the Woman's Film*, ed. Christine Gledhill, 43–69. London: British Film Institute, 1987.

Eng, David, and David Kazanjian, eds. *Loss: The Politics of Mourning*. Berkeley: University of California Press, 2003.

Engels, Friedrich. "Socialism: Utopian and Scientific." (1880). *The Marx/Engels Reader*, 2nd ed., ed. Robert C. Tucker, 683–717. New York: Norton, 1978.

Faderman, Lillian. *Odd Girls and Twilight Lovers: A History of Lesbian Life in Twentieth-Century America*. New York: Columbia University Press, 1991.

Faulkner, William. *Absalom, Absalom!* (1936). New York: Modern Library, 1993.

Felski, Rita. *Doing Time: Feminist Theory and Postmodern Culture*. New York: New York University Press, 2000.

——. "Nothing to Declare: Identity, Shame, and the Lower Middle Class." PMLA 115, no. 1 (January 2000): 33–45.

Ferguson, Frances. "Sade and the Pornographic Legacy." *Representations* 36 (1991): 1–21.

Ferguson, Margaret, ed. *Feminism in Time*. Special issue of *Modern Language Quarterly* 65, no.1 (2004).

Ferguson, Roderick A. *Aberrations in Black: Toward a Queer of Color Critique*. Minneapolis: University of Minnesota Press, 2003.

Firestone, Shulamith. *The Dialectic of Sex: The Case for Feminist Revolution*. New York: Morrow, 1970.

Fleissner, Jennifer. *Women, Compulsion, Modernity: The Moment of American Naturalism*. Chicago: University of Chicago Press, 2004.

Fletcher, Angus. *Allegory: The Theory of a Symbolic Mode*. Ithaca, N.Y.: Cornell University Press, 1964.

Floyd, Kevin. "Making History: Marxism, Queer Theory, and Contradiction in the Future of American Studies." *Cultural Critique* 40 (1998): 167–201.

Foucault, Michel. "The Life of Infamous Men." *Michel Foucault: Power, Truth, Strategy*, ed. Meaghan Morris and Paul Patton, 76–91. Amherst, N.Y.: Prometheus Books, 1979.

Fradenburg, Louise (now L. O. Aranye). *Sacrifice Your Love: Psychoanalysis, Historicism, Chaucer*. Minneapolis: University of Minnesota Press, 2002.

Fradenburg, Louise (now L. O. Aranye), and Carla Freccero. "The Pleasures of History." *GLQ* 1, no. 4 (1995): 371–84.

Fradenburg, Louise (now L. O. Aranye), and Carla Freccero, eds. *Premodern Sexualities*. New York: Routledge, 1996.

Frank, Adam, and Eve Kosofsky Sedgwick. "Shame in the Cybernetic Fold: Reading Silvan Tompkins." *Critical Inquiry* 21, no. 2 (1995): 496–522.

Freccero, Carla. *Queer/Early/Modern*. Durham, N.C.: Duke University Press, 2006.

Freeman, Elizabeth. "Queer Belongings: Kinship Theory and Queer Theory." *A Companion to Lesbian, Gay, Bisexual, and Transgender Studies*, ed. George Haggerty and Molly McGarry, 295–314. Malden, Mass.: Blackwell Press, 2007.

——, ed. *Queer Temporalities*. Special issue of *GLQ* 13, no. 2–3 (2007).

——. *The Wedding Complex: Forms of Belonging in Modern American Culture*. Durham, N.C.: Duke University Press, 2002.

Freud, Sigmund. *The Ego and the Id*. Trans. Joan Riviere and ed. James Strachey. New York: W. W. Norton, 1962.

——. "On Narcissism: An Introduction." (1914). Trans. Cecil M. Baines. *General Psychological Theory*, intro. Philip Rieff, 56–82. New York: Macmillan, 1963.

——. "Remembering, Repeating, and Working-Through." (1914). *The Standard Edition of the Complete Psychological Works of Sigmund Freud*, trans. and ed. James Strachey, 147–56. London: Hogarth Press and the Institute of Psycho-Analysis, 1958.

——. *Three Essays on the Theory of Sexuality*. Trans. and ed. James Strachey. New York: Basic Books, 1975.

Garrison, Ednie Kaeh. "U.S. Feminism—Grrrl Style! Youth (Sub)Cultures and the Technologics of the Third Wave." *Feminist Studies* 26, no. 1 (spring 2000): 141–70.

Gilligan, Carol. *In a Different Voice: Psychological Theory and Women's Development.* Cambridge, Mass.: Harvard University Press, 1982.

Gillis, John. "Making Time for Family: The Invention of Family Time(s) and the Reinvention of Family History." *Journal of Family History* 21, no. 1 (January 1996): 4–21.

———. "Ritualization of Middle Class Life in Nineteenth Century Britain." *International Journal of Politics, Culture, and Society* 3, no. 2 (1989): 213–36.

Girard, René. *Violence and the Sacred.* Trans. Patrick Gregory. London: Continuum International Publishing Group, 2005.

Goode, Mike. "Dryasdust Antiquarianism and Soppy Masculinity: The Waverley Novels and the Gender of History." *Representations* 82 (spring 2003): 52–86.

———. *Sentimental Masculinity and the Rise of History, 1790–1890.* Cambridge: Cambridge University Press, 2009.

Gordon, Angus. "Turning Back: Adolescence, Narrative, and Queer Theory." *GLQ* 5, no. 1 (1999): 1–24.

Gordon, Avery. *Ghostly Matters: Haunting and the Sociological Imagination.* Minneapolis: University of Minnesota Press, 2007.

Gorfinkel, Elena. "The Future of Anachronism: Todd Haynes and the Magnificent Ambersons." *Cinephilia: Movies, Love and Memory*, ed. Marijke de Valck and Malte Hagener, 153–67. Amsterdam: Amsterdam University Press, 2005.

Graves, Robert. "It's a Queer Time." (1915). Typescript at the University of Oxford First World War Poetry Digital Archive, http://www.oucs.ox.ac.uk/ww1lit/collections/document/1125/1097?REC=1#page-image. Also published in *Modern British Poetry*, ed. Louis Untermyer, 226–27. New York: Harcourt Brace, 1920.

Grosz, Elizabeth. *The Nick of Time: Politics, Evolution, and the Untimely.* Durham, N.C.: Duke University Press, 2004.

———. *Space, Time, and Perversion: Essays on the Politics of Bodies.* New York: Routledge, 1995.

———. *Time Travels: Feminism, Nature, Power.* Durham, N.C.: Duke University Press, 2005.

Habermas, Jürgen. *The Structural Transformation of the Public Sphere.* Trans. Thomas Burger. Cambridge, Mass.: MIT Press, 1991.

Halberstam, Judith. "Forgetting Family: Queer Alternatives to Oedipal Relations." *A Companion to Lesbian, Gay, Bisexual, Transgender, and Queer Studies*, ed. George Haggerty and Molly McGarry, 315–24. Malden, Mass.: Blackwell, 2007.

———. *In a Queer Time and Place: Transgender Bodies, Subcultural Lives.* New York: New York University Press, 2005.

———. *Skin Shows: Gothic Horror and the Technology of Monsters*. Durham, N.C.: Duke University Press, 1995.

Hall, Radclyffe. "Miss Ogilvy Finds Herself." (1934). *Women, Men, and the Great War: An Anthology of Stories*, ed. T. Tate, 127–35. Manchester and New York: Manchester University Press, 1995.

Hanna, Kathleen. "Gen X Survivor: From Riot Grrrl Rock Star to Feminist Artist." *Sisterhood Is Forever: The Women's Anthology for a New Millennium*, ed. Robin Morgan, 131–37. New York: Washington Square Press, 2003.

Hareven, Tamara K. *Family Time and Industrial Time: The Relationship between the Family and Work in a New England Industrial Community*. New York: Cambridge University Press, 1982.

Harris, Bertha. "Introduction to *Lover*." *Lover* (1976), xvii–lxxviii. New York: New York University Press, 1993.

———. *Lover*. First ed. Plainfield, Vt: Daughters, Inc., 1976.

Harris, Geraldine. *Staging Femininities: Performance and Performativity*. New York: Manchester University Press, 1999.

Hart, Lynda. *Between the Body and the Flesh: Performing Sadomasochism*. New York: Columbia University Press, 1998.

Hartman, Sadiya V. *Scenes of Subjection: Terror, Self-Making, and Slavery in Nineteenth-Century America*. New York: Oxford University Press, 1997.

Hebdidge, Dick. *Subculture: The Meaning of Style*. New York: Routledge, 1981.

Hegel, G. W. F. "Preface." *Elements of the Philosophy of Right* (1820), trans. H. B. Nisbet, 9–23. New York: Cambridge University Press, 1991.

Heller, Dana. "The Anxieties of Affluence: Movements, Markets, and Lesbian Feminist Generation(s)." *Generations: Academic Feminists in Dialogue*, ed. Devoney Looser and E. Ann Kaplan, 309–26. Minneapolis: University of Minnesota Press, 1997.

Hénaff, Marcel. *Sade: The Invention of the Libertine Body*. Trans. Xavier Callahan. Minneapolis: University of Minnesota Press, 1999.

Hendricks, Wanda A. *Gender, Race, and Politics in the Midwest: Black Club Women in Illinois*. Bloomington: Indiana University Press, 1998.

Hennessy, Rosemary. "Queer Theory, Left Politics." *Rethinking Marxism* 7 (spring 1995): 85–111.

Hilderbrand, Lucas. "Retroactivism." GLQ 12, no. 2 (spring 2006): 303–17.

Hirsch, Marianne. *Family Frames: Photography, Narrative, and Postmemory*. Cambridge, Mass.: Harvard University Press, 1997.

Holland, Sharon. *Raising the Dead: Readings of Death and (Black) Subjectivity*. Durham, N.C.: Duke University Press, 2000.

Howard, John. *Men Like That: Southern Queer History*. Chicago: University of Chicago Press, 1999.

Howard, June. *Publishing the Family*. Durham, N.C.: Duke University Press, 2001.

Hunt, John. "A Thing of Nothing: The Catastrophic Body in Hamlet." *Shakespeare Quarterly* 39, no. 1 (1988): 27–44.

Irigaray, Luce. "Questions to Emmanuel Levinas." *The Irigaray Reader*, ed. Margaret Whitford, 178–89. New York: Blackwell, 1991.

———. "Sexual Difference." *An Ethics of Sexual Difference*, 5–19. Ithaca, N.Y.: Cornell University Press, 1993.

Ivy, Marilyn. "Have You Seen Me? Recovering the Inner Child in Late Twentieth-Century America." *Childhood and the Politics of Culture*, ed. Sharon Stephens, 79–102. Princeton, N.J.: Princeton University Press, 1995.

Jackson, Shannon. *Lines of Activity: Performance, Historiography, Hull-House Domesticity*. Ann Arbor: University of Michigan Press, 2000.

Jagose, Annamarie. *Inconsequence: Lesbian Representation and the Logic of Sequence*. Ithaca, N.Y.: Cornell University Press, 2002.

James, Nick. "I Forgot to Remember to Forget." *Sight and Sound* 14, no. 5 (May 2004): 14–18.

Jameson, Fredric. "Cognitive Mapping." *Marxism and the Interpretation of Culture*, ed. Cary Nelson and Lawrence Grossberg, 347–57. Urbana-Champaign: University of Illinois Press, 1988.

———. "The End of Temporality." *Critical Inquiry* 29, no. 4 (summer 2003): 695–718.

———. "Pleasure: A Political Issue." *The Ideologies of Theory: Essays 1971–1986*, 61–74. Minneapolis: University of Minnesota Press, 1988.

———. *The Political Unconscious: Narrative as a Socially Symbolic Act*. Ithaca, N.Y.: Cornell University Press, 1981.

Johnson, Walter. "Time and Revolution in African America: Temporality and the History of Slavery." *Rethinking American History in a Global Age*, ed. Tom Bender, 148–67. Berkeley: University California Press, 2002.

Julien, Isaac. "Confessions of a Snow Queen: Notes on the Making of *The Attendant*." *Critical Quarterly* 36, no. 1 (1994): 120–26.

Kennedy, Elizabeth, and Madeline Davis. *Boots of Leather, Slippers of Gold: The History of a Lesbian Community*. New York: Routledge, 1993.

Kotz, Liz. "Inside and Out: Lesbian and Gay Experimentals." *Afterimage* 19 (December 1991): 3–4.

Krauss, Rosalind. "The Originality of the Avant-Garde: A Postmodernist Repetition." *Art after Modernism: Rethinking Representation*, ed. Brian Wallis, 13–29. New York: New Museum of Contemporary Art, 1984.

Kristeva, Julia. "Women's Time." *The Kristeva Reader*, ed. Toril Moi, 187–213. New York: Columbia University Press, 1986.

Landsberg, Alison. *Prosthetic Memory: The Transformation of American Remembrance in the Age of Mass Culture*. New York: Columbia University Press, 2004.

Landy, Marcia. "'The Dream of the Gesture': The Body of/in Todd Haynes's Films." *boundary 2* 30, no. 3 (fall 2003): 123–40.

Laplanche, Jean, and J. B. Pontalis. "Binding." *The Language of Psychoanalysis*, 50–52. New York: W. W. Norton, 1973.

———. "Deferred Action." *The Language of Psychoanalysis*, 111–14. New York: W. W. Norton, 1973.

Lentricchia, Frank, and Andrew DuBois, eds. *Close Reading: The Reader*. Durham, N.C.: Duke University Press, 2003.

Lichtman, Chelsey. "Deeply Lez: Allyson Mitchell." Interview. *Trade* 5 (winter 2004): 21–23.

Lochrie, Karma. "Mystical Acts, Queer Tendencies." *Constructing Medieval Sexuality*, ed. Peggy McCracken, Karma Lochrie, and James A. Schultz, 180–200. Minneapolis: University of Minnesota Press, 1997.

Lorde, Audre. "The Uses of the Erotic." *The Lesbian and Gay Studies Reader*, ed. Henry Abelove, Michèle Aina Barale, and David Halperin, 339–43. New York: Routledge, 1994.

Love, Heather. *Feeling Backward: Loss and the Politics of Queer History*. Cambridge, Mass.: Harvard University Press, 2007.

———. "'Spoiled Identity': Stephen Gordon's Loneliness and the Difficulties of Queer History." *GLQ* 7, no. 4 (2001): 487–519.

Lucey, Michael, and Didier Eribon. *Insult and the Making of the Gay Self*. Durham, N.C.: Duke University Press, 2004.

Luciano, Dana. *Arranging Grief: Sacred Time and the Body in Nineteenth-Century America*. New York: New York University Press, 2007.

———. "Coming Around Again: The Queer Momentum of *Far from Heaven*." *GLQ* 13, no. 2–3 (2007): 249–72.

Lyotard, Jean-François. *The Differend: Phrases in Dispute*. Trans. Georges van den Abbeele. Minneapolis: University of Minnesota Press, 1988.

Mackinnon, Catharine. *Feminism Unmodified: Discourses on Life and Law*. Cambridge, Mass.: Harvard University Press, 1988.

Mansbridge, Jane J. *Why We Lost the E.R.A.* Chicago: University of Chicago Press, 1986.

Marks, Laura. *The Skin of the Film: Intercultural Cinema, Embodiment, and the Senses*. Durham, N.C.: Duke University Press, 2000.

Martin, Biddy. "Extraordinary Homosexuals and the Fear of Being Ordinary." *Feminism Played Straight: The Significance of Being Lesbian*, 45–70. New York: Routledge, 1997.

Marx, Karl. *Capital, Volume One*. *The Marx-Engels Reader*, ed. Robert C. Tucker, 294–442. New York: W. W. Norton, 1978.

Mauss, Marcel. "Body Techniques." *Sociology and Psychology: Essays*, trans. Ben Brewster, 97–123. London: Routledge and Kegan Paul, 1979.

McClintock, Anne. *Imperial Leather: Race, Gender, and Sexuality in the Colonial Contest*. New York: Routledge, 1995.

McGarry, Molly. *Ghosts of Futures Past: Spiritualism and the Cultural Politics of Nineteenth-Century America*. Berkeley: University of California Press, 2007.

McKay, Sally. "Allyson Mitchell: *The Fluff Stands Alone*." Review. *Canadian Art* 21, no. 2 (summer 2004): 47–49.

Mercer, Kobena. "Imaging the Black Man's Sex." *Photography/Politics: Two*, ed. Pat Holland, Jo Spence, and Simon Watney, 61–69. London: Comedia, 1986.

——. "Skin Head Sex Thing: Racial Difference and the Homoerotic Imaginary." *How Do I Look: Queer Film and Video*, ed. Bad Object-Choices, 169–210. Seattle: Bay Press, 1991.

Miriam, Kathy. "From Rage to All the Rage: Lesbian-Feminism, Sadomasochism, and the Politics of Memory." *Unleashing Feminism: Critiquing Lesbian Sadomasochism in the Gay Nineties*, ed. Irene Reti, 7–70. Santa Cruz: Herbooks, 1993.

Moon, Michael, and Eve Kosofsky Sedgwick. "Divinity: A Dossier, a Performance Piece, a Little-Understood Emotion." Sedgwick, *Tendencies*, 211–45. Durham, N.C.: Duke University Press, 1992.

Moraga, Cherríe. *Giving up the Ghost: Teatro in Two Acts*. New York: West End Press, 1986.

——. *Loving in the War Years: Lo Que Nunca Pasó Por Sus Labios*. Boston: South End Press, 1983.

Moraga, Cherríe, and Gloria Anzaldúa, eds. *This Bridge Called My Back*. New York: Kitchen Table/Women of Color Press, 1983.

Moraga, Cherríe, and Amber Hollibaugh. "What We're Rollin' around in Bed With: Sexual Silences in Feminism." *Powers of Desire: The Politics of Sexuality*, ed. Ann Snitow, Christine Stansell, and Sharon Thompson, 440–59. New York: Monthly Review Press, 1983.

Morrison, Paul. "End Pleasure." *GLQ* 1, no. 1 (1993): 53–78.

Morrison, Toni. *Love*. New York: Alfred A. Knopf, 2003.

Morton, Donald. "Changing the Terms: (Virtual) Desire and (Actual) Reality." *The Material Queer: A Lesbigay Cultural Studies Reader*, ed. Donald Morton, 1–33. Boulder, Colo.: Westview, 1996.

——. "Pataphysics of the Closet: Spectral Queer Theory as the Art of Imaginary Solutions for Unimaginary Problems." *Marxism, Queer Theory, Gender*, ed. Donald Morton, Dana L. Cloud, Bob Nowlan, Jennifer Cotter, Huei-ju Wang, Rob Wilkie, and Teresa L. Ebert, 1–70. Syracuse, N.Y.: Red Factory, 2001.

Muñoz, José Esteban. *Cruising Utopia: The Politics and Performance of Queer Futurity*. New York: New York University Press, 2009.

——. "Dead White: Notes on the Whiteness of the New Queer Cinema." *GLQ* 4, no. 1 (1998): 127–38.

——. *Disidentifications: Queers of Color and the Performance of Politics*. Minneapolis: University of Minnesota Press, 1999.

Nealon, Christopher. *Foundlings: Lesbian and Gay Historical Emotion before Stonewall*. Durham, N.C.: Duke University Press, 2001.

Negri, Antonio. *Marx beyond Marx: Lessons on the Grundrisse*. New York: Autonomedia, 1989.

Negrón-Muntaner, Frances. "Racing *The Sticky Fingers of Time*." *GLQ* 5, no. 3 (1999): 425–35.

Nicolson, Nigel. *Portrait of a Marriage: Vita Sackville-West and Harold Nicolson.* New York: Atheneum, 1973.

Nietzsche, Friedrich. *On the Advantage and Disadvantage of History for Life.* Trans. Peter Prauss. Indianapolis: Hackett, 1980.

Nissenbaum, Stephen. *The Battle for Christmas: A Cultural History of America's Most Cherished Holiday.* New York: Random House, 1996.

Nora, Pierre. "Between Memory and History: Les Lieux de Mémoire." *Memory and Counter-Memory.* Special issue of *Representations* 26 (spring 1989): 7–24.

Nugent, Richard Bruce. "Smoke, Lillies, and Jade." (1926). *Gay Rebel of the Harlem Renaissance: Selections from the Work of Richard Bruce Nugent,* ed. Thomas Wirth, 75–87. Durham, N.C.: Duke University Press, 2002.

Nussbaum, Martha. "The Professor of Parody: The Hip Defeatism of Judith Butler." Review. *New Republic,* February 22, 1999, 37–45.

O'Malley, Michael. *Keeping Watch: A History of American Time.* Washington, D.C.: Smithsonian Institution Press, 1996.

O'Neill, Edward. "Traumatic Postmodern Histories: Velvet Goldmine's Phantasmatic Testimonies." *Camera Obscura* 19, no. 3 (2004): 156–85.

Orgeron, Devin. "Re-Membering History in Isaac Julien's *The Attendant.*" *Film Quarterly* 53, no. 4 (2000): 32–40.

Osborne, Peter. *The Politics of Time.* New York: Verso, 1995.

Patel, Geeta. "Ghostly Appearances: Time Tales Tallied Up." *Social Text* 64 (2000): 47–66.

Pellegrini, Ann. "Touching the Past; or, Hanging Chad." *Journal of the History of Sexuality* 10, no. 2 (2001): 185–94.

Pendleton, David. "Out of the Ghetto: Queerness, Homosexual Desire and the Time-Image." *Strategies* 14, no. 1 (2001): 47–62.

Pinnock, Andrew. "'Unscarr'd by turning times'?: The Dating of Purcell's *Dido and Aeneas.*" *Early Music* 20, no. 3 (1992): 373–90.

Povinelli, Elizabeth. "Notes on Gridlock: Genealogy, Intimacy, Sexuality." *Public Culture* 14, no. 1 (2002): 215–38.

Price, Curtis. "*Dido and Aeneas* in Context." *Dido and Aeneas: An Opera,* ed. Curtis Price, 3–41. New York: W. W. Norton, 1986.

Probyn, Elspeth. "Suspended Beginnings: Of Childhood and Nostalgia." *Outside Belongings: Disciplines, Nations, and the Place of Sex,* 93–123. New York: Routledge, 1996.

Rambuss, Richard. *Closet Devotions.* Durham, N.C.: Duke University Press, 1998.

Ransom, John Crowe. *The New Criticism.* Norfolk, Conn.: New Directions, 1941.

Reckitt, Helena. "My Fuzzy Valentine: Allyson Mitchell." Online at http://www.allysonmitchell.com. Also published in *C Magazine* 89 (spring 2006).

Reese, A. L. "Siting the Avant-Garde." *A History of Experimental Film and Video,* 1–14. London: British Film Institute, 1999.

Renan, Ernest. "What Is a Nation?" *Becoming National,* ed. Geoff Eley and Ronald Grigor Suny, 42–55. New York: Oxford University Press, 1996.

Reti, Irene. "Remember the Fire: Lesbian Sadomasochism in a Post Nazi Holocaust World." *Unleashing Feminism: Critiquing Lesbian Sadomasochism in the Gay Nineties*, ed. Irene Reti, 79–97. Santa Cruz: Herbooks, 1993.

Ricco, John. *The Logic of the Lure*. Chicago: University of Chicago Press, 2002.

Rich, B. Ruby. *Chick Flicks: Theories and Memories of the Feminist Film Movement*. Durham, N.C.: Duke University Press, 1998.

Richter, Gerhardt. *Walter Benjamin and the Corpus of Autobiography*. Detroit: Wayne State University Press, 2000.

Roach, Joseph. *Cities of the Dead: Circumatlantic Performance*. New York: Columbia University Press, 1996.

Robinson, Amy. "It Takes One to Know One: Passing and Communities of Common Interest." *Critical Inquiry* 20, no. 4 (1994): 715–36.

Rohy, Valerie. "Ahistorical." *GLQ* 12, no. 1 (2006): 61–83.

Roof, Judith. "Generational Difficulties; or, The Fear of a Barren History." *Generations: Academic Feminists in Dialogue*, ed. Devoney Looser and E. Ann Kaplan, 69–87. Minneapolis: University of Minnesota Press, 1997.

Rosen, Philip. *Change Mummified: Cinema, Historicity, Theory*. Minneapolis: University of Minnesota Press, 2001.

Rosenbaum, Jonathan. "Remaking History." Review of *Shulie*. *Chicago Reader* 20 (November 1998): 48–49.

Ross, Andrew. "The Uses of Camp." *No Respect, Intellectuals and Poplar Culture*, 135–70. New York: Routledge, 1989.

Rubin, Gayle. "Of Catamites and Kings: Reflections on Butch, Gender, and Boundaries." *The Persistent Desire: A Femme-Butch Reader*, ed. Joan Nestle, 466–82. Boston: Alyson Publications, 1992.

Russo, Vito. *The Celluloid Closet: Homosexuality in the Movies*. New York: Harper and Row, 1981.

Samois, ed. *Coming to Power: Writings and Graphics on Lesbian s/m*. Boston: Alyson Publications, 1987.

Schneider, Rebecca. "Still Living: Performance, Photography, and *Tableaux Vivants*." *Point & Shoot: Performance and Photography*, ed. France Choinière and Michéle Thériault, 61–71. Montreal: Dazibao, 2005.

Scott, Joan. "Fantasy Echo: History and the Construction of Identity." *Critical Inquiry* 27, no. 2 (January 2001): 284–304.

Sedgwick, Eve Kosofsky. *Between Men: English Literature and Male Homosocial Desire*. New York: Columbia University Press, 1985.

——. *The Coherence of Gothic Conventions*. New York: Methuen, 1976.

——. *Epistemology of the Closet*. Berkeley: University of California Press, 1990.

——. "Paranoid Reading and Reparative Reading; or, You're So Vain, You Probably Think This Introduction Is about You." *Novel Gazing: Queer Readings in Fiction*, ed. Eve Kosofsky Sedgwick, 1–37. Durham, N.C.: Duke University Press, 1997.

———. "Queer Performativity." *GLQ* 1, no. 1 (1993): 1–16.

Shakespeare, William. *Hamlet*. Arden Shakespeare Edition, third series, ed. Neil Taylor and Ann Thompson. London: Cengage Learning EMAE, 2006.

———. *A Midsummer Night's Dream*. Arden Shakespeare Edition, ed. Harold F. Brooks. New York: Routledge, 1994.

Shelley, Mary. *Frankenstein, or, The Modern Prometheus*. (1831). New York: Modern Library, 1999.

Siegel, Lee. "The Gay Science: Queer Theory, Literature, and the Sexualization of Everything." *New Republic*, November 1998, 30–42.

Smith, Bonnie. *The Gender of History: Men, Women, and Historical Practice*. Cambridge, Mass.: Harvard University Press, 1998.

Smith, Mark M. *Mastered by the Clock: Time, Slavery, and Freedom in the American South*. Chapel Hill: University of North Carolina Press, 1997.

Smith, Shawn Michelle. *American Archives: Gender, Race, and Class in Visual Culture*. Princeton, N.J.: Princeton University Press, 1999.

Somerville, Siobhan. *Queering the Color Line: Race and the Invention of Homosexuality in American Culture*. Durham, N.C.: Duke University Press, 2000.

Spivak, Gayatri Chakravorty. "The Staging of Time in *Heremakhonon*." *Cultural Studies* 17, no. 1 (2003): 85–97.

Star, Susan Leigh. "Swastikas: The Street and the University." *Against Sadomasochism: A Radical Feminist Analysis*, ed. Darlene R. Pagano, Robin Ruth Linden, Diana E. H. Russell, and Susan Leigh Star, 131–35. San Francisco: Frog in the Well Press, 1982.

Stevens, Jacqueline. *Reproducing the State*. Princeton, N.J.: Princeton University Press, 1999.

Stockton, Kathyrn Bond. *Beautiful Bottom, Beautiful Shame: Where Black Meets Queer*. Durham, N.C.: Duke University Press, 2006.

———. "Eve's Queer Child." *Regarding Sedgwick: Essays on Queer Culture and Critical Theory*, ed. Stephen M. Barber and David L. Clark, 181–99. New York: Routledge, 2002.

———. "Growing Sideways, or Versions of the Queer Child: The Ghost, the Homosexual, the Freudian Child, the Innocent, the Interval of Animal." *Curiouser: On the Queerness of Children*, ed. Stephen Bruhm and Natasha Hurley, 277–315. Minneapolis: University of Minnesota Press, 2004.

Stone, Lawrence. *The Family, Sex, and Marriage in England, 1500–1800*. New York: Penguin, 1990.

Subrin, Elisabeth. "Trashing *Shulie*: Remnants from Some Abandoned Feminist History." *F Is for Phony: Fake Documentary and Truth's Undoing*, ed. Alexandra Juhasz and Jesse Lerner, 59–66. Minneapolis: University of Minnesota Press, 2006.

Taormino, Tristan, and Karen Green, eds. *A Girl's Guide to Taking over the World: Writings from the Girl Zine Revolution*. New York: St. Martin's Griffin, 1997.

Taussig, Michael. *Mimesis and Alterity: A Particular History of the Senses*. New York: Routledge, 1993.

Taylor, Diana. *The Archive and the Repertoire: Performing Cultural Memory in the Americas*. Durham, N.C.: Duke University Press, 2003.

Terdiman, Richard. *Present Past: Modernity and the Memory Crisis*. Ithaca, N.Y.: Cornell University Press, 1993.

Thompson, E. P. "Time, Work-Discipline, and Industrial Capitalism." *Past and Present* 38, no. 1 (December 1967): 56–97.

Thompson, Mark, ed. *Leatherfolk: Radical Sex, People, Politics, and Practice*. Boston: Alyson Publications, 1991.

Torok, Maria. "The Illness of Mourning and the Fantasy of the Exquisite Corpse." *The Shell and the Kernel: Renewals of Psychoanalysis*, vol. 1, ed. Nicholas T. Rand, 107–24. Chicago: University of Chicago Press, 1994.

Treichler, Paula. *How to Have Theory in an Epidemic: Cultural Chronicles of AIDS*. Durham, N.C.: Duke University Press, 1999.

Tuhkanen, Mikko. "Binding the Self: Baldwin, Freud, and the Narrative of Subjectivity." *GLQ* 7, no. 4 (2001): 553–91.

Tweedie, James. "The Suspended Spectacle of History: The *Tableau Vivant* in Derek Jarman's *Caravaggio*." *Screen* 44, no. 4 (winter 2003): 379–403.

Vivien, Renée. *The Muse of the Violets: Poems*. Tallahassee, Fla.: Naiad Press, 1982.

Voloshinov, V. N. *Marxism and the Philosophy of Language*. New York: Seminar Press, 1973.

Weston, Kath. *Gender in Real Time: Power and Transience in a Visual Age*. New York: Routledge, 2002.

Wiegman, Robyn. "Feminism's Apocalyptic Futures." *New Literary History* 31, no. 4 (2000): 805–25.

———. "On Being in Time with Feminism." *Modern Language Quarterly* 65, no. 1 (2004): 161–77.

Williams, Linda. *Hard Core: Power, Pleasure, and the "Frenzy of the Visible."* Expanded ed. Berkeley: University of California Press, 1999.

Williams, Raymond. "Structures of Feeling." *Marxism and Literature*, 128–35. Oxford: Oxford University Press, 1977.

Wings, Mary. "A Maverick among Mavericks: Cecilia Dougherty Brings New Form and Content to Video." *Advocate*, September 10, 1991, 82–83.

Woolf, Virginia. *Orlando: A Biography*. (1928). New York: Harcourt Brace Jovanovich, 1973.

Young, Elizabeth. *Black Frankenstein: The Making of an American Metaphor*. New York: New York University Press, 2008.

Zaretsky, Eli. *Capitalism, the Family, and Personal Life*. Rev. ed. New York: HarperCollins, 1986.

Zerubavel, Eviatar. "The French Republican Calendar: A Case Study in the Sociology of Time." *American Sociological Review* 42, no. 6 (December 1977): 868–77.

———. *Hidden Rhythms: Schedules and Calendars in Social Life*. Chicago: University of Chicago Press, 1981.

———. "The Language of Time: Toward a Semiotics of Temporality." *Sociological Quarterly* 28, no. 3 (1987): 343–56.

Žižek, Slavoj. *The Plague of Fantasies*. New York: Verso, 1997.

index

1940s, 36; Hollywood melodramas of, 31; women's films of, 40

1950s, 111–12, 123, 126–28, 130–32; girlhoods of, 81; Hollywood cinema of, 31, 39; women's films of, 40

1960s, 68, 72, 75; audio clips of, 66; detritus of, xv; feminist position of, 79; figurines of, 89; *jouissance* of, 58; Now generation of, 65; revolutions in, xiv

1970s, 128, 129–33; costumes of, 166; as embarrassment, xiv; feminism in, 59, 61, 68, 76, 79; girlchild of, 85; texts by lesbians in, xxiii; gay men in, 13

1980s, 66, 75; feminism in, 61, gay men in, 13; lesbian subcultures of, 61; movements of, xiv; projects of, xv; queer cinema in, 26; sex wars of, 145; style, 25; television shows of, 29

1990s, 66, 75, 111–12, 122, 127–28, 130; audiences of, 146; drag of, 62; lesbian filmmakers of, 31; lesbian presses of, 117; lesbian subcultures of, 61; movements of, xiv; nostalgia and, 82; queer subculture of, 24; queer cinema in, 26; queergirl and, 71; Riot Grrrl and, 72, 83; sex wars of, 145; style in, 25, 66; texts by lesbians in, xxiii; transgender movement of, 66; yoga craze of, 132

Abraham, Karl: on mania, 119

Abraham, Nicholas, and Maria Torok: incorporation, theory of, 118–19

Accent: theory of, 29–30

ACT UP, xiv, 61, 84; die-ins, 59; understanding of AIDS, xv

Activism, 67, 123; African American, 80; AIDS, xiii; feminist, 66; grassroots, xv; queer, xiv; retro, 85; street, xix; transgender, 60

Africa, 108, 158, 166

African Americans, 80, 132

Afro-futurism: theory of, 132

Agamben, Giorgio: on pleasure in relation to time, 118

AIDS: activism, xiii, xiv; deaths, xxi, 181 n. 41; epidemic, xv, 171; era before, 167; late capitalism and, 64; Memorial Names Quilt, xxi; stigmatization of, 11

Allegory, 70, 158, 167, 184 n. 21; drag and, 69. *See also* Butler, Judith; Melancholia

Alterity, 72; temporal, 16, 124. *See also* Otherness

Altman, Meryl, 59, 65

America. *See* United States

Amnesia, 51, 55; historical, 158; as trope, 50; white, xxiii

Anachronism, xi, xxii, 95, 101, 133–34;

Anachronism (*cont.*)
in art, xvii, 60–61, 79; body as, 91;
disruptive, 70–71; feminism and,
62–63; racial difference as, 80
Analog technology, 110
Anastrophe, xxii
Antiracism: accusations of, 146; causes
of, 80; movement, 84; organizing
and, 91
Anxiety of Influence, The (Bloom), 54
Ars erotica, 100, 106, 169
Art Institute of Chicago, 65, 67–68, 73
Asynchrony, xxii, 19; historical, 139
Atavism, 133; fantasies of, 86
Attendant, The (Julien), xxiii–xxiv,
137, 144–69, 171
Avant-garde, xiii, 31

Barnes, Djuna: critical response to, 38;
on Robin Vote, 7. *See also individual
works*
Barthes, Roland: on cinematography
as mimesis, 125; *jouissance*, theory of,
58
Beckett, Samuel, xix
Becoming: historical, xxi; lover, 52–
53; narratives of, xv; object, 109;
process of, 142; queer, 11, 135; of
substance, 54; tableau, 152
Beecher, Catherine: *Treatise on Domestic Economy*, 39–41
Being, 11; ahistorical, 168; alive, ix;
anachronism, 133; comes into, 78;
dead, 43, 62; forms of, xiii, 71; generational, 75; historical, xviii, xxi,
104; knowing and, 144; long, 13;
lover, 57; modern, xii; queer, xxi, 45;
question of, 74; seen, 10; in time, 76,
116; truths of, 4; victimized, 143;
ways of, 32, 44
Belated, xxi–xxii; as new now, xxiv;
lesbian feminist, quality of, 92

Belonging, xiii, 4, 18, 71; class, 30; cultural, xi; families and, 28; middle-
class, xxii; modes of, xx, 13, 172; narratives of, xv, xx; national, 6; queer
theory and, 11; structures of, xi
Beloved (Morrison), 81
Benjamin, Walter, 122, 158, 165; angel
of history, 131, 154; on Baudelaire,
123; on commodity culture, 152; on
historical materialism, 162, 192 n.
67; on homogenous time, xxii; mimesis, theory of, 124–27; optical unconscious, theory of, 114; on shock,
10; technology and, 131, 134. *See
also individual works*
Berlant, Lauren, 179 n. 5; on fat,
92–93
Bersani, Leo: on *askesis*, 45; on ego,
142; on sadomasochism, 140–41
Bhabha, Homi: distinction between
linear and cyclical time by, 6; on synchrony, 28
Biard, F. A.: *The Slave Trade, Scene on
the Coast of Africa*, 145, 148, 150–54,
156, 158, 161
Bikini Kill, 84
Binding, 7, 113, 160; cross-temporal,
49; in Freud, xvi; gaze, xviii; historiographical, 118; history, 172; to
manage excess, xvi; as rebound effect, xvi; temporal, 85, 125; theory
of, 3. *See also* Freud, Sigmund
Bisexuality, 96; identity of, xv
Blackness, 134; discourse on, 135; racialized, 80
Bloom, Harold, 54. *See also individual
works*
Body, 3; cognition and, 99; derangement of, 3; erotohistoriography and,
95; film and, 1; Frankensteinian,
134; Freudian, 8; history and, 10;
Jameson on, 11; Kristeva on, 45,

118; lesbian, 123; mother as, 46;
politic, 14; queer, 163; slave, 151;
time and 3, 14, 46
Body theory: Jameson on, 10–11
Bonder, Diane, 48; *The Physics of Love*,
xxiii, 31–34, 36–39, 41–47, 50–51,
53–55, 70, 122
Bourdieu, Pierre: on accent, 29; on
habitus, xx, 3–4, 18–19, 167
Bourgeois, xx, 42, 144; household, 43;
merchants, 90; mothers, 40
Brougher, Hillary: *The Sticky Fingers of
Time*, xxiii, 111–18, 120–24, 126,
130, 133, 162, 164
Burke, Edmund, 105–6; on sympathy
and historiography, 99, 101, 104,
109, 117
Butch/femme, 61, 120, 129; styles, 66,
130
Butler, Judith, 12, 118; on allegory, 70;
on gender performativity, 4, 62, 63;
on melancholia, xiii, 68–69; on psychic life, 64; on trauma, 11. *See also
individual works*

Camp, x, 68, 71, 133, 155; performance, 120; sensibility, 52
Capital, xvi; Firestone on, 78; logic of,
xx; secular rhythms of, 40; social relations and, 48
Capitalism, 19, 51; effect on family
economy of, xx; failure of, xvi; free-
market, 159; industrialization and, 7,
10, 39, 66, 153, 168; inevitability of,
xx; influence on cinema of, xviii; late,
63–64; multi-national, 57; temporality and, xvi, 54
Carthage, 158–59
Caruth, Cathy: on trauma, 142
Casarino, Cesare: on pleasure and desire, 55; clinamen, theory of, 53–54
Castration, 108, 113; complex, 107

Chakrabarty, Dipesh: on affective histories, xx; on analytic social norms, xix
Chicago, 66, 68; Westside group, 77
Childbirth, 49, 53; as grand narrative,
21; pain of, 115
Christianity, 36; Catholicism and, 16,
25, 37, 49; Christ and, 49, 69, 115;
Sabbath and, 39, 138; saints and, 33,
37, 39, 47, 49
Chronobiopolitics, 3–5, 10
Chrononormativity, xxii, 10, 35, 44;
class and, 39; definition of, 3; fat
and, 92
Cinema, 44, 74, 132, 149, 151; Hollywood, 1, 39; Marxist vision of, 78;
as mimetic technology, 127; as optical consciousness, 114; queer, 27,
144, 145, 150
Cinematography, 125, 127
Citizenship, 4; as modernizing narrative, xx
Class, 48, 98, 173; accent, 29, 57; binding sexuality and, 53; consciousness,
28; differences in, 46; middle, 22, 25,
51; struggle, 19; time and, 18–19;
working, 26
Climax. *See* Orgasm
Clinamen: theory of, 53–54. *See also*
Bloom, Harold; Casarino, Cesare
Close reading: as historiography, xvii;
as process, xvi–xvii. *See also* Historiography
Closet, 24
"Coal Miner's Daughter" (Lynn), 24,
28
Coal Miner's Granddaughter (Dough-
erty), xxiii, 24–29, 31–32, 38, 48, 53,
122
Consumption, 51; history of, 2; production and, 58
Corporeality. *See* Body
Counterpolitics, xi

Coupledom. *See* Couplehood

Couplehood, xv, 3, 122; white, 130

Crimp, Douglas, xiii

Critical race theory, xxiv, 140–41

Cross-dressing, 70

Culture, xi, xiv, xvi, xix, xxiii, 4, 18, 24, 29, 57, 64, 70, 83–84, 93, 104, 132, 165, 171; African, 159; Anglo-American, 90; commodity, 152; cowboy, xi; dominant, xxii, 68; feminist, 82; genocidal, 140; human, 101; logic of, xix; lesbian, 85; middle-class, 27; popular, 40, 50; queer, xiii; s/m, 139, 149; sentimental, 11, 142; of simulation, 58. *See also* Subculture

Cvetkovich, Ann: on sadomasochism, 142

Cyborg: future and, 129; reproduction, 66, 75

Daguerreotypes, 21–22

Daughters, 31, 33, 37, 38, 42–43, 45–46, 48, 50–52, 55, 106, 122; binding with mothers of, 47; erotics between, 35; lesbian, 44; wayward, xiv; 81. See also *Coal Miner's Granddaughter*

Daughters, Inc., 31, 35

de Beauvoir, Simone, 66; on sadomasochism, 138–40, 142, 149–50

de Sade, Marquis, 138, 144–45, 149, 150, 153; ekphrastic sex scenes and, 151

Decadence, 7

Deconstruction, 12, 112; politics of, xvi; as queer, xxi; queer studies and, 62; queer theory and, 9; reading practices of, xv

Deep Lez, xxiii; definition of, 85. *See also* Temporal drag

Defiguration, xxi

Degeneration, 23

Delay, 4, 161

Deleuze, Gilles, 156; on cinema, 132; on masochism, 153

Deleuze, Gilles, and Félix Guattari: on body-without-organs, 53; on minor literature, xix

D'Emilio, John, xx

Democracy: liberal, 159; socialist, 19

Depression, 24

Derangement: of bodies, 3; narratives of, 28

Derrida, Jacques, 11, 14; on diastema, 121; history and; 10; on nostalgia, xiv. *See also* Gothic; Marxism

Dery, Mark, 132

Desire, 13, 42, 52–53, 76, 82, 84, 95; homosexual, 70, 82; interracial, 146; mourning and, 119; object of, 46, 153; queer theory and, 9; race and, 167

Desocializing: as aesthetic, xviii

Deterritorialization, xii

Diachrony, xxiii

Dialectic of Sex, The (Firestone), 65–66, 73, 77–78, 82–84

Dialectics of feeling: theory of, 123, 127

Dido and Aeneas (Purcell), 157–58, 166

Difference: temporal, 38

Digital technology, 144; description of, 110

Dimock, Wai Chee, 167

Dinshaw, Carolyn, 114

"Divinity" (Moon and Sedgwick), 90–91

Doane, Mary Ann, 32; on *Life of an American Fireman*, 22; on visual technologies, 21

Domesticity, xxii, 41, 50; antebellum, 7; discourse of, 5, 39–40; domestic life, 22, 43; melodrama and, 42; middle-class, 39–40, 45

Domestic partnership: as privatized, 4

Domestic time, 40, 42, 50–51; theory of, 39, 44–45

Double, xviii, 35, 98, 103, 119, 126, 150, 153; back, 12, 114; body's, 6; exposure, 13; modernity's, 169

Double time, 7, 23

Dougherty, Cecilia, 28, 31; on her own work, 27, 32. *See also individual works*

Drag, 62, 172; allegory and, 69; culture, xi; fat, 90; gender-transitive, 63; as obstacle to progress, 64; self-presentation, xxi; Shakespearean, 14; skin, 135. *See also* Temporal drag

Drag performance, xxiii, 58, 67, 91; Judith Butler on, 62, 69

Du Bois, W. E. B.: "Sociology Hesitant," 171

Duration, 1, 124, 149, 161; structures of, xi

Dworkin, Andrea: male sexuality, theory of, 140

Dyke: fat, 91; feminist, 86; hairy, 93; working-class politics, xxiii, 22; urban, 30

Edelman, Lee, 130; on *askesis*, 45. *See also individuals works*

Ego, 8, 11, 12, 49, 58, 140; Bersani's theory of, 142

"Ego and the Id" (Freud), 12

Eighteenth century: Burkean ideal of, 109; erotic life and, 8; historiography and, 116–17; secular time and, 189 n. 6

Eliot, T. S.: on sexual alienation, 7

Elsassaer, Thomas: on still life, 40, 42

Embodiment, 3, 4, 12, 24, 99; history and, 103, 134; male, 74; modes of, 91; new forms of, 46; queer, 65; split, 45; transgender, 91

Empire, 158–59; British, 169. *See also* Imperialism

Engels, Friedrich, 76–77

England: church of, 16; Elizabethan, 107; first bill of rights of, 159; slavery and, 166

Epistolarity, 96–97

ERA (Equal Rights Amendment), 59–61, 68, 72, 79, 184 n. 3

Eroticism, 66, 117, 127, 140, 148, 150, 160; anal, 50; history and, 141; homo-, 27, 137; interracial, 165; as queer, 143–45

Erotohistoriography, 105, 132, 135, 163; *Frankenstein* and, 96; lesbian, 110; noir, 131; *Orlando* and, 109–10; theory of, xxiii, 95, 120; tools and, 134. See also *Frankenstein*

Essentialism, 39, 44, 49

Eternity, 5, 43, 70; secularized, 42. *See also*; Temporality; Time

Ethnicities: African American, 80, 113, 129–30, 132, 164–65; Anglo-American, 22, 90, 99; Asian, 131; Jewish, 67, 143; Native American, 131. *See also* Race

Fabulous, xxi–xxii

Familial arrhythmia, 22–21, 44, 53

Family, xv, xxii, 7, 22, 24–25, 27, 29, 30, 32–33, 36, 48, 128, 150, 173; categories of, 52; circle, 53; economy, xx; generation and, 64–65; *Frankenstein* and, 96–97, 99, 114; heritage, 160; as heteronormative, 28, 50; period and, 21; photography, 49, 56; portraits of, 23; ritualization of, 39, 42; s/m and, 143; status of, 45; temporality of, 31, 37, 40, 51; women's rights movement and, 79

Family time. *See* Domestic Time

Fantasy, 82; of immediacy, 172; political, 65; queer theory and, 9; racial, 86–87; rebound into, xxi; s/m, 79, 160; time of, x

Fat aesthetic, 93, 119; in work of James Joyce, xix

Fatness, 90–91; feminism and, xi, 89; theory of, 92

Femininity, 4, 63, 105; middle-class, 39; nonhegemonic, 81; outmoded, xxiii; symbol and, 69–70

Feminism, 59, 66, 70, 79, 83, 84–85, 143; art history and, 74; black, 130; discarded, 86; equality and, 60; generational model and, 64–65; history of, 79; lesbian, 32, 61–62, 76, 91–92, 140; as movement, xiv; radical, 65, 68, 72, 76, 81; of waves, xiv, xxiii, 75, 79, 141; white, 80, 91; women of color and, xiv

Feminist theory, 11, 76, 89

Ferguson, Roderick A.: on queer-of-color critique, 191 n. 67

Fetish, 8–9, 76, 147, 155; belief, 14; childhood and, 84; clothing, 163; of color, 165; commodity, 63, 151; word, 119

Film, xiv, xvii, 31, 38, 48; *The Attendant* and, 137, 144–52, 154–59, 162–69; Benjamin on, 124; *Coal Miner's Granddaughter* and, 27–28; experimental, xi, 2, 13; history and, xviii; lesbian-feminist, 76; mimesis and, 127; noir, 122; *The Physics of Love* and, 32–34, 43, 50–51, 54–55; properties of, 32; *Shulie* and, 65–68, 74, 76–77, 79, 80; *The Sticky Fingers of Time* and, 110, 112–17, 121–23, 126, 128–34; technology and, 22–23; time and, 1, 21, 24, 38, 124; women's, 40–41

Firestone, Shulamith, 86; allegiance to dialectical materialism of, 77–78; on children, 81–82; on cyborg reproduction, 75; feminism, theory of, 74, 79; life of, 65, 184 n. 14; *Shulie* and, 65–66, 68, 71–72, 74, 76

First World War, x; modernity and, xii

Fisting, 114, 172

Foreplay, xxii, 2; Henry Abelove and Paul Morrison on, 8

Foucault, Michel, xii, 100, 103; on *ars erotica*, 169; discourse and, xix, 8

Frankenstein (Shelley), xvii, xxiii, 95–105, 108, 114, 117, 120, 132, 134–35, 165, 187 n. 15. *See also* Shelley, Mary

Freccero, Carla, 108–9, 147

French Revolution, xii, 138, 145, 153, 189 n. 6

Freud, Sigmund, 107, 114, 118, 120, 122, 140; on binding, xvi; melancholia, theory of, 119; *Nachträglichkeit*, theory of, 64; perversion, definition of, 160–161; repetition in, 22–23; on trauma, 11–12; unconscious, theory of, 7–8. *See also individual works*

Futurity, 123; concept of, 11; melancholic, 120; view of, xv

Gay. *See* Queer

Gays, xx; violence against, 11

Gaze, 46, 74, 146, 156; binding, xviii; of cinematic spectator, 151; of queer archivalist, 19

Gender Trouble (Butler), 62

Gender, 70, 74–75, 78, 83, 98, 173; constructedness of, 106, 112, as historically contingent, 108. *See also* Butler, Judith

Ghosts, 15 10, 98; of chattel slavery, 139; stories about, 96. *See also* Gothic

Gillis, John: ritualization of family life, 39–40

Giving Up the Ghost (Moraga), xiii

Goode, Mike: on Burkean historicism, 102; on gothic, 98; on history as crisis of masculinity; 99–101; on Paineite subject, 103; on sentimental history, 187 n. 8

Gordon, Avery: ghosts, theory of, 98

Gothic, 82, 104, 117, 186 n. 46; theory of, 97–98

Graves, Robert: "It's a Queer Time," ix–xii, xx

Guerilla Girls, xiv, xv

Habermas, Jürgen: on epistolary conventions, 97. *See also* Epistolarity

Habitus, 32, 39, 65, 71, 191 n. 62; ancestral, 154; class and, 44, 137; definition of, 3; normative, 52; rhythm and, 167

Halberstam, Judith: critical response to *Frankenstein* of, 96; on temporal binding, 85–86

Hamlet (Shakespeare), 14–16, 43, 69, 126

Harris, Bertha, 58; critical response to, 32; life of, 52; on *Lover*, 31. *See also individual works*

Hart, Lynda: sadomasochism, theory of, 142, 147, 152

Hartman, Saidiya, 137, 144, 162

Hauntology, 166; Derridean, 162; erotics of, 14; hauntological call to action, 61

Hayes, Sharon, 66, 84, 93, 119, 129. *See also individual works*

Hegel, G. W. F.: master/slave dialectic, theory of, 152

Hénaff, Marcel: Sadean tableaux, 150–53

Hermeneutics, xix

Heterogendered, 25, 39, 44, 47

Heteronormativity, xxiii, 35, 49, 56, 58; reading, 115; timings, 45–46

Heterosexist, 44, 54, 150

Heterosexuality, xx, 115, 128, 192 n. 67; bodily potentiality and, 19; genital, 8

Heterotemporality, 28

Higgins, William: as director, 2, 181 n. 41

Hilderbrand, Lucas: retroactivism, theory of, 85

Hirsch, Marianne: on photography, 22, 39

Historical consciousness, 99, 117, 120, 144, 147

Historical dissidence, 14

Historical materialism, 12, 118, 162, 192 n. 67

Historicism, 141, 162–63; affective, 102

Historicity, 115; of bodily response, 141; photographic media and, xviii

Historiography, xxiii, 11, 27, 107, 161; affective, 104; binding and, 118; bottom, xxiv, 120; close reading and, xvii; corporealized, 117; film and, 124; haptic, 123; intervention on, xvii; mimetic, 127; modes of, 115; performance, 86; queer, 92–93, 95, 164; Romantic, 103; s/m as device for, xxiii; sex as, 139

"History 2" (Chakrabarty), xx

History of the Kings of Britain (Monmouth), 158

History, x–xii, xv–xvi, xx–xxi, 9, 24, 27, 43, 50, 57–58, 65, 70, 84, 95–98, 123–25, 136, 138; activist, 81; African, 159; African American, 80; *The Attendant* and, 149–51, 163, 165–66; Benjamin on, 155, 162; body as, 107; border as, xiii; *clinamen* and, 54; consciousness and, 117; of consumption, 2; crisis of masculinity and, 100; digital, 110; discourse of, 93; Engels on, 77; English, 14, 102, 106, 158; eroticism and, 141; European, 159; of feminism, 64, 66–68, 74, 79, 86, 89, 91; filmmaking as, xvii–xviii; *Frankenstein* and, 101,

History (*cont.*)
103–5; gay, 122; *Hamlet* and, 15–16; heterosexist, 44; HUAC and, 60; hurt as, 10, 55; of industrialization, 154; lesbian, 122, 131; linear, 40, 139; Marxist, 28, 53, 78; mimesis and, 126–27; national, 115; *Orlando* and, 106, 108; political, 63; queer and, 21, 27, 32, 109, 169; S/M and, 141–44, 153, 161, 168; as signifier, 62; of slavery, 81; social, 26; *The Sticky Fingers of Time* and, 115–18, 134; time and, xxii, 6–7, 23, 46, 133; trope for, 121; unconscious and, 140; working-class, 30; writing, 139

HIV: deaths from complications of, xxi, 181 n. 41; drugs for, xv

Hollywood, xvii, 1, 26, 32, 39; melodrama, 31, 42; women's films, 40

Holocaust, 140, 143, 160

Homoerotic, xxiv, 27, 135, 166; bibliomania, 100

Homogenous time, xxii, 22, 51. *See also* Benjamin, Walter

Homophobia, ix

Homosexuality. *See* Queerness

Homosexuals. *See* Gays; Lesbians; Queers

Homosocial, x–xii, 82, 115

Hunt, John: on *Hamlet*, 15

Hypotaxis: Deleuze and Guattari on, xix

"I am Woman [Hear Me Roar]" (Reddy), 86

Identity, xxii, 7, 49, 64, 84, 95; constructed, 27; femme, 70; gender, 69; as girl, 82; lesbian, 25; queer, 179 n. 5; sexual, 27

Ideology: carnal aspect of, 172; demystifying, xix; of familial history, 32; of normative domesticity, 40; revolutionary, 155. *See also* Marxism

"Illness of Mourning and the Fantasy of the Exquisite Corpse, The" (Torok), 119

"Imitation and Gender Subordination" (Butler), 68

Imperialism: British, 166; histories of, 138. *See also* Empire

Incest: sadomasochism and, 142–43

Incorporation, 70; Abraham's and Torok's theory of, 118–19; Carla Freccero on, 108–9; Maria Torok on, 120–21, 125; as queer, 119

Industrialization, 6, 11, 48; history of, 154; United States and, 5, 7. *See also* Capitalism

Inheritance, 5, 27, 64; genetic, 49; junk, xxii–xxiii, 21, 47, 52; Marquis de Sade and, 158; revolution as, 84; troped as rhythm and sequence, 44

In the Near Future (Hayes), 59–61, 67–68, 72, 79, 128

Installations, xvii–xviii, xxiii, 86–87, 89, 138

Intimacy, xxii, 23, 40, 96; familial, 30–33, 44; synchronous, 47

Introjection: Maria Torok on, 119, 125; theory of, 118

Irigaray, Luce: on bodily pleasure and temporality, 49–50; of *poesis*, 54; theory of time, 49

"It's a Queer Time" (Graves), ix, xxi

"It's a queer time": as refrain, ix–xi, xiii, xvii

Jagose, Annamarie, 120, 178 n. 38, 182 n. 13

James, Henry, 82

Jameson, Fredric: on cognitive mapping, 144; on culture of simulation 58; on modernity, 10, 57–58; on queer theory, 11

Johnson, Walter: on resynchronization and slavery, 153

Jouissance, 58, 104, 120

Joyce, James, xix

Julien, Isaac, 138, 147, 150, 161–62, 164; critical response to, 145. *See also individual works*

Kinship, 14, 18, 49, 96; anthropology on, 37; biological, 58; corporeal, 116; heteronormative, 28

Kinship diagram, 37–38, 53, 57. *See also* Belonging; Family

K.I.P. (Nguyen), 1, 64, 181 n. 41; alternative to reprofuturity of, 19, 21; close reading of, 1–2; as hauntology, 13–14; as Shakespearean referent, 16–18

Kip Noll, Superstar (Higgins), 2, 13, 43

Kristeva, Julia, 49; on *askesis*, 45; on body, 46, 118; on cyclical time, 5–6, 38; on "women's time," 6, 44. *See also individual works*

Kruger, Barbara, 72–73

Labor, 6, 18, 24, 39, 41, 51, 54, 159; abstract, xx, activist, 63; black, 154; body and, xxiii; domestic, 149; exploitation of, 153; forms of, 138; gendered, 78; histories of, 138; household, 48; industrial, 44; movement, 60; power, 19; servant, 40; time and, xviii

Lacan, Jacques, xxi, 122, 140; future interior and, 142

Landsberg, Alison: prosthetic memory, 159–60

Law, 5, 138, 171; ERA and, 60; kinship under, 18; Newtonian, 32, 52

Lesbian-feminism, 61–62, 81, 91; belated quality of, 92; film, 76; middle-class ideal and, 32; s/m and, 140; theoretical move, 143. *See also* Feminism

Lesbianism, 35, 38, 44, 57, 62, 122, 126; black, 130

Lesbians, 27; accent, 30; activism, 60; culture, 85; ego of, 12, feminist, 62, 76; history and, x, xii, 32, 122; identity of, mainstreamed, xv; middle-class, 32; sex and, 111, 113, 126, 182 n. 13, 187 n. 23; style, 25, 66; violence against, 11

Levine, Sherry, 72–73

Libido, 121; Freud on, 12, 140; Maria Torok on, 119

Live performance, xix, 44

Lochrie, Karma: female saints, theory of, 49

Looking for Langston (Muñoz), 147

Lorde, Audre: "The Uses of the Erotic," 53

Lover (Harris), xvii, xxiii, 31–32, 35–39, 41–46, 48–49, 52–53, 56–58, 70

Luciano, Dana, 7, 10; on chronobiopolitics, 3–4, 6; sentimental culture, 142; on separate spheres, 5

Lynn, Loretta: "Coal Miner's Daughter," 24, 27

Lyotard, Jean-Francois: on the *differend*, 10

MacKinnon, Catherine: male sexuality, theory of, 140

Manhood: white, 113

Mania, 119; as melancholia, 120

Manifest Destiny, xi

Mapplethorpe, Robert, 147; "Man in the Polyester Suit," 156

Market, 8; capitalism, 159; niche, xvi; penetration, 84; slave, 145; time, 154. *See also* Capitalism

Marks, Laura, 165; haptic historiography, theory of, 123

Marriage, xv, 4, 22, 128; arranged, 17; fleshly bond of, 14; martyrdom and, 43, 48; as plot or narrative, 15, 21

Marx, Karl, xix, 9, 53, 78, 151–52, 192 n. 67

Marxism, 84; class struggle and, 1; commodity fetish, 151–52; orthodox, 114; queer theory and, 9; vision of history, 78. *See also* Capitalism

Masculinity, 4, 162; Christian, 115; crisis of, 100; female, 191 n. 65; forms of, 105; outmoded, xxiii; studies, 74; symbol and, 69–70

Mass cinema: capitalism and, xviii. *See also* Cinema

Maternity, 37, 42, 57. *See also* Mothers

Mauss, Marcel: on accent, 29; on habitus, 18

Melancholia, xiii, 9, 104, 153, 172; Abraham and Torok on, 118–19; collective, 70; Freud on, 119; Judith Butler on, 69–70; Maria Torok on, 120–21, subjectivity and, 114. *See also* Butler, Judith

Melodrama: domestic, 42–43; maternal, 50; mother-daughter, 31; plots, 48; theory of, 149

Memory, 33, 36, 46, 110; family, 22; historical, 50, 144; maternal, 51; political, 158; prosthetic, 159–61; racial, 161; skin, 168; technologies of, 39

Mercer, Kobena, 164; critique of Mapplethorpe, 147

Midsummer Night's Dream, A (Shakespeare), 16–18, 28

Microtemporalities: of body, xii, 59; reappropriation of, 52

Mimesis, 124–27, 165

"Mimetic Faculty, The" (Benjamin), 124

Mitchell, Allyson, 119: art installations of, xxiii; on Deep Lez, 85; *Barb and Barb*, 86; *Big Trouble*, 87; *Fluffer Nutter*, 89; *The Fluff Stands Alone*, 89, 91, 93; *In a Wiccan Way*, 87; *It Ain't Gonna Lick Itself*, 87; *Lady Sasquatch*, 86–87, 89, 93; "The Michigan Three," 91–93; *Rugburn #1*, 89; *Shebacca*, 87; *Venus of Nudiesque*, 89. *See also* Deep Lez

Modernism, 7

Modernity, 8, 10, 23, 80, 139, 154, 161, 171; capitalist, 172; dialectic of, 138; double, 169; Euro-American, 9; failure of, xvi; progress and, 134; as queer, 30; twentieth-century and, xii

Modern time: violence of, xii

Monmouth, Geoffrey of: *History of the Kings of Britain*, 158

Monsters, 116, 134; in *Frankenstein*, 96–105, 108, 114, 120, 132, 134–35; primeval, 86; in *The Sticky Fingers of Time*, 115. See also *Frankenstein*; Gothic

Moon, Michael: on "Divinity," 90–91

Moraga, Cherríe: *Giving Up the Ghost*, xiii

Morrison, Toni: *Beloved*, 81; on skin memory, 168

Motherhood. *See* Maternity

Mothers, 22, 37–38, 44–45, 51; binding with daughters of, 47; bourgeois, 40; erotics between, 35; times associated with, 42; working-class, 31

Muñoz, José Esteban: on *Looking for Langston*, 147

Mysticism: female saints, 43, 47–49, 55; feminized, 163. See also *Lover*

Nahum, Tate, 158–59

Narrative, 24–25, 28, 44, 68, 70, 95, 97, 103, 116, 119, 150–51; battle and, 115; of belonging, xv; coming-out, 27; continuity of, 156; conventions of, 1; genres, 126, 149; as historical, xi, 28, 163; linear, 132; memories, 8; of modernity, xii, xx; of movement, 4, 15; Oedipal, 108,

113; progress, 80, 106; space, 43; suspension of, 159; syncopated, 69; texture, 6; time, 41; voice, 53; working-class dyke, 22

Nationalism: homosocial, xi; modern, 21

Nationality, 6

Nationhood, xxii, 28; histories of, 138

Negrón-Muntaner, Frances: critical response to *The Sticky Fingers of Time*, 129, 134

Neologism: Deleuze and Guattari on, xix

New England, 42

New Queer Cinema, 144–45, 150; description of, 26–27

New York: performance art in, 59–60; radical feminist groups and, 65

Nguyen, Hoang Tan, 1, 13, 28, 43, 64. *See also individual works*

Nietzsche, Friedrich: on monumental time, 4

Nightwood (Barnes), 38

Nihilism, xx

Nineteenth century, 24, 107, 116; antebellum, 23; decadence of, 7; film technologies and, 23; historicist methods of, 104; invention of match in, 124; letters of, 97; novel and, 99; perverts and, 9; photograph and, 22; sentimental culture of, 142; sentimental history of, xii; separate spheres and, discourse of, 5; sexologists and, 63, 182 n. 13; *tableau vivant* and, 150; women's rights movement and, 79, 86

No Future (Edelman), xxi, 19; on futurity, 140

Noll, Kip, 2–3; name, 13

Nostalgia: for another revolution, xvi; Derrida on, xiv; sadomasochism and, 144

Obesity. *See* Fatness

Oedipus complex, 69; oedipal drama, 114; oedipal narrative, 108, 113

"On Narcissism" (Freud), 12

Orgasm, 1, 2, 8, 109; genitalized, 123; male, 161

Orgy: interracial sex and, 146; sadomasochistic, 161–62. *See also* Sadomasochism

Orlando (Woolf), xvii, xxiii, 105–13, 117–18, 121, 124, 132–34, 164, 187 n. 21

Otherness, 24; Derrida on, 9–10, feminism and, 62; racial, 24; time of the other, 45

Paine, Thomas: on male sensibility and history, 99, 102–3, 162

Parataxis: as thin aesthetic, xix

Pause, xxiii, 4, 6, 41, 131, 152–53, 169; historicized, 155, 165

Penetration, 2, 49, 114, 128, 163; endless, 9; market, 84

Peoplehood, 6, 21

Performativity, 63, 191 n. 62; familial, 43; gender, xiii, 4; queer, 62, 65–66, 68, 70, 72; theory of, 64

Personhood, 4, 46–47, 54; gendered, 82

Perversion, 47; definition of, 160; sexual, 100

Phallus, 114, 118, 122, 133, 158, 162; black, 129; lesbian, 12; sexuality and, 45

Photographic media, xviii, 22; middle-class domesticity and, 59

Photography, 21; domestic, 22, 33–34, 36, 38–39; pornographic, 164; time and, 124

Physics of Love, The (Bonder), xxiii, 31–34, 36–39, 41–47, 50–51, 53–55, 70, 122

Playboy, 89–91

Pleasure, xii, xiv, xvii, xix, xxiii, 1, 14, 49–50, 53–55, 58, 63, 82, 118–20, 169, 173; Agamben on, 118; analog, 110; bodies and, 16, 47, 131; digital, 110; derangement of, 3; erotic, 13, 106; of figuration, xxi; future imagined as, 118; history and, 95, 129, 168; idiom of, 138; illicit, 122; melancholia and, 119; memory of, 166; physical, 10, 51; queer, 117; of queerness, x; of reading, 123; sadomasochism and, 143–144, 158, 161, 169; sexual, 57, 105, 162; voyeuristic, 22; white, 130. *See also* Sexuality

Pornography, xvii, 2; genre of, 3; photographic, 164

Postfeminism, xvi, 74, 76, 84

Postmodernism, 27–28, 45, 57, 66–67, 80; freeplay and, 46; gender and, 112; queer and, 47; relationship to technology, 66; as simulacrum, 57–59; strategies of, 74

Poststructuralism, 49, 122; Marxism and, 16; queer theory and, 11

Prefeminist, 74, 76

Premodernity, 138, 154

Prolepsis, xxii, 10, 60, 73, 80, 103, 111, 133

Psychic Life of Power, The (Butler), 11, 68–69

Psychoanalysis, 64, 70, 125; conventional, 114

Purcell, Henry: *Dido and Aeneas*, 157–58, 166

Queen, x, 62; drag, 68

Queer, 27, 62, 76; activism, xiv; affect, 8, 145; archivalism, xi, 19; as class, 19; culture, xiii; definition of, 44; generation, 84; history, xi, 109, 123; identity, 7; movement, xiv; as organizing term, xxi; past, xvii, 157; point of, xiii; as polymorphous, 82; as premise for TV shows, xv; as queer, xiii, 98; subculture, 24; as subject position, 19; temporalities, x, xxii; time-binding, 130; world of, x; youth, xv

Queering, 30; family, 24, as semiotic warfare, xiv; time, 42

Queer Nation, xv, 61, 179 n. 5; archived, xv; groundwork for, xv

Queerness, xvi; 18, 24, 82, 100, 105, 179 n. 5; analysis of, 27; future and, 130; obesity and, 90; pleasures of, x; power of, 130; temporal crossing and, 70

Queer politics, xix, 3, 62, 82; class-conscious and, 48; melancholy and, 69; of time, 28

Queers, xxi–xxii, 19, 32, 117, 132, 164, 169

Queer studies, 62, 169

Queer theory, xv, 45, 62, 68, 95, 104, 112, 179 n. 5; as academic subspecialty, xv; dominant strains of, xiii; drag and, 62–63; lesbian, 142, 143; lesbian stigma and, 91; "ludic," 9; melancholia and, 11; sadomasochism and, 139–141; without social justice, xx; time and, xii, 10

Queer time, x–xii, xxiv, 23, 109. *See also* "It's a Queer Time"

"Questions to Emmanuel Levinas" (Irigaray), 49

Race, 80, 173; birthright and, 167; degeneration and discourse of, 23; difference, xxiii, 80, 86, 87, 135; discrimination and, 80; histories of, 138, 150; interracial contact, 91, 155, 165; justice and, 132; memory and, 162; multiracial, 129, 151; politics and, 13, 167; primitive, 89; purity and, 22, 155; segregation and, 131; superstructures and, 140–44

Racism, 80, 129, 132, 147, 167, 192 n. 67; as fetish, 165; s/m and, 164; trope, 108

Reddy, Helen: "I am Woman [Hear Me Roar]," 86

Reflections on the Revolution in France, The (Burke), 101

Renan, Ernest, 29

Repertoire, 133; theory of, 71

Repetition, 5, 13; difference and, 62; in Freud, 8, 23; gender performance, 63; identity and, 4; as thin aesthetic, xix

Reproduction, 4, 33, 49, 52, 151; biological, 26, 123; bodily experience of, 45; cultural logic of, 74; cybernetic, 66; cyclical, 115; heterosexual, 51; mechanical, 47; modes of, 127; rhythms of, 169; technological, 36; unnatural, 57

Reprofuturity, 19, 21

Revolution: class, xiv; failed, xxii, 172; libidinalized, 168; of past, xvi

Rhythm, 4, 21, 167, 171; of body, 1; of capital, 40; factory, 39; of gift exchange, 4; of habitus, 18; hidden, 3; of household, xxii; natural, 7; quotidian, 154; of reproduction, 169; routinized, 6; of Sabbath, 138; spoken, 29; troped as, 44

Rich, B. Ruby, 27, 76

Riggs, Marlon: *Tongues Untied*, 147

Riot Grrrl, 72, 84; style, 81; zines, 82

Roach, Joseph: critical response to *Dido and Aeneas*, 158, 166

Romantic era, 104–5. *See also* History

Rosen, Philip: on film and history, xvii–xviii

Royal African Company, 159

Sackville-West, Vita, 106

s/m. *See* sadomasochism

Sadomasochism, xxiii, 50, 61, 79, 136, 143–44, 147–49, 152, 156–58, 165, 168, 172; culture of, 139, 149; destruction of subject and, 141–42; as dialectic, 153; erotohistoriography and, 138; interracial, 135, 137, 146, 168; orgy and, 151, 163; play and, xii, 137, 161; prosthetic memory and, 161; as racialized practice, 164; sex and, 138–40, 147; skin and, 164–65; slavery and, 150; temporal aspects of, 169

San Francisco, 24, 30; Castro district of, 2

Sedgwick, Eve, 82; on "Divinity," 90–91; paranoid and reparative criticism and, xiii; queer inner child and, xii

Segregation: of children, 83; racial, 131

Sentimentalism, 123, 154, 168

Sequence, 3, 5, 13, 22, 27, 32, 36–38, 55, 128–29, 182 n. 13; genealogical, 47; generational, 43, 44; historical, 148; reproductive, 123; of *tableau vivants*, 152

Sexual dissidence, xii, xxi, 27, 48, 171; queer, 1; temporality and, 7

Sexuality, 47, 53, 103, 114, 182 n. 13; constructedness of, 112; dissident, 27; female, 62, 162; histories of, 108, 138, 150; male, 140; memory and, 166; phallic, 45; politics of, 90; Sadean, 153

Shakespeare, William, 14, 122, 130. *See also individual works*

Shelley, Mary: allusion to, 114; heterosexual logic and, 115; life of, 96; sympathy and, 100. See also *Frankenstein*; Gothic

Sherman, Cindy, 72–73

Shulie (Subrin), xxiii, 65–68, 71–81, 83, 128–29, 185 n. 23

Simulacrum, 71; postmodernism and, 57–59

Singer, Leslie, 25, 28, 30

Slave Trade, Scene on the Coast of Africa, The (Biard), 145, 148, 150–54, 156, 158, 161

Slavery, 151, 163; auction, 152; capitalism and, 153, 159; chattel, 135, 139, 144; history and, 81, 150, 164; race, 150; S/M and, 140, 162, 163; slaveholders in, 154; slave trade, xxiv, 145, 150–51, 159; transatlantic, 138, 145, 157; wage, 24, 191 n. 47

Smith, Shawn Michelle: on photography, 22

Social justice: cycle of, 76; projects and theories of, xxii; queer theory and, xx

"Sociology Hesitant" (Du Bois), 171

"Something's Got to Give" (Sinatra), 32

Soss, Kim, 67, 71, 74, 83

Space, xii, 22, 38, 41, 48, 53, 56–57, 93, 126, 155; classical, 154; diegetic, 96; extensions of, 161; fat and, 92; of home, 39; Kristeva on, 45; narrative, 43; pure, 59; queer theory and, 3, 179 n. 5; reification of, 7; safe, 87; time and, xviii, xix, 54, 135, 147; virtual, 97. *See also* Domesticity; Habitus

Spanish Inquisition, 138, 140, 160

Spectatorship, 2–3, 13, 23, 147, 151, 165

Specters of Marx (Derrida), 10, 13–14

Stein, Gertrude, xix

Stevenson, Robert Louis: *Treasure Island*, xi

Sticky Fingers of Time, The (Brougher), xxiii, 111–18, 120–24, 126, 130, 133, 162, 164

Stockton, Kathryn Bond: critical response to *Nightwood*, 38

Stowe, Harriet Beecher: *Uncle Tom's Cabin*, 103

Straight, 69; feminist past, 129; identity of, xv; passing for, x; temporalities of, x; women, xv

Subculture, 52; commodified, 72; gay, x; lesbian, 61; queer, 24

Subjectivity, 4, 11, 64, 92, 117; historical, 160; melancholy and, 69–70, 114; new forms of, 57, 123; subject-position and, xx, 54, 68, 70, 85

Subrin, Elisabeth, 93, 119, 129; critical response to, 75–76. *See also individual works*

Surrealism, 125, 133

"Surrealism" (Benjamin), 125

Swallow (Subrin), 82, 186 n. 48

Synchronicity, 39–40, 96

Synchrony, xxiii, 28, 48

Tableau vivant, 146, 148, 150–52, 161, 163

Taussig, Michael: mimesis, theory of, 126–27, 133

Taylor, Diana: repertoire, theory of, 71, 184 n. 22

Technology, 110–11, 131, 134; digital, 112, 144; film, 23; mimetic, 127; visual, 40

Television, 1, 29, 32, 43, 44

Temporal dissonance, 1, 48, 142

Temporal drag, 95, 119, 135, 167; Deep Lez and, 85, theory of, xxiii, 62, 65, 78

Temporal heterogeneity, 14–15, 89, 116, 179 n. 4; Fredric Jameson on, 11

Temporality, xii, xxiii–xxiv, 54–55, 138; of body, 49–50; Derrida and, 121; domesticity as, 45, epidermal, 134; family, 31; film and, xviii, 1; influence of; linear, 41; modern, 7,

10; queer corpus and, 116; queer theory and, 9; Sedgwick's work concerned with, 82; sexual dissidence and, xxiv; suspended, 153; trans-, 92

"Theses on the Philosophy of History" (Benjamin), 19, 124, 155

Third World, xiv, 143

Time, xi, 6, 39–40, 48, 123; as asynchronous, xii; as body, 14; as border, xiii; black social, 129; as cyclical, 5, 44, 115; digital era and, 111; as eschatological, x; feudal era and, 139; filmic, 1; as foreshortened, x; generational, 38; heterogeneous, 138; history and, xxii, 9, 21, 54, 130; as industrial, 22, 145; as linear, 7, 13, 23, 37–38, 133; leisure, xviii; as millennial, xi; modern, xxii, 145, 154; as monumental, 5, 42, 51, 57; as nationalist, x; organizational strategies of, xii; politics of, 48; as productivity; 53; as progressive, 32; as quality, 40, 43; as queer, x; as rational, 21; as sacred, 5, 33, 49; as secular, xi, 23; as sequential, 3; synchronic, 42, 59; wage, xv; Western, 158

Time travel, xxiii, 111–14, 117, 123, 132, 143, 145

Tongues Untied (Riggs), 147

Torok, Maria, 119, 125: melancholia, theory of, 120

Transgender, 62, 161; activism, 60; movement, 74

Trauma, 11, 92, 119, 120; individual, 143, 160; sexual, 142

Treasure Island (Stevenson), xi

Treatise on Domestic Economy (Beecher), 39–41

Tweedie, James: on *tableau vivant*, 150

Twentieth century, 107, 116, 130; dialectic of time and, 22; fisting and,

114; modernity and, xii; 114; quality time and, 40; Sabbaths and, 39; still life aesthetics of, 40; women of, 183 n. 36

Twinning, 42, 44. *See also* Double

Uncle Tom's Cabin (Stowe), 103

United States, xiii–xiv, 4, 6, 32, 132, 134, 172; AIDS normalized in, xv; industrialization and, 5–6, 39; Holocaust Museum in, 160. *See also* Capitalism; Industrialization

Utopia, xiii, 140, 162, 192 n. 67

Vampires, 86, 98; Sapphic, 7. *See also* Gothic

Vaudeville, 32, 44

Victorian era, 102–3

Video, xiv, xxiii, 1–2, 31; *Coal Miner's Granddaughter*, 24–30; diaries, 83; home, 45; independent, 24; *K.I.P.*, 3, 12–13, 64; as minor literature, xvii; as mode of close reading, xviii; *The Physics of Love*, 33, 38, 41–42, 46, 50–51; *Shulie*, 65–68, 71–72, 76–77, 80–81

Vietnam, 59–60; escalation of war in, xiv

Virgil: *Aeneid*, 158–59

Voloshinov, V. N.: on multiaccentuality, 29

Wedding Complex, The (Freeman), xxi

West Indies, 159, 166

WHAM (Women's Health Action Mobilization), 61

"What Is a Minor Literature" (Deleuze and Guattari), xviii–xix

Wiegman, Robyn, 62, 64, 76

Williams, Raymond, 10, 127

Womanhood, 47, 70; black, 113

Women's Liberation, xvii, 80

Women's Rights Movements (WRM), 79

Women's time, 6, 23, 44. *See also* Kristeva, Julia

"Women's Time" (Kristeva), 45

Woolf, Virginia, 123; heterosexual logic and, 115. *See also individual works*

"Work of Art in the Age of Mechanical Reproduction, The" (Benjamin), 124

Working class, 29, 62; family, 24; history, 30; sociability, 25; solidarity, 30; as subject position, 19. *See also* Class

World War I. *See* First World War

Young, Elizabeth: on black underclass and *Frankenstein*, 135

Zerubavel, Evitar: on hidden rhythms, 3–4

ELIZABETH FREEMAN is a professor of English at the University of California, Davis. She is the author of *The Wedding Complex: Forms of Belonging in Modern American Culture*, also published by Duke (2002).

Library of Congress Cataloging-in-Publication Data
Freeman, Elizabeth, 1966–
Time binds : queer temporalities, queer histories / Elizabeth Freeman.
p. cm. — (Perverse modernities)
Includes bibliographical references and index.
ISBN 978-0-8223-4790-3 (cloth : alk. paper)
ISBN 978-0-8223-4804-7 (pbk. : alk. paper)
1. Time — Social aspects. 2. Homosexuality — Social aspects. 3. Queer theory. I. Title. II. Series: Perverse modernities.
HM656.F74 2010
306.76′601 — dc22
2010005251